Global Contexts

D1314167

THE ALLYN AND BACON SERIES IN TECHNICAL COMMUNICATION

SERIES EDITOR: SAM DRAGGA, TEXAS TECH UNIVERSITY

Thomas T. Barker
Writing Software Documentation:
A Task-Oriented Approach

Dan Jones
Technical Writing Style

Charles Kostelnick and David D. Roberts
Designing Visual Language: Strategies for
Professional Communicators

Carolyn D. Rude
Technical Editing, Second Edition

Deborah S. Bosley
Global Contexts: Case Studies in
International Technical Communication

Paul M. Dombrowski
Ethics in Technical Communication

Laura J. Gurak
Oral Presentations for
Technical Communication

Global Contexts

Case Studies in International Technical Communication

Deborah S. Bosley

University of North Carolina at Charlotte

Allyn and Bacon

Boston • London • Toronto • Sydney • Tokyo • Singapore

*To my husband, Marty, for his continued support;
to my daughter, Hannah, for giving up spending time with me;
and to the hundreds of students who have taught me how to be a better teacher*

Vice President, Humanities: Joseph Opiela
Executive Marketing Manager: Lisa Kimball
Editorial Production Service: Chestnut Hill Enterprises, Inc.
Manufacturing Buyer: Suzanne Lareau
Cover Administrator: Jennifer Hart

Copyright © 2001 by Allyn & Bacon
A Pearson Education Company
160 Gould Street
Needham Heights, MA 02494

All rights reserved. No part of the material protected by this copyright notice may be reproduced or utilized in any form or by any means, electronic or mechanical, including photocopying, recording, or by any information storage and retrieval system, without written permission from the copyright holder.

Internet: www.abacon.com

Between the time Website information is gathered and published, some sites may have closed. Also, the transcription of URLs can result in typographical errors. The publisher would appreciate notification where these occur so that they may be corrected in subsequent editions.

Library of Congress Cataloging-in-Publication Data

Global contexts : case studies in international technical communication / [edited by] Deborah S. Bosley.
    p. cm.
    Includes bibliographical references and index.
    ISBN 0-205-28682-8
    1. Communication of technical information—Case studies.   I. Bosley, Deborah S.

T10.5 G64 2000
601'.4—dc21
                                  00-025301

Printed in the United States of America
10 9 8 7 6 5 4 3 2 1   05 04 03 02 01 00

Contents

Foreword by Series Editor   vii

Introduction:

> **Welcome to the New Global Village:**
> **Our Changing Global Worldview**   1
> by Deborah S. Bosley, *University of North Carolina at Charlotte*

1 **A Visit to the Forbidden City: A Sign of the Times**   10
   by Sam Dragga, *Texas Tech University*

2 **Multilevel Challenges for Technical Documentation:**
   Encountering Chinese Culture   19
   by Craig J. Hansen, *Metropolitan State University*

3 **High-Context and Low-Context Cultures:**
   How Much Communication Is Too Much?   27
   by Emily A. Thrush, *University of Memphis*

4 **Usage as an Interactive Strategy for International**
   Team-Building: The Never-Ending Story   42
   by Boyd H. Davis, *University of North Carolina at Charlotte*,
   Jeutonne Brewer, *University of North Carolina at Greensboro*, and
   Ye-Ling Chang, *National Kaohsiung Normal University*

5 **Resolving Cultural Misunderstandings in Crisis Situations:**
   The Case of the Inexperienced Entrepreneurs   52
   by Jayne A. Moneysmith, *Kent State University at Stark*

6 Translating User Manuals: A Surgical Equipment
   Company's "Quick Cut"   64
   by Bruce Maylath, *University of Wisconsin at Stout*

7 Adapting to South American Communication Patterns:
   Odyssey's Proposal to Remedy Inconsistent Car Sales   81
   by Barry. L. Thatcher, *Ohio University*

8 Cultural Issues in Corporate Hierarchies:
   Keeping Your Distance Isn't That Simple   96
   by Roger Baumgarte, *Winthrop University,* and
   Philippe Blanchard, *Rio de Janeiro*

9 A Venture between American Academe and Corporate
   Malaysia: The CyberUniversity Blues   113
   by Thomas F. Lannin, *CyberInstitute Inc.*

10 Human Error, Communication Failures, and the Sinking
    of the M/S *Estonia:* Recipe for Disaster   127
    by Elizabeth M. Lynn, *Kettering University*

11 Risk-Based Design in a Pipeline Engineering Project
    for Colombia: First Do No Harm   148
    by Linda Driskill, *Rice University,* and
    Frank Driskill, *Brown & Root Energy Services*

12 Communicating the Risks of Natural Hazards:
    The World-at-Large Is at Stake   174
    by Nancy L. Hoft, *Michigan Technological University*

List of Contributors   209

Index   213

Foreword by the Series Editor

The Allyn and Bacon Series in Technical Communications is designed for the growing number of students enrolled in undergraduate and graduate programs in technical communication. Such programs offer a wide variety of courses beyond the introductory technical writing course—advanced courses for which fully satisfactory and appropriately focused textbooks have often been impossible to locate. This series will also serve the continuing education needs of professional technical communicators, both those who desire to upgrade or update their own communication abilities as well as those who train or supervise writers, editors, and artists within their organization.

The chief characteristic of the books in this series is their consistent effort to integrate theory and practice. The books offer both research-based and experienced-based instruction, describing not only what to do and how to do it but explaining why. The instructors who teach advanced courses and the students who enroll in these courses are looking for more than rigid rules and ad hoc guidelines. They want books that demonstrate theoretical sophistication and a solid foundation in the research of the field as well as pragmatic advice and perceptive applications. Instructors and students will also find these books filled with activities and assignments adaptable to the classroom and to the self-guided learning processes of professional technical communicators.

To operate effectively in the field of technical communication, today's students require extensive training in the creation, analysis, and design of information for both domestic and international audiences, for both paper and electronic environments. The books in the Allyn and Bacon Series address those subjects that are most frequently taught at the undergraduate and graduate levels as a direct response to both the educational needs of students and the practical demands of business and industry. Additional books will be developed for the series in order to satisfy or anticipate changes in writing technologies, academic curricula, and the profession of technical communication.

Sam Dragga
Texas Tech University

Acknowledgments

Thank you to my friends and family, who gave me the encouragement and the needed support to complete this book.

The Department of English and the College of Arts and Sciences at the University of North Carolina at Charlotte gave me the precious gift of time through a research and development leave during spring 1998.

Throughout the development of this book, I received necessary and intelligent feedback from the following reviewers: Deborah C. Andrews, University of Delaware; Karla Saari Kitalong, Michigan Technological University; Bille Wahlstrom, University of Minnesota; and TyAnna K. Herrington, Georgia Institute of Technology.

Allyn and Bacon's continued encouragement and support enabled me to complete this project. In particular, thank you to Joe Opiela, vice president and editor-in-chief, humanities, for having the insight to understand the relevance of this project to the field of technical communication.

Finally, my deepest gratitude to Sam Dragga, who encouraged me to take on this project and who, throughout the entire process, guided me, supported me, and kept me focused on the task at hand. Without his assistance and insight, this book would not have been possible.

Introduction

Welcome to the New Global Village

Our Changing Global Worldview

DEBORAH S. BOSLEY
University of North Carolina at Charlotte

With the rapid expansion of corporate interests worldwide and the unparalleled explosion of the Internet and the World Wide Web, the field of technical communication needs to keep up with new possibilities and opportunities for creating effective documentation. The world has become a global village. An increasing number of corporations are doing business in overseas markets, with employees from countries outside the United States and with documents that span multiple cultures. With this expansion and with new employee populations, however, comes the difficulty of educating students and employees to be effective professional and technical communicators in a world of international readers and users. Added to this situation is the fact that the number of university students from international cultures is increasing nationwide, thereby populating courses with students whose diverse cultural backgrounds enrich the classroom environment.

The Need to Adjust the Technical Communication Curriculum

Meeting the needs of diverse international audiences can be a daunting task for communicators. Professors, students, and practitioners often have been unable to keep up because so few resources have been available to this new field. Although, books, articles, and textbooks focused on international technical communication have proliferated. However, these items tend to fall into two categories: (1) scholarly books and articles and (2) textbooks that either isolate international issues by sprinkling information throughout their chapters or that confine the discussion to a separate chapter. The tendency is to discuss international issues as if they functioned separately from our own cultural assumptions and, therefore, separately from the backgrounds of students. This book provides an alternative that allows readers to understand the *context* in which international technical communication occurs and to uncover their own cultural assumptions that affect documentation.

Students graduating into their professional lives are entering a world remarkably different from the world that educated their professors and their corporate counterparts. The worldwide tendency toward westernization has meant that the English language and U.S. attitudes, behaviors, and icons are moving closer to the center of many other countries. McDonald's is in China, and the business suit is becoming universal. Part of the responsibility of technical communication teachers is to prepare students for the twenty-first century and to help shape the definitions of what it means to be a professional. Clearly, giving students access to and experience with other cultures is a necessity to their professional development, and "world knowledge" is a necessary component of technical communicators (Boswood, 1999, p. 121).

Technical communication professors and professionals have a responsibility to go "beyond instructing our students to acquire information about cultures; we need to equip them with more rhetorically sensitive strategies and processes for evaluating cultural interactions and for adapting their communications to the needs of particular situations" (Lovitt, 1999, p. 7). By using a case approach, this book provides such rhetorical situations.

Definitions of Culture

Culture could be defined as the way in which a group of people solve problems; or the patterns of thinking, feeling, and acting that form a group's mental programming; or the political, religious, ethical, educational, economic, and social system; or as "a system of competence shared in its broad design and deeper principles, and varying between individuals in its specificities . . . the way the human brain acquires, organizes, and processes information and creates 'internal models of reality' " (Keesing, 1974, p. 89).

Others suggest that culture is a symbolic system (Geertz, 1973), or that it is so intricately bound up with communication that the two are interchangeable (Hall, 1959). Regardless of the definition, all cultures and the individuals that inhabit them are influenced by politics, religion, the linguistics of their primary language, social organization, the educational system, beliefs in gender similarities and differences, nonverbal behavior, relationship with the environment, and economic foundations.

Defining *culture* and determining which factors influence how an individual communicates are complex activities. Identifying the factors that influence a culture's general modes of thinking, feeling, acting, and knowing can best be described using the analogy of an iceberg (Hoft, 1995, p. 113): 80 percent of what exists is below the surface.

Perhaps the best we can do as professors and as students is to try to uncover the 20 percent above the surface. Despite the naïveté in focusing primarily on the visible, we have to begin somewhere. For the purpose of this book, then, *culture* is a system created from the multitude of influences that shape our perceptions of the world, our beliefs about the world, and our behavior in it.

Disclaimers

Three disclaimers need to be made at this point: First, calling attention to differences in cultures in no way implies a hierarchy of accepted behavior. All cultures tend to be ethnocentric—that is, all tend to cling to the belief that their own culture is the standard by which others are to be judged. Some people subscribe to a "universalist's" notion that purports that people from different cultures nevertheless behave (or should behave) the same way. Other adhere to a "relativist's" perspective, which suggests that differences in cultures can be understood only within the context of the particular cultures. The cases in this book attempt to give readers a sense of cultural influences.

Second, it is difficult to speak of the behavior of any one individual by generalizing to his or her entire culture. However, individuals from different cultures do have tendencies to behave in identifiable ways referred to as "the characterization of character" (Hall, 1976).

Finally, most attempts to discuss cross-cultural communication are overly simplified because it is often difficult to ascribe concrete reasons to thoughts, feelings, and behaviors. However, every discussion has to start somewhere, and the authors here are attempting to generalize with the best of intentions: to lead readers to further understanding, not just to classify and stereotype differing behaviors.

How This Book Can Help

This book provides readers with the following:

1. Fictionalized and nonfictionalized scenarios that uncover issues relevant to international technical communication
2. Strategies for recognizing behaviors and patterns of thinking and feeling that affect technical documentation
3. Issues relevant to the new field of international technical communication
4. References for additional research and reading
5. Assumptions and presumptions about the cultures from which we each come.

These narratives allow readers to wrestle with the intricacy and complexity of documentation they will produce for the twenty-first century.

Who Should Use This Book

This book is intended for multiple audiences. To satisfy the needs of those who have had experience with international communication and those who have not, each case includes an extensive analysis of the case, questions for discussion, and writing and communication assignments. The analyses are appropriate for professors and students who have little knowledge of and/or experience with international issues. By expanding on the cultural contexts relevant to understanding the cases, readers learn to analyze the cases as well as respond to issues inherent in the cases themselves.

These cases will help the following audiences understand the complexities of international contexts:

- *Undergraduates in introductory technical communication courses.* Currently, 400,000 undergraduates are enrolled in introductory technical communication courses. Many of them are introduced to international issues by brief material presented by a book or a professor, if they are introduced to it at all.
- *Advanced technical communication students in undergraduate, graduate, and/or certificate programs.* As the number of students studying to become technical communicators increases, books such as this one will provide the material they need to gain some understanding of international cross-cultural communication and documentation issues.
- *Technical communications practitioners.* Technical communicators themselves need to upgrade their skills and gain additional insight into international issues as more corporations do business with international companies or find themselves exporting their documentation.
- *Technical or professional communications professors.* Many of today's communication professors were educated in a world that maintained the illusion of centrality—the ethnocentric belief that the culture of the United States was (or should be) the culture of the world. Many are underprepared to educate students about new global markets and communities.
- *Technical communications trainers.* Trainers working with either international corporations' documentation for their products or with documentation services companies themselves need materials to teach international concepts before employees go overseas or prepare documentation for international export.

What Are Case Studies, and Why Use Them?

A case study is a narrative (either fiction or nonfiction) describing a situation that reflects issues and problems that students may encounter during their professional lives. Using cases allows professors and students to discuss these issues, identify problems, and propose solutions in ways they cannot by examining documents, discussing rhetorical situations in the abstract, or providing guidelines for professional communication. Although cases may involve fictionalized companies and situations, they also may tell about historical events. Whether history or fiction, they let students and professors simulate participation in real-life situations, apply theory to practice, and develop analytical skills by proposing viable solutions to the problems presented in the cases. In addition, both students and professors can discover the complexity of situations compounded by the demands of understanding intracultural and intercultural behavior and motivation. The best these cases can do is to expose readers to some of the elements they are likely to encounter in the internationalized workplace.

How Can Readers Use These Cases?

Reading a case study is different than reading fiction or a more traditional textbook. The following guidelines will help readers understand and discuss the cases:

- Read the case once to get an overall sense of the characters, the plot, and the issues. Then, read it a second time, taking notes on the critical features and facts of the situation. In particular, spend time on the background for analysis and on the analysis of each case, where the authors explain some of the cultural elements that affect the scenarios.
- Assume that all the information relevant to understanding the case may not necessarily be presented. At the end of each case, authors have provided additional readings that make it possible to research the issues in more depth. In addition, technical communication courses often contain students from a multitude of cultural backgrounds. Sometimes students themselves can best explain particular behavior patterns or actions. However, no student should ever be assumed to represent a particular culture.
- Understand that communication of any kind is complex. Added to that complexity is the difficulty of understanding cultural behavior and motivation. Therefore, assume that there generally are no right answers, nor only one approach to identifying problems or providing suggestions for solutions. All of us read cases through our own cultural lens. One of the values of these cases is to help us uncover our own cultural assumptions and presumptions.

The Issues in The Cases

The cases are arranged from least complex to most complex, allowing students and professors to build on concepts and issues from one case to the next. For example, the last three cases are derived from historical and current information about actual situations in which communication played a pivotal role. They introduce ethical, managerial, professional, cultural, and political situations as each affects technical communication.

All the cases contain similar elements: Each introduces background information helpful for an analysis, provides questions for discussion, suggests writing assignments, and includes references for students and professors who want to read more about the issues developed in the case.

In "A Visit to the Forbidden City: A Sign of the Times," Sam Dragga narrates the story of a technical communicator traveling in China who volunteers to rewrite a sign for tourists at a museum entrance. He notices several grammatical and style problems and believes that he could design a better sign. Using the Confucian virtues of goodness (*ren*), wisdom (*zhi*), and righteousness (*yi*), Dragga explicates the cultural elements that influenced Chinese officials to incorporate only a few of the technical communicator's suggestions.

Craig J. Hansen, in "Multilevel Challenges for Technical Documentation: Encountering Chinese Culture," introduces us to Evans Vacuum Modules Corporation in the Midwest United States, which produces computerized control systems for manufacturers. When the company expands business interests to the Pacific Rim, a senior technical writer is charged with developing a combined operations manual with her counterparts in Taiwan. In addition, she is asked to look over and comment on the business plan. Faced with differences in cultural expectations, the writer has to negotiate issues of effective document design as well as the collaboration process and translation.

Emily A. Thrush, in "High-Context and Low-Context Cultures: How Much Communication Is Too Much?" tells the story of a collaboration between the TEFL (Teaching English as a Foreign Language) programs of the University of West Bohemia (UWB) in Pilson, Czech Republic, and the University of Memphis, Tennessee. This program provides teachers from the United States with the opportunity to gain experience in an environment where English is not the primary language. This situation focuses on a series of letters between a U.S. teacher and the program director at UWB as teachers try to discover the information they need to participate in the program. Thrush introduces us to Edward T. Hall's concepts of high-context and low-context cultures, the relationship between these concepts, and expectations for the amounts and types of information included in professional communication. For example, Thrush discusses the reliance on oral versus written communication and individual versus group emphasis on control, and the expectations for what occurs during a business relationship. Hall's concept reappears in other cases (see Chapters 7 and 8 in particular).

Boyd H. Davis, Jeutonne Brewer, and Ye-Ling Chang, in "Usage as an Interactive Strategy for International Team-Building: The Never-Ending Story," examine choices in gender pronoun usage among U.S. and Taiwanese businesspeople. A junior technical writer is asked to develop training materials for the new Pizza-for-Us franchise opening in Taipei, Tokyo, and Seoul. Knowing that the manuscript will be translated, the writer tries to be scrupulously detailed. Working closely with a cross-cultural trainer, the writer wanders into what U.S. citizens consider to be sexist usage. A series of e-mail exchanges illuminate these differences in pronoun usage.

Jayne A. Moneysmith, in "Resolving Cultural Misunderstandings in Crisis Situations: The Case of the Inexperienced Entrepreneurs," describes the attempts of college students to develop a new computer start-up company, NetRider. NetRider computers (NRC) provides Internet connections only, and the students believe that there is a burgeoning market for this one feature. Orders pour in, and they receive heavy national exposure just when their supplier cannot fill their order for needed microchips. This problem leads to negotiations with International Chips in Seoul, Korea. A series of faxes illustrates differences in directness and more subtle forms of concurrence.

Bruce Maylath, in "Translating User Manuals: A Surgical Equipment Company's 'Quick Cut,' " narrates the story of Cordpatch, a company that produces a synthetic heart patch to seal heart perforations. Taking us inside the company, he shows us the communication that occurs between Cordpatch and Language-Crossing, a translation company hired to translate the manual for the heart patch. Maylath explicates the translation procedure from product manufacturing to the users (heart surgeons), focusing on three dimensions that affect translation: (1) time, (2) quality, and (3) cost. Technical writers find themselves caught in "ethics of shortchanging quality for timely delivery at the expense of patients' lives." When instructions for product use can mean the difference between life and death, technical writers become the watchdogs of consumer safety. This case shows how such ethical concerns affect technical communication in a translation company.

In "Adapting to South American Communication Patterns: Odyssey's Proposal to Remedy Inconsistent Car Sales," Barry L. Thatcher focuses on the Odyssey Automobile Company, which has made its greatest penetration into the northern South American market in Ecuador. A decrease in automobile sales forces the company to challenge property tax laws that affect the cost of the car to the consumer. According to the law, the consumer pays an entire year's worth of property taxes regardless of the time of year in which he or she buys the car. The Ecuador Transit Company publishes a letter supporting and explaining suggested changes in the tax law. A technical writer at Odyssey translates the letter into English and, at the same time, decides to write a proposal to the Ecuadorian government arguing for a change in the tax law. The writer struggles with differences in audience expectations. Thatcher extends Hall's concepts of high-context and low-context cultures, paying particular attention to "the whirlpool approach" (solve the problem as quickly as possible despite the chaos such an approach generates) employed by many U.S. businesspeople.

Roger Baumgarte and Philippe Blanchard, in "Cultural Issues in Corporate Hierarchies: Keeping Your Distance Isn't That Simple," illustrate the concept of high and low proximity, which affect a technical translator's ability to manage a project team at a company in South American. Despite fluency in Spanish, the translator finds himself baffled by issues of hierarchy and authority as they relate to his ability to work closely with the documentation team. Using Hofstede's four typologies of (1) individual versus collective, (2) high- and low-uncertainty avoidance, (3) masculine and feminine approaches, and (4) power distance, Baumgarte and

Blanchard give students theories to frame and understand the problems facing this technical translator. This case works well as a way of comparing high- and low-context cultures with high- and low-proximity cultures.

In Thomas F. Lannin's "A Venture Between American Academe and Corporate Malaysia: The CyberUniversity Blues," a university professor of technical communication is hired as a consultant to develop a virtual university for a Malaysian company. Lannin details the history of the political, social, and communication styles of representatives of the company that brought the project to a halt.

Elizabeth M. Lynn, in "Human Error, Communication Failures, and the Sinking of the M/S *Estonia:* Recipe for Disaster," narrates the sinking of the *Estonia*. Departing from many historical narratives about this event, she focuses on the role of communication in risk management. She looks at problems of communication moving across multiple organizations and the minimization of actual risk levels, focusing on the company that owned the *Estonia*. We learn that the company's monopoly, demands to increase tourism, and worries over flaws in the ship's design were factors in the disaster. Lynn proposes that differences in what nations consider to be *communication* in terms of communication methods, types of messages, and language usage also added to the disaster.

In "Risk-Based Design in a Pipeline Engineering Project for Columbia: First Do No Harm," Linda Driskell and Frank Driskell take us into multinational petrochemical companies. Two companies collaborate on a project (one company handles the front-end design, the other handles the design detail) and attempt to develop a set of universal standards. In a land of guerilla warfare, kidnapping, and uncertainty, we discover differences in attitudes about technology, nature, and communication. Because of the complexity of this case, the authors have divided it into three parts, each of which includes questions for discussion and writing assignments.

Nancy L. Hoft, in "Communicating the Risks of Natural Hazards: The World-at-Large Is at Stake," focuses on risk communication, specifically volcanic hazard communication about the Santa María volcano in Guatemala, near the Venezuelan border. She shares her struggles to help the Guatemalan people by promoting extraordinary communication between the government and the people. She develops the concept of the *multiplicadore*—the person who spreads the word in a specific field of knowledge—and she discusses how *multiplicadores* develop in international scientific communities, developed nations, local governments and agencies, educational communities, and on the World Wide Web. The latter, she contends, will be the technological communication tool by which knowledge on risk communication will be generated and spread worldwide.

A Final Story

Several years ago, in an introductory course in technical communication, I assigned students to a group project and asked them to evaluate one another's level of responsibility to the project; it was a fairly common assignment in technical communication classes. When I read the individual evaluations, I noticed that two of the Vietnamese students and one Japanese student had given all groups members the highest scores. I knew, however, that two members of the two different groups were highly recalcitrant. Later, when I was able to speak discreetly with these Asian students, I asked about their responses. Each one indicated that he or she could never have confronted other students about their behavior or point out where group members fell short of expectations. Nor could either expound on his or her own valuable contributions to group efforts. Such comments would have been anathema in their cultures (Bosley, 1993).

Because of their responses, I was forced to confront my own lack of cultural sensitivity and my own ethnocentrism. I had merely assumed that all students carried with them the same model of standards for team and classroom behavior. I recognized that I was going to have to rethink each of my writing assignments in order to uncover my own cultural assumptions and to provide opportunities in class to discuss international issues that were affecting students and the classroom environment. That was the beginning of my journey of discovery into international communication patterns, in which I learned to respect them and, at times, use them.

I continue to be fascinated by communication complexities. I hope readers will find themselves looking at the world with a wider cultural lens and that they will experience ideas and examples that will make them better informed international technical communicators and, ideally, better people.

Additional Readings: Issues Relevant to the Introduction

Andrews, D. C. (Ed.) (1996), *International dimensions of technical communication.* Arlington, VA: Society for Technical Communication Press.

Bosley, D. S. (1993). Cross-cultural collaboration: Whose culture is it, anyway? *Technical Communication Quarterly, 2*(1), 51–62.

Boswood, T. S. (1999). Redefining the professional in international professional communication. In C. Lovitt with D. Goswami (Eds.), *Exploring the rhetoric of international professional communication: An agenda for teachers and researchers,* Amity, NY: Baywood, 11–138.

Geertz, C. (1973). *The interpretation of culture.* New York: Basic Books.

Gudykunst, W. B. & Kim, Y. Y. (1992). *Communicating with strangers: An approach to intercultural communication.* New York: McGraw-Hill.

Hall, E. T. (1959). *The silent language.* New York: Doubleday.

Hall, E. T. (1976). *Beyond culture.* New York: Anchor Press.

Hofstede, G. & Bond, M. (1984). Hofstede's cultural dimensions. *Journal of Cross-Cultural Psychology, 15,* 417–433.

Hoft, N. L. (1995). *International technical communication: How to export information about high technology.* New York: Wiley.

Keesing, R. (1974). Theories of culture. *Annual Review of Anthropology, 3,* 73–97.

Lovitt, C. with Goswami, D. (Eds.). (1999). *Exploring the rhetoric of international professional communication: An agenda for teachers and researchers.* Amity, NY: Baywood.

Chapter 1

A Visit to the Forbidden City:

A Sign of the Times

SAM DRAGGA
Texas Tech University

Abstract: On a visit to Beijing, China, a technical communicator offers to revise the English-language version of a sign at the Forbidden City that explains the significance of the historic site to foreign tourists. Initially, the job seems simple enough as he focuses on meeting the information needs of the designated audience. He soon realizes, however, that his revision ignores the genuine complexities of Chinese culture.

Note: The following case is fictitious. However, Figure 1.1 replicates a real sign previously on public display at the Forbidden City, and Figure 1.3 replicates a real sign exhibited today at this historic site.

Background for the Case

Thomas Wild is chief executive officer of Wild Solutions, Inc., in Seattle, Washington. Wild Solutions is a small company that employs five writers, a supervisor/editor, and two artists/designers. Wild started the company in 1990, after he graduated from the University of Washington with a bachelor's degree in psychology and a master's degree in technical communication. The company specializes in devising communication solutions for business organizations. More and more of the clients are multinational corporations.

Wild does a little international traveling, chiefly in Asia, soliciting business for his company and meeting with existing clients. He has been to India, Japan, and once to the People's Republic of China, specifically Shanghai.

In 1996, he visits Beijing. While in the capital city, at the urging of his client, Gu Baohui of Xinghua Computer Corporation, Wild decides to delay their business meeting a day while he visits a major attraction for millions of foreign tourists—the Forbidden City, once the imperial palace of the emperors of China. He enjoys his visit to this historic site, but like a good technical communicator, he notices that the sign explaining the museum to foreign visitors is defective and could be revised. On the left side of the gate to the palace is a wooden sign with painted Chinese characters. On the right side is a wooden sign with the painted English translation (see Figure 1.1). At least Wild assumes it is a translation: although he speaks a little Chinese (chiefly common greetings), Wild has a quite limited understanding of Chinese characters and has hired a local interpreter for his business negotiations.

Aside from the grammatical and spelling errors, Wild notices immediately that the English translation displays several hyphenation errors. Thus, at the end of a line, instead of dividing words between syllables, the sign divides words arbitrarily (e.g., "re/sidence" and "pala/ce"). In addition, the use of all uppercase letters makes the sign difficult to read. And the sign offers a lot of information that typical tourists might consider unnecessary, such as both the Chinese and English names for each of the buildings.

At a meeting with his client on the following day, Wild mentions how delighted he was with his visit to the Forbidden City. Mr. Gu is obviously pleased. In his limited English, he reveals that his sister, Zhou Peiya, is a supervisor at the museum. Mr. Gu also explains that the museum exhibits only a fraction of the available imperial treasures and, according to his sister, will soon be receiving major new funding from private and public sources. Wild confesses that he thought the English language signs could be revised and proposes that his company would be willing to do the writing as a donation to the museum. Mr. Gu declares that he will notify his sister of Wild's generous offer.

Revising the Sign

Later that afternoon, Ms. Zhou telephones Wild at his hotel and invites him to a meeting the next morning at the Forbidden City. On arrival at the palace, Wild receives a private guided tour of the facility from Ms. Zhou. He is ushered through buildings typically closed to the public—rooms of furniture, clothing, jewelry, porcelain, and mechanical toys. After the tour, Wild is guided to a lovely meeting room filled with exquisite paintings and embroideries. He is introduced to several museum officials and served tea. "The new sign must help tourists appreciate the treasures of Chinese civilization." Ms. Zhou explains. "Millions of people come every year. We have audiotapes in several languages and players. . . ."

Yes, I did the audio tour yesterday, Wild interrupts. "It's really good. Quite informative!"

Ms. Zhou smiles. "It was all that was possible with so little money."

"Oh, is that right?" commiserates Wild.

Ms. Zhou looks at the museum officials, looks at Wild, and smiles again. She proceeds, "We have domestic tourists and foreign tourists. The majority of the

THE PALACE MUSEUM

THE IMPERIAL PALACE, POPULARLY KNOWN AS THE FORBIDDEN CITY, WAS THE PERMANENT RE-SIDENCE OF THE EMPERORS OF THE MING AND QING DYNASTIES. BUILT IN 1406–1420, THE IMPERIAL PALACE HAS A HISTORY OF 560 YEARS. OCCUPYING AN AREA OF 720,000 SQUARE METRES WITH OVER 9000 ROOMS THE IMPERIAL PALACE IS THE LARGEST AND MOST COMPLETE GROUP OF ANCIENT BUILDINGS WHICH CHINA HAS PRE-SERVED TO THE PRESENT. IN 1961, THE IMPERIAL PALACE WAS LISTED BY THE STATE COUNCIL AS ONE OF THE IMPORTANT HISTORICAL MONUMENTS UNDER THE PROTECTION OF THE GOVERNMENT.

THE BUILDINGS OF THE IMPERIAL PALACE ARE DIVIDED INTO TWO PARTS. THE FRONT PART, OR THE OUTER COURT, CONSISTS OF THE THREE GREAT HALLS—TAI HE DIAN (HALL OF SUPREME HARMONY), ZHONG HE DIAN (HALL OF MIDDLE HARMONY), AND BAD HE DIAN (HALL OF PRE-SERVING HARMONY), WHERE THE EMPEROR HELD IMPORTANT CEREMONIES. THE REAR PART, OR THE INNER COURT, CONSISTS OF THE THREE REAR PALACES—QIAN QING GONG (PALACE OF HEAVENLY PURITY), JIAO TAI DIAN (HALL OF UNIION), KUN NING GONG (PALACE OF EARTHLY TRANQUILITY), YANG XIN DIAN (HALL OF MENTAL CULTIVATION), PLUS THE SIX EAST PALACES, THE SIX WEST PALACES AND YU HUA YUAN (IMPERIAL GARDEN), WHERE THE EMPEROR HANDLED ROUTINE AFFAIRS AND WHERE THE EMPEROR AND HIS EMPRESS AND CONCUBINES LIVED AND SPENT THEIR LEISURE HOURS. FROM MING TO QING DYNASTIES, A TOTAL OF 24 (14 MING AND 10 QING) EMPERORS LIVED HERE AND EXERCISED SUPREME FEUDAL AUTOCRATIC POWER OVER THE COUNTRY. THE QING DYNASTY WAS OVERTHROWN IN THE REVOLUTION OF 1911. IN 1914, THE MUSEUM OF ANTIQUITIES WAS HOUSED IN THE THREE GREAT HALLS OF OUTER COURT. IN 1925, THE WHOLE REAR PART OF THE PALACE WAS TURNED INTO THE PALACE MUSEUM. IN 1947, THE MUSEUM OF ANTIQUITIES WAS MERGED INTO THE PALACE MUSEUM.

SINCE THE FOUNDING OF THE PEOPLE'S REPUB- LIC OF CHINA IN 1949, NOT ONLY THE ANCIENT BUILDINGS HAVE BEEN REPAIRED, BUT ALSO A LARGE AMOUNT OF WORK IN THE ACQUISITION, AR-RANGEMENT, RESTORATION AND EXHIBITION OF CU-LTURAL RELICS HAS BEEN MADE. AT PRESENT, FOR DISPLAY SOME OF THE HALLS ARE KEPT AS THEY WERE ORIGINALLY FURNISHED, AND OTHERS ARE USED TO EXHIBIT SPECIAL COLLECTIONS: ANCIENT PAINTINGS, BRONZES, CERAMICS, ARTS AND CRAFTS, JEWELRY, CLOCKS AND WATCHES, ETC., WHICH SHOW THE SPLENDID ACHIEVEMENTS OF TRADITIONAL CHINESE CULTURE.

FIGURE 1.1   Original Sign at the Palace Museum

foreign tourists will speak or read English, so we have only two signs: Chinese for the Chinese and Japanese, and English for the Americans, Australians, Indians, Africans, and Europeans who visit. So the English sign is important," Ms. Zhou explains. "The people reading the English sign usually have little understanding of China."

"I will write you a good sign." Wild promises.

He exchanges business cards with the museum officials, adopting the Chinese practice of offering and receiving the cards with two hands.

On returning to Seattle, Wild immediately starts to read about the Forbidden City, quickly finishing several books, and to write a new sign. After a couple of weeks of sporadic writing and editing six different drafts, he produces a version he considers satisfactory (see Figure 1.2).

He e-mails his version of the new sign to Ms. Zhou.

She replies quickly. "The new sign arrived today. My colleagues and I are pleased to receive it. We appreciate your generous gift."

Two weeks later, Wild e-mails again to ask Ms. Zhou if she has questions about the new sign.

"It is not so long," she notes.

The Palace Museum

Built in 1406–1420, the Imperial Palace, popularly known as the Forbidden City, was the permanent residence of the emperors of the Ming and Qing dynasties. Its buildings are divided into two parts. The front part, or the "outer court," consists of the Hall of Supreme Harmony, Hall of Middle Harmony, Hall of Preserving Harmony, which are taken as its main body. The rear part, or the "inner court," consists of the Palace of Heavenly Purity, Hall of Union, Palace of Earthly Tranquility, Hall of Mental Cultivation plus the six east palaces, the six west palaces and the Imperial Garden, where the emperor handled routine affairs and he with his empress and concubines lived or spent their leisure hours. A total of 24 Ming and Qing emperors lived here.

Since the founding of the People's Republic of China in 1949, not only the palace buildings have been repaired, but also a vast amount of work has been performed on the arrangement, restoration, collection and exhibition of precious cultural relics. Today, some of the halls or palaces are kept as they were originally furnished, and the others are used to exhibit special art treasures of the Chinese nation, such as jewelry, ancient paintings, bronzes, ceramics, and clocks and watches.

The Imperial Palace is the largest and most complete group of ancient buildings that China has preserved to the present. It embodies the fine tradition and national style of ancient Chinese architectural art.

FIGURE 1.2   Proposed Revision to the Sign

"Yes," Wild explains. "I focused on the essential information. That will make hurried tourists more likely to read the sign."

She also questions the use of lowercase letters.

"It's easier to read this way," Wild explains. "The similar size and shape of uppercase letters makes it difficult for readers to distinguish one letter from the next."

"We'll consider this important change," Ms. Zhou replies.

"I am so pleased you like it," answers Wild. "I was working on the revision day and night and keeping my usual clients waiting."

Wild is initially pleased with his effort. But the newly hired editor at Wild Solutions, Sylvia Jiang, a technical communication graduate from Miami University and the granddaughter of Chinese immigrants, thinks that Wild's version sacrifices a clear sense of the culture for readability. "You've eliminated the Chinese voice, the Chinese feeling of the original sign," she claims. "It's more American and less Chinese. I don't think they'll like it."

Wild is encouraged, however, because three months later, Ms. Zhou e-mails again to notify Wild that new signs will soon be installed at the Forbidden City.

On a business trip to Beijing later that year, Wild stops again at the Forbidden City. His visit is chiefly to see the new sign, but he is also meeting with Ms. Zhou to raise the possibility of his writing additional materials for the museum—brochures, funding proposals, and fliers for special exhibits.

On seeing the sign, Wild is simultaneously disappointed and irritated. The sign is substantially as he revised it, but previously deleted information has been reinserted and Chinese names have been substituted for the English names of buildings. It also uses all uppercase letters and includes obvious errors in spelling, punctuation, and grammar (see Figure 1.3). And though the original sign was painted wood, the new sign is engraved bronze; it is unlikely to be revised again soon. He sighs.

Wild has a meeting with Ms. Zhou in five minutes. He is unsure of how to approach this meeting. He thought the museum officials liked his revised version of the sign, but obviously he was wrong.

Background for Analysis

If he is to develop a solid working relationship with his Beijing clients, Wild must achieve a better understanding of the cultural differences dividing China and America, especially regarding the ethics and etiquette of social and business relationships. For example, unlike the United States with its Judeo-Christian heritage, China adopts a chiefly Confucian perspective on ethics. According to Confucius, the ethical individual develops and exercises virtues such as goodness *(ren)*, wisdom *(zhi)*, righteousness *(yi)*, and trustworthiness *(xin)*.

Goodness is not doing to others what you would not want done to yourself, but goodness to others is usually offered according to the goodness you have received. Instead of treating all people equally, therefore, you give family and friends special privileges. It is especially important to be polite so that nobody is embarrassed or

THE PALACE MUSEUM

BUILT IN 1406–1420, THE IMPERIAL PALACE, POPULARLY KNOWN AS THE FORBIDDEN CITY, WAS THE PERMANENT RESIDENCE OF THE EMPERORS OF THE MING AND QING DYNASTIES. ITS BUILDINGS ARE DIVIDED INTO TWO PARTS. THE FRONT PART, OR THE "OUTER COURT", CONSISTS OF TAI HE DIAN HALL, ZHONG HE DIAN HALL AND BAO HE DIAN HALL, WHICH ARE TAKEN AS ITS MAIN BODY, PLUS WEN HUA DIAN HALL AND WU YING DIAN HALL, WHICH ARE TAKEN AS ITS TWO WINGS, WHERE THE EMPEROR HELD IMPORTANT CEREMONIES. THE REAR PART, OR THE "INNER COURT", CONSISTS OF QIAN QING GONG PALACE, JAO TAI DIAN HALL, KUN NING GONG PALACE, YANG XIN DIAN HALL PLUS THE SIX EAST PALACES, THE SIX WEST PALACES AND YUHUA YUAN GARDEN, WHERE THE EMPEROR HANDLED ROUTINE AFFAIRS AND HE WITH HIS EMPRESS AND CONCUBINES LIVED OR SPENT THEIR LEISURE HOURS.

THE IMPERIAL PLACE IS THE LARGEST AND MOST COMPLETE GROUP OF ANCIENT BUILDINGS WHICH CHINA HAS PRESERVED TO THE PRESENT. IT EMBODIES THE FINE TRADITION AND NATIONAL STYLE OF ANCIENT CHINESE ARCHITECTURAL ART. IN 1961 THE IMPERIAL PALACE WAS LISTED BY THE STATE COUNCIL AS ONE OF "THE IMPORTANT HISTORICAL MONUMENTS UNDER THE PROTECTION OF THE GOVERNMENT", AND, IN 1987, IT WAS AFFIRMED BY THE UNESCO AS "THE WORLD HERITAGE".

FROM MING TO QING DYNASTIES, A TOTAL OF 24 EMPERORS LIVED HERE. THE QING DYNASTY WAS OVERTHROWN IN THE REVOLUTION OF 1911 FROM THEN ON, AS THE FEUDAL IMPERIAL PALACE, THE FORBIDDEN CITY COMPLETED ITS HISTORICAL MISSION. IN 1914, THE MUSEUM OF ANTIQUITIES WAS HOUSED IN THE OUTER COURT. IN 1925, THE PALACE MUSEUM WAS ESTABLISHED.

SINCE THE FOUNDING OF THE PEOPLE'S REPUBLIC OF CHINA IN 1949 NOT ONLY THE PALACE BUILDINGS HAVE BEEN REPAIRED, BUT ALSO A VAST AMOUNT OF WORK ON THE ARRANGEMENT, RESTORATION, COLLECTION AND EXHIBITION OF PRECIOUS CULTURAL RELICS HAS BEEN MADE. TODAY, SOME OF THE HALLS OR PALACES ARE KEPT AS THEY WERE ORIGINALLY FURNISHED, THE OTHERS ARE USED TO EXHIBIT SPECIAL ART TREASURES, SUCH AS JEWELLERY, ANCIENT PAINTINGS, BRONZES, CERAMICS, ARTS AND CRAFTS, CLOCKS AND WATCHES, ETC, WHICH SHOW THE AGE-OLD AND SPLENDID HISTORICAL CIVILIZATION OF THE CHINESE NATION.

FIGURE 1.3   Revised Sign

humiliated. If you give a gift, for example, the recipient will thank you, but ordinarily won't open it in your presence. If the recipient dislikes the gift or considers it too much or too little, she or her might be embarrassed or you might be embarrassed. If the recipient really likes the gift, she or he will thank you again later.

Because Wild was introduced to Ms. Zhou by a family member, the resulting business association is special. It is a personal relationship of reciprocal obligations linking Mr. Gu, Ms. Zhou, and Wild. By offering a gift, Wild solidifies that important relationship. Wild's e-mail, however, essentially asks Ms. Zhou to unwrap the gift publicly and later calls attention to the cost of the gift (i.e., "I was working on the revision day and night and keeping my usual clients waiting.").

The virtue of wisdom is acquired chiefly through schooling, not from experience. Most critical is knowledge of people because human behavior is the chief variable in life. Study of the humanities, as a consequence, is considered superior to study of science or technology. Wild's graduate education might be the important credential that encourages Mr. Gu to hire Wild and to introduce Wild to his sister. Technical communication as a discipline, however, is relatively new in the People's Republic of China; writers of signs would ordinarily be trained in history or literature. Wild's revision focuses chiefly on the mechanical issues of display as opposed to clarification or elaboration of the information itself.

Righteousness is trying to be as good a man or woman as possible without looking for praise or glory. If you are ethical, therefore, you always speak and act with modesty about your accomplishments. For example, you must be unassuming about a gift you give, regardless of the price, and claim that it is nothing—a trifle. In receiving compliments, similarly, you must always be modest. If a dinner guest, for example, said he or she liked a dish you served, you would tell the guest "I'm afraid that it is not so good," or "I am still learning how to prepare this dish properly," because the receipt of such praise must never be the object of having guests to dinner. You have guests because sharing food with friends is itself a good thing to do and solidifies the friendship. If the guest really liked your dinner, however, he would dismiss your objections and reinforce the compliment: "No, no, the dinner is delicious. It is cooked just right." Wild, however, never denies the compliments he receives. Though he compliments the audio tour of the Forbidden City, once that compliment is denied by Ms. Zhou, he never reinforces it. As indicated earlier, he also emphasizes to Ms. Zhou the cost of the gift he has given.

Trustworthiness is matching your words with your deeds. The ethical individual never makes claims or promises until a deed is already or almost accomplished. Wild, however, almost immediately promises to deliver a good sign. If he disappoints, his reputation is damaged.

While more and more Chinese people are adopting new ideas and developing new habits, the majority nevertheless honor the traditional ways. The ancient ideals of Confucius still dominate their daily lives.

It is important to realize, however, that as Westerners such as Wild try to adapt themselves to Chinese perspectives and practices, Chinese officials such as Mr. Gu and Ms. Zhou are trying to adapt themselves to Western attitudes and behaviors. Communicating effectively and ethically through the multiple filters of differing expectations is a continuous challenge for both sides.

Questions for Discussion

1. Why did the museum officials modify Wild's revision of the sign? Does his sign omit information that the Chinese would like tourists to know about this historic site? By omitting the Chinese names for the various buildings, for example, is he implying that the Chinese names are unimportant or that the English names are the real names? Why did Ms. Zhou never inform Wild of the changes?

2. Should Wild question Ms. Zhou about this misunderstanding? If so, how does he raise the issue without humiliating either himself or Ms. Zhou? If not, how will he avoid making similar mistakes on subsequent projects?

3. How damaged is Wild's credibility with Ms. Zhou? How damaged is his credibility with Mr. Gu? How does Wild restore his credibility?

4. Should Wild speak to Ms. Zhou about the problems he has noticed with the new sign? Why? If he doesn't, what should he do? If he does, which of the following should be the focus of their discussion?

   - The use of all uppercase letters
   - The spelling error
   - The punctuation error
   - The grammatical errors
   - The newly inserted information
   - The issue of cultural integrity versus readability
   - All of the above.

5. What additional revisions could Wild have made to the original sign to make it more readable and accessible to tourists? To make it more acceptable to the museum officials? What information, if any, could he have deleted? What information, if any, could he have added? How could he improve the organization, style, or design?

6. Are Jiang's objections to Wild's revision valid? Is Wild sacrificing cultural integrity for readability? Does his revision conceal the complexity of Chinese culture? Will tourists reading his sign come away with a genuine appreciation of the cultural differences or the incorrect impression that all cultures are basically similar? By making his sign easy to read, is he conveying the message that China is easy to understand? By Americanizing his sign, is he also Americanizing the Forbidden City?

7. How would Jiang revise the original sign? Is she sacrificing readability for cultural integrity?

8. Is it ethical for Wild to compose and design a sign that is fully adapted to tourists? Will tourists thus receive a diminished sense of the culture and derive a false impression of universality? Or is it ethical for Wild to compose and design a sign that incorporates the rhetorical practices of Chinese culture? While doing so might be difficult or distracting for tourists, does it provide a compensating accuracy in their understanding and appreciation of cultural differences? In short, should the technical communicator try to represent the interests of the tourists (the readers) or the local culture (the writers)? Should such international communication be reader-based or writer-based?

9. What additional revisions could be made to the revised sign to make it more readable and accessible but still preserve a sense of the Chinese culture? Is it possible to achieve

such a balance? What information, if any, would you delete? What information, if any, would you insert? How would you improve the organization, style, or design?

Writing Assignment

Compose a three-page memo to Ms. Zhou from Wild, proposing the additional materials he would like to design for the museum. In this memo, restore Wild's credibility and demonstrate the better understanding he has developed of Chinese ethics and etiquette.

Additional Reading: Issues Relevant to the Case

Alston, J. P., & Yongxin, H. (1997). *Business guide to modern China.* East Lansing; MI: Michigan State University Press.

DeMente, B. L. (1989). *Chinese etiquette and ethics in business.* Lincolnwood; IL: NTC.

Confucius (1979). *The analects.* (D. C. Lau, Trans.). New York: Penguin.

Confucius. (1997). *The analects of Confucius: Lun Yu.* (C. Huang, Trans.). New York: Oxford University Press.

Huang, Q., Andrulis, R. S., & Chen, T. (1994). *A guide to successful business relations with the Chinese: Opening the Great Wall's gate.* New York: International Business Press.

Irwin, H. (1996). *Communicating with Asia: Understanding people and customs.* St. Leonards, Australia: Allen & Unwin.

Kam, L. (1980). *Critiques of Confucius in contemporary China.* Hong Kong: Chinese University of Hong Kong Press.

Tung, R. L. (1996). Managing in Asia: Cross-cultural dimensions. In P. Joynt & M. Warner (Eds.), *Managing across cultures: Issues and perspectives* (pp. 233–245). London: International Thomson Business Press.

Tu, W. (1990). The Confucian tradition in Chinese history. In P. S. Ropp (Ed.), *Heritage of China: Contemporary perspectives on Chinese civilization* (pp. 112–137). Berkeley: University of California Press.

Yum, J. O. (1998). The impact of Confucianism on interpersonal relationships and communication patterns in East Asia. *Communication Monographs, 55,* 374–388.

Chapter *2*

Multilevel Challenges for Technical Documentation

Encountering Chinese Culture

CRAIG J. HANSEN
Metropolitan State University

Abstract: This case presents a technical communicator who encounters Chinese culture for the first time. As a result of a business partnership, she must negotiate a combined set of manuals and other product documentation. Her management also asks her to edit an important document from their Taiwanese partner. Both tasks present unfamiliar challenges. Some are rooted in language and translation. But the more difficult originate from significant cultural differences that include issues of politeness, hierarchy, rhetoric, and even writing systems. The case raises several key questions: How does a technical communicator balance the expectations of different cultures? How can a technical communicator be successful in this type of international collaboration? And, more specifically, what should a technical communicator know about Chinese culture to develop and maintain effective working relationships?

Note: This case is based on experience and documents gathered from years of work with Chinese students and businesses. It should not be construed to represent Chinese culture and business practice in any absolute sense, as they are highly diverse. Rather, it is designed to be illustrative, to introduce some of the more common challenges and rewards that a technical communicator might encounter in working with Chinese culture counterparts.

Background for the Case

Evans Vacuum Modules (EVM) Corporation, located in the midwestern United States, produces computerized control systems for manufacturing equipment. The company has done very well in U.S. markets for more than thirty years and, in the last decade, has been reasonably successful in marketing its products in Europe. For some time, top management has eyed the lucrative Pacific Rim market. However, attempts to market products in Japan, Taiwan, and Malaysia have not met expectations. Management has decided to try a different approach.

EVM has established a preliminary agreement with Star Technical Products Manufacturing (STPM), headquartered in Taipei, Taiwan. STPM has agreed to purchase manufacturing control products from EVM, combine them with some of their own products, and market them in the Pacific Rim. Management in both corporations see advantages in the relationship, though some details remain unresolved.

Sonya Josephs is a senior technical writer in the Information Services Department at EVM. Sonya works closely with the company's development and marketing organizations to produce some of EVM's product documentation. She also develops technical sales and promotional material for one of EVM's product lines (since EVM does not develop products for the general consumer market, all of its customers are, in a sense, technical). Sonya reports to Mary Karras, the Director of Information Services.

"Have I got something interesting for you," Mary tells Sonya, handing her a stack of papers. After explaining the new relationship between STPM and EVM, she adds, "What I would like you to do is work with the publications people in Taiwan to come up with a combined operations manual, one that integrates our operations processes with theirs. And probably some new, joint promotional material, too. I'd like to see your proposal for the joint documentation in, oh, three weeks or so. One other thing: STPM sent us a business plan. Randy upstairs thought it could use a little editing before he presented it to the board. Could you look it over for him?"

The Business Plan

That afternoon, Sonya receives the business plan. In preparation, she has looked over two business plans prepared by EVM and has glanced at a technical communication textbook. She believes she has some idea about the form and expectations for the document. The plan in front of her now looks professional—nicely bound, and good paper, with sharp graphics. She scans the table of contents:

Executive Summary
Chapter One: Introduction
Chapter Two: Reviews of Research and Data—SWOT
Chapter Three: Chances for Current Expectations

Chapter Four: STPM's Plan to Meet Taiwan's and EVM's Needs in the Twenty-First Century

Chapter Five: Summary and Conclusions

Appendix: Sources of Data

Sonya finds some of the chapter titles a little surprising. She opens the plan and samples a few pages:

From the Executive Summary
"People think there is demand for combined, coordinated product line in the aspect of manufacturing control systems."

From Chapter Two
"The trend to competitiveness in computerized control is fostered by the forces of economics, demand, which is epitomized by the multinational corporation entry into global marketplace and sources of advantage garnered from efficiencies of manufacturing, and supply, in which the same multinational entry introduces many product systems of similar form. In which follows the Strength, Weakness, Opportunity, Threat analysis of the proposed business cooperation . . . "

From Chapter Four
"Our country and company are now turning point. As we look for the future in areas such as Taiwan, Singapore, etc., we hope a plan which can do justice to the manufacturing control market and embrace positive impact on competition."

As Sonya reads, she registers the surface errors—dropped articles or verb endings, some strained or erroneous grammar. These can be fixed. However, what she finds more troublesome, daunting even, is that the meaning of whole passages seems to float just out of her reach. She isn't sure she can edit the text because she isn't always sure what it means to communicate.

Negotiating a Joint Documentation Plan

A few days later, Sonya finds herself in Taipei. It has been a long trip, and she arrives late at night and exhausted. She is met at the airport by two pleasant STPM employees, both of whom speak excellent English. On the way to the hotel, Sonya is briefed on the schedule for her four-day visit. At 8 A.M. sharp the next morning, the STPM employees pick her up at the hotel and bring her to company headquarters in the outskirts of Taipei. Sonya comments on what she sees as they drive, and the employees eagerly provide information about their city.

STPM headquarters is a large, impressive building. Sonya is hurried to to a conference room on the top floor, where nearly a dozen people are waiting. They briefly applaud when she enters the room. There is a quick exchange of business cards, and tea is served. One of her escorts acts as translator:

"We are so happy that you have come to Taiwan. Our vice president of development would like to thank you with this very small gift." A distinguished-looking man rises and hands Sonya a heavy box wrapped in red paper. Sonya is unsure what to do: Open it? Carry it? She is very conscious that she has no gift to return.

Her translator continues, "I would now like to introduce you to some of the people whom you will work with during your visit." Sonya is quickly confused by a flurry of unfamiliar names. Eventually, two people rise, one man and one woman.

Ming Te Wang is the supervisor of publications. "You will spend much of your time in his area. Neiling Dai works in his area and will help you." Ming Te introduces himself as Roger, Neiling as Alice.

"Now we would like to take you on a tour of STPM," Roger (Ming Te) continues.

What follows is a tour not just of the headquarters building but, after several long car rides, of three manufacturing facilities. Along the way, her escorts stop at places of interest: a museum, a Chinese opera school, an arts center. It is late-afternoon when the tours are over. Her escorts return Sonya to her hotel and announce they will be back in an hour to take her to a banquet.

The next morning, Alice picks Sonya up at the hotel, drives her to headquarters, and takes her to the publications area. Once again, there is a gathering of people, tea, introductions, another gift, and another tour—this time of the publications' area, which includes not only writers and illustrators but a complete print shop. Sonya begins to wonder if she will ever get to the work she is supposed to do.

Finally, Roger and Alice invite Sonya to join them in a conference room. Spread across the table are samples of STPM documents. Sonya sees brightly colored brochures (one features a picture of STPM headquarters backed by a particularly vivid rainbow), technical reference materials, and what appear to be operations manuals. She picks one of these up. She feels a sense of relief as she pages through it. It is clearly an operations manual, and the look of it is familiar. It features crisp line drawings of machinery, clear labeling of parts, and direction arrows to help illustrate process.

She also notices differences. Each page is divided into six panels. In each panel is a fairly small illustration and brief text (in both Chinese and English). Sonya is not clear on the order of the overall procedure—do the panels read left to right, or top to bottom? Numbered steps appear in each panel. Still, Sonya is pleased; she had no clear expectation, but she envisioned far greater difference than what she is seeing. She quickly imagines how this format could blend with EVMs. She visualizes a hybrid style—perhaps keep the panels but clearly number them (or maybe reduce the page size and put one panel on each page); keep the line drawings, but maybe supplement them with photos. Clarify the English—make it parallel and consistent and use imperative sentences. She will leave the Chinese up to them.

She smiles at Roger and Alice. This will be a piece of cake, she says. Roger's own smile dims for a second, and he says, "I don't understand."

Alice, too, looks surprised. She says, "May we see the documents you have brought with you?"

Sonya has the feeling she has done something wrong, but quickly retrieves her samples—operations manuals, technical brochures, and data sheets.

Alice looks them over. "We could never hope to do so well," she says.

"Yes," agrees Roger. "These are so very, very good."

Encouraged, Sonya quickly outlines her idea for merging formats. While she emphasizes some the advantages of EVMs' approach to operation manuals, she is careful to note that lots of details need to be worked out and that she is open to other opinions.

"Yes, yes," Roger says, "very good ideas. Why don't you and Alice talk about it?"

Alice and Sonya spend the better part of two days working out the details for Sonya's plan. Sonya notices that Alice defers to her frequently, but Sonya is pleased with the rapid, smooth progress. They plan a pilot project, melding their operations procedures for the first of the combined EVM/STPM products. After more thought, Sonya advocates a three-column page instead of panels, with line drawings (two or three on each page, depending on the complexity of the operation) taking up two columns of space and instructions, the third. They agree that Sonya will forward mock-up drawings and finished text to STPM, where Alice's illustrators will render the final drawings. Further, Alice's group will produce a very limited run of the first combined manual for review and approvals.

Back in the United States, Sonya tells her supervisor about her successful trip. She produces the text and drawings that are her responsibility, sends them to STPM, and eagerly awaits the first combined draft.

Some weeks later, she receives the draft. She opens the manual to find six panels per page, in the exact format she had seen in the STPM manuals. Her text is where it should be and her drawings have been expertly rendered, but this is definitely not her concept for combining the manuals.

Background for Analysis

In terms of the business plan, Sonya is faced with a multilevel challenge. Not only are there significant differences in the English and Chinese languages, but the cultural expectations that surround a document like a business plan are also widely divergent. In terms of language, the transition from a nonalphabetic language like Chinese to English is very difficult. Some errors are almost unavoidable, especially those concerning punctuation, use of articles (e.g., *a, an, the*), and inflected endings (like the -ed that indicates past tense). These and other features of English have no clear counterparts in written Chinese.

In terms of style, English speakers value direct, succinct writing in business and technical communication. Chinese culture, on the other hand, favors a less direct style of expression, one characterized by analogy, proverbs, double meanings, and, to Western eyes, an exaggerated politeness. It places more emphasis on the interpretive powers of the reader than on the writer's efforts toward explicitness and clarity. Written Chinese conveys reader-responsible messages efficiently; a few Chinese characters in combination can express ideas of richly layered meaning. (In fact, Chinese text translated into English almost always becomes substantially longer.)

Chinese communicators also may perceive argumentation and logic differently than Western readers and writers. Western audiences want directly stated main ideas supported by data. Chinese communicators may present the data first and then present an idea drawn from it—or leave interpretation up to the audience. Further, what makes up data or evidence can be understood differently by Chinese and Western audiences. For some Chinese audiences, an idea or plan might be good because it furthers harmony among participants; a company may be a good business partner because it is loyal; a product may be a good choice because people like it.

Cultural differences that are separate from professional communication strategies also affect technical communicators, as evidenced by the pilot documents that resulted from Sonya's trip to Taiwan. Sonya spent hours with Alice working out the details of the joint documentation plan. Why did Alice and Roger use their format and ignore all her work? Several types of cultural misunderstanding probably contributed to this result.

The Slow Start

Sonya grew impatient with how long it took to actually get to work. There were introductions, tours, tea, gifts, and banquets. None of these fit with her experience in an American corporation. By the time she finally met with Roger and Alice, Sonya was becoming impatient and ready to get things done. She did not want to return to EVM without a clear direction for the joint documentation effort. However, to the STPM employees, Sonya's trip had a somewhat different meaning. First, they were very conscious of the delicacy of a joint effort between the two companies. Not sure about the structure of EVM or, for that matter, the relative status of Sonya and her projects, they treated her as an honored guest—a practice with deep roots in Chinese culture and a standard business practice. Second, they assumed she would desire what they would desire—that is, to know something about the company and the people with whom she was dealing: hence the careful introductions and the tours. They also felt it was important for her to experience something of their culture: thus, part of her work time was given to tourist trips and elaborate meals.

Standards of Politeness

Once she did get to work, Sonya made a number of errors that also contributed to her frustrated expectations. Following Roger's and Alice's praise of EVM's documentation, politeness demanded that she compliment their work as they complimented hers. Similarly, Chinese ideas of politeness demanded that she move slowly and carefully in offering her ideas for the joint documentation. Instead, her "take charge" actions fit some of the commonly held Chinese stereotypes of Americans as abrupt, pushy, and rude. The support Roger and Alice exhibited for Sonya's ideas was meant to comfort her, to help her maintain "face" as she dealt with an unfamiliar organization. The actions did not mean that Roger and Alice necessarily agreed with Sonya's opinions. To directly disagree with Sonya would have been rude.

Issues of Hierarchy

Sonya assumed that meeting with Alice meant that she had the warrant to develop a plan that both departments would follow. In fact, there was no such agreement about procedure. Sonya needed to be sensitive to hierarchy at STPM. Alice, though a senior member of staff and in many ways equivalent to Sonya's own supervisor, was not the final decision maker. Roger, the final decision-maker, did not work with Sonya and simply accepted the plan when it was presented to him by Alice as a recommendation. Roger chose to follow the format with which he was familiar.

Questions for Discussion

1. Translation is not easy. The translator faces difficult choices. To translate Chinese into English word-for-word does not work well at best; at worst, it produces unintelligible "word soup." A translation that keeps the spirit of Chinese expression but renders it more grammatically correct can also be problematic. Why? What considerations are involved if the translator chooses to do a loose translation, essentially rewriting the document for a different audience? What kind of translation happened with the business plan? What do you think would be the best kind of translation, given this situation? Who is the primary audience for this particular business plan? What are their needs and expectations? Who is responsible to see that those needs are met?

2. Common misconceptions about the nature of writing and editing play a role in the production of the business plan. Explain.

3. What role do power and hierarchy have here? How should Sonya proceed as editor of the business plan? What problems does she face, and from whom? What are her alternatives? How can she succeed in this situation?

4. Does Sonya face any ethical problems with the business plan? Gift-giving is important in many Asian cultures. If, like Sonya, one does not have a return gift (the expected behavior), what should the person do?

5. The arrangement of panels and illustrations in STPM's documentation may have cultural roots. What could Sonya have done to better understand the reasons behind this format?

6. Sonya noticed inconsistent use of imperative mood in the Chinese documentation. Why might that be? How could Sonya accommodate those concerns in her documentation plan?

7. What issues beside cultural differences could have contributed to the misunderstanding about the design of the documentation?

Writing Assignments

1. Review the section on background for analysis and at least one of the suggested readings listed below (or a similar relevant reading). In a brief essay, explain what was the root cause of the misunderstanding.

2. How could Sonya have acted differently to help ensure a shared understanding of the goals and procedures for the project? Sonya hears that STPM will send Alice to visit EVM to continue work on the joint documentation project. In a brief essay, discuss the following:

   • How might Sonya structure Alice's visit?
   • How might Sonya address the misunderstanding over the first pilot manual?
   • How might Sonya try to minimize any misunderstandings in this visit and in subsequent collaboration?

Additional Readings: Issues Relevant to the Case

Beamer, L. (1994). Teaching English business writing to Chinese-speaking business students. *The Bulletin of the Association of Business Communication, 7*(1), 13–18.

Kincaid, D. L. (Ed.). (1987). *Communication theory: Eastern and western perspectives.* San Diego: Academic Press.

Ling, C. (1997). How we know what we know about Americans: Chinese sojourners account for their experiences. In A. Gonzalez, M. Houston, & V. Chen, *Our voices: Essays in culture, ethnicity, and communication* (pp. 177–186). Los Angeles: Roxbury.

Yum, J. O. (1994). The impact of Confucianism on interpersonal relationships and communication patterns in East Asia. In L. Samovar & R. Porter (Eds.), *Intercultural communication: A reader* (pp. 75–86). Belmont, CA: Wadsworth.

Chapter *3*

High-Context and Low-Context Cultures
How Much Communication is Too Much?

EMILY A. THRUSH
University of Memphis

Abstract: This case study looks at the anthropological concept of high- and low-context cultures as it applies to business negotiations. It describes a series of incidents that occurred when Americans signed up for a summer program in the Czech Republic. The American representing the program was caught between the expectations of the low-context Americans for information and written documents and the assumptions of the high-context Czechs based on their normal business practices. The case study shows that mere knowledge of the differences in culture does not always ease the strain of negotiations or decrease the level of frustration felt by the participants.

Note: While the situation described below actually happened, the names of the individuals involved have been changed. Also, the documents represent a compilation from several people over the seven years of history of this agreement.

Background for the Case

The University of West Bohemia (UWB), in Pilsen, Czech Republic, holds a Summer Institute in languages each year, with classes in Czech, Russian, German, and French. In 1990, a faculty member from the University of Memphis (UOM) in

Tennessee started an English track as part of this Summer Institute. While the majority of students who study in the Institute are Czech, others come from all over Europe and, occasionally, Asia. Students from outside the Czech Republic are important to UWB because they pay in hard currencies and are charged more for classes as well as room and board in the dormitory. Their fees support the program for the Czech students, who can't afford to pay very much. The average monthly salary in the Czech Republic is around $200.

As part of the English track, the University of Memphis offers two courses in Teaching English as a Foreign Language (TEFL). Students in TEFL program pay the same fees as the language students, but they spend three hours every morning learning the methodology of teaching. In the afternoons, they take a class in the Czech language, then teach two hours of English conversation to students from around the world. This program has been popular because it gives prospective teachers experience teaching English in an environment where English is not the primary language. It also gives them credentials in the teaching of English. Participants in the TEFL program often go on to teach at schools and universities in many parts of the world.

The agreement between the University of West Bohemia and the University of Memphis is important to both schools. UWB supplies a wonderful experience to the Americans in living and working overseas, while UOM provides teachers for many of the English classes in the Summer Institute—teachers who actually pay for the privilege of teaching. In 1993, the rector (head) of UWB visited Memphis and signed a formal agreement of cooperation between the two schools.

The Situation

In 1994, the director of the Summer Language Institute decided to advertise the TEFL program in the United States to capitalize on American's interest in former Eastern Bloc countries that had opened up for tourism and business. He hoped to attract other prospective English teachers from around the United States to join those from Memphis.

Since communication is still difficult between Central Europe and the United States, a faculty member at the University of Memphis agreed to be the contact point for people who wanted more information about the program. This representative, Helen Cornwall, was to respond to initial queries resulting from the ads by sending a brochure about the program. The brochure included an application form that asked applicants to indicate which area of the institute they wanted to attend (Czech, Russian, French, English, or TEFL) and housing preferences, in case they wanted to designate a suite mate or request placement on the nonsmoking floor. Part of the brochure is reproduced in Figure 3.1.

The dates of the Institute that year were July 7–August 5. The brochure included the information that participants would be met at the airport in Prague on July 5 and taken to Pilsen by bus. All flights from the United States land at the Prague airport before 2:00 in the afternoon. Participants were told to plan to arrive

Area of Study: Czech
(Circle one)
                   Russian

                   French

                   English

                   Teaching English as a Foreign Language

Housing will be provided in a University dormitory. Participants will have private rooms, but will share a bathroom with a suite mate.

Do you have a preferred suite mate?
If so, write their name here _____

Do you prefer a non-smoking floor?   _____ yes   _____ no

$650 program fee includes housing, 3 meals a day in the cafeteria, and 2 bus trips a week to various sights around the Czech Republic. You may pay with dollars, Czech crowns, or travelers' checks on arrival.

PLEASE DO NOT SEND MONEY IN ADVANCE!

We cannot process American checks.

FIGURE 3.1   Section of Application for the Summer Institute

on July 5 or, if they wanted to spend a few days in Prague before the Institute started, to meet the group at the Prague airport by 3:00. P.M.

Helen Cornwall received many requests for the brochure. The ad had her school address and phone number on it as well as her e-mail address. She was in touch with the people in Pilsen who run the Institute mostly by e-mail. She would send e-mail to the English-speaking director of the English program, who would contact the Czech-speaking officials at the university. Phone contact was difficult because of the time and language differences and the cost. Mail into and out of the Czech Republic was still slow and somewhat unreliable. Neither Helen nor the officials at UWB had easy access to a fax machine at that time.

Problems Arise

In April, Helen received a phone call at her office. It was Madeleine Hartwell, a teacher in Indiana who had requested one of the brochures. Madeleine told Helen that she had sent her application for the Summer Institute TEFL program to the Czech Republic, but had not received a response. Helen said she was sure there was no problem. She told Madeleine about the communication difficulties and explained that the Czech officials were probably not sending any mail because of the expense. Madeleine was concerned, so Helen promised to e-mail her contact in Pilsen to check on the status of Madeleine's application. She did so the next day. In response, the director sent a list of all the people who had sent applications and who were expected for the Institute that summer. Madeleine's name was among them. Helen notified Madeleine that her application had been received and a place was reserved for her.

Over the next month, Helen received several more calls from people who were worried about what had happened to their applications. In each case, Helen was able to assure them that they were on the list sent from Pilsen and that there should be no problems. With each caller, she discussed travel arrangements and made sure the individual planned to be at the Prague airport on July 5.

The Phone Call

On May 6, Helen was surprised to get a phone call at home at 10:30 P.M. It was Madeleine Hartwell. The following conversation ensued:

MH: "This is Madeleine Hartwell. I talked to you last month about my application to the program in Pilsen."

HC: "Yes, I remember. Have you changed your plans?"

MH: "No, but I still haven't gotten anything from the university."

HC: "I don't think they're sending anything. It's too expensive for them to send mail to the United States."

MH: "But I have plane tickets reserved, and my travel agents says I have to pay for them this week or lose my reservation. Are you sure it's all right?"

HC: "Yes. As I told you, I got a list from them by e-mail with the names of all the Americans who are going to the program. Your name was on it."

MH: "So you're sure I've been accepted?"

HC: "Yes. There's no reason why you wouldn't be. They need as many people to participate in the TEFL program as possible. You have a college degree—that's all that's required."

MH: "But are you sure there will be a room for me?"

HC: "Yes, the housing is no problem. There are plenty of dorm rooms available in the summer."

MH: "Well, I'm afraid that I'll get there and find there's no place for me."

HC: "The university will find a place for everyone attending the program."

MH: "OK. Well, I'll go ahead and get my tickets then."

HC: "Good. Let me know if you have any other questions."

There were a few other calls from applicants with similar concerns. Some, like Madeleine, called information to get Helen's home phone number to call her there.

The Letters

On June 9, Helen received the letter shown in Figure 3.2. She was a little surprised to read that Madeleine had sent a check to UWB although the brochure clearly explained that UWB could not process American checks, there was no way to deposit them or convert them to Czech crowns.

She responded with the letter in Figure 3.3.

In Prague

On July 5, participants met at the Prague airport. Madeleine Hartwell was there, but she was still worried and nervous. Participants were taken to the university and checked into their rooms. They were shown where to get dinner and to meet for orientation the next morning.

Orientation consisted of a discussion of the testing and placement of students in the English classes and a Czech lesson for the Americans. Just before lunch, the participants started asking questions: When did they need to pay for the program?

June 8, 1994

Dear Ms. Cornwall:

As I told you on the telephone, I sent a registration form for the Language Institute at the University of West Bohemia last March. I still have not received anything from them confirming that I am accepted in the program or that they have reserved a room for me. My concern is that I have a non-cancelable plane ticket and no information from the University. It seems strange to me that they didn't want a deposit sent with the application, and I was afraid that I had not received a request for payment, so I mailed a check for 25% of the fees to the Director. My check has not cleared my bank yet, so I don't know if the University ever received it.

Another thing that crosses my mind is the possibility that my registration might have gone astray somewhere. Despite your reassurances, I'm quite concerned that I will arrive in the Czech Republic and have no place to stay for 3 weeks.

I have sent a similar letter to the University of West Bohemia. If you are in touch with the Registrar, please ask him to send me a written confirmation as soon as possible.

Sincerely,

Madeleine Hartwell

FIGURE 3.2   Letter from program applicant to University representative

June 10, 1994

Dear Madelaine:

Sorry you haven't heard anything from the University of West Bohemia—I can imagine it must be very worrying. But there really is no need for concern. As I told you when you called, I e-mailed the Director, and confirmed that your application had been received.

The reason they haven't asked for any payment of the fees at this point is that the University has no way to deposit U.S. checks yet. They would like you to pay for the course when you get there, either in Czech crowns or with travelers' checks. I imagine they are holding your check—you can probably get it back when you get here.

I've e-mailed the Registrar to make sure that he's reserved a room for you. Other-wise, there's no problem even if they didn't receive your application. There are other people who are just now making up their minds to go. We're used to western bureaucracy with lots of paperwork and deadlines, but they don't operate that way—yet! Anyway, they will be happy to have you there, so don't worry—just be ready to have a good time!

Sincerely,

Helen Cornwall

FIGURE 3.3   Reply from University representative to applicant

Where could they change money? Where could they buy bottled water (tap water is not drinkable because of pollution)? Where could they get something to heat water in and detergent to wash clothes? Unfortunately, very little was open on the weekend, and the few stores that did open on Saturday closed at noon. After lunch, one of the Czech students took the Americans on a walk to a place where they could buy water and pointed out the little grocery store and produce market that would be open on Monday. Participants were told that on Monday they could take the trolley to the new K-Mart to buy anything else they needed. When they asked which trolley to take, they were told that someone would accompany them on Monday afternoon.

Monday morning's TEFL class was almost entirely taken up with complaints from the Americans about the lack of information they had received. They still didn't know where or how to get bus passes, where to buy things, where to change money, and so on. Over the next week, they were taken to all the neces-sary offices and shops, and they slowly settled into the routine. At the end of the Institute, most of the participants reported finding the program worthwhile, good value for the money, and generally well run, although they still had complaints about the lack of written information they had received. Many suggested handouts with information about transportation, shopping, school activities, schedules for classes, and other events.

When the director and Helen Cornwell discussed continuing their arrangement for the following summer, Helen complained that she had been badgered at all hours by phone calls and faxes from applicants worried about the status of their applications. She asked the director to develop some follow-up materials, including a letter of confirmation of registration and a schedule of classes and activities. The director was puzzled by the request. She didn't understand why people had been so concerned, pointed out that all the necessary information was in the brochure, and stated that the program could not afford to mail materials to the United States. Helen suggested that the university raise the fees to Americans to cover the cost of mailing and of printing informational materials. The director said she would look into it.

The following spring, the same situation occurred. Helen herself wrote up some materials for the participants on where to find things they needed in Pilsen and gave these out during orientation. But the general unease of the American continued, spoiling their enjoyment of an otherwise good experience.

What happened in this situation? Do we know anything about cultural differences that explains both the seeming inattention to business details by the Czech organizers and the sometimes severe state of discomfort experienced by the Americans?

Background for Analysis

Anthropologists say that all cultures fall somewhere on a continuum:

|———|

High Context   Low Context

In a high-context culture, most of the members have the same religion, education, ethnic or national background, and history. That means that they usually share the same values and attitudes, and assume that other members of their culture think the same way they do. In a low-context culture, however, members are very different in all of the ways listed above, so they may have different values and different ideas about all areas of life.

Think about how you communicate in your personal life. Are there things you can say to your family or your friends that they would understand immediately, although outsiders would need an explanation? In the following conversation, Roman and his friend, Bettina, are talking to Roman's father.

Roman: "I'm going out with some friends, Dad. Can I borrow your car?"
Father: "No, it's Wednesday."

Roman: "Oh, yeah. OK. we'll take the bus."

Bettina: "Why can't we borrow the car?"

Roman: "Because on Wednesday nights, my father goes to business group meetings, and he needs the car."

Roman and his father understood each other because they are members of a very high-context culture—a family. Bettina does not have the background knowledge shared by Roman's family, so she needs a more specific explanation of why Roman can't borrow the car.

Figure 3.4 gives more information about the differences between high-context and low-context cultures.

High-context cultures often have developed in places where the people were isolated from outside contact except when they were under attack. Being part of a close-knit cohesive group was vital for survival. Members of these cultures also try to avoid conflict with each other, which often results in well-defined rules of politeness that help maintain civility. For example, requests and orders may be couched in such indirect language that an outsider barely recognizes the nature of the communication. Similarly, members of such cultures avoid giving negative responses to requests if possible, so that the requester won't "lose face" by being turned down. It has been said that Japanese doesn't have a word for *no*. While this is not true, it *is* true that the Japanese, like many other people, are reluctant to give a direct refusal. Look at the following conversation that took place between Helen and the director from the Czech Republic:

H: "As I mentioned before, the American participants really need to get some response from you to feel sure that they've been accepted for the program."

D: "You know the problem—it's very expensive to mail materials to the United States."

H: "But the program is very inexpensive for Americans. You could easily increase the fees a little for Americans to cover the postage costs."

D: "Well, I don't know if we can do that."

H: "Will you think about it and see if it's possible?"

D: "Yes, I'll think about it."

Both Helen and the director knew that the answer to Helen's request was "no." When Helen heard the director hesitate, she gave the director a way to avoid giving a direct refusal by asking her to think about it. This gave the director a chance to give a positive response so that both she and Helen would feel good about the exchange. It worked in this case because Helen understood that she had been told that the fees would not be raised and information would not be mailed to the Americans.

This sort of subtle, indirect communication is easier in oral interactions, so people in high-context cultures often prefer this mode of communication to written

FIGURE 3.4   Characteristics of High- and Low-Context Cultures

	Low-Context Cultures	High-Context Cultures
Affiliation	Part of many groups.	Part of one predominant in-group—identifies strongly with the group.
Concept of Self	Individual goals separate from group members.	Group goals.
Trust	More open because of variety of group affiliations.	Unlikely to trust someone outside the in-group.
Expected Behavior	Independent. Emphasis on personal enjoyment and fulfillment.	Dependence on others. Compliance with in-group norms.
Work/Play	Kept separate.	Integrated.
Approach to Disagreement	Seeks resolution through conflict.	Seeks resolution through consensus.
Relationship to Nature	Separate. Believes humans can control environment.	Integral part of nature. Prefers to adapt to it.
Achievement	Reached by individual effort.	Fate determines path of life.
Valued Activity	Doing	Being
Motivation	Competition individual goals.	Good of the group.
Interpersonal Relationships	Informal.	Formal.
Status in Relationships	Egalitarian belief.	Hierarchical.
Resolution of Conflict	Face-to-face.	Through intermediary.
Business Relationships	Based on bottom-line benefits.	Based on history, personal relationships.
Time Orientation	Future.	Present and past.

Note: There are, of course, individual and other differences that affect an individual's communication style. For example, research on how American women and men communicate and negotiate suggests that women are more likely to seek consensus than men and are often more comfortable with cooperation than competition. In other ways, however, American women also exhibit the attitudes and behaviors associated with low-context cultures (Tannen, 1994).

documents. This explains, to some extent, why the Czechs did not understand the need for written information and did not want to communicate with the Americans that way. Once things are set down in writing, they are no longer open to negotiation.

On the other hand, low-context cultures are usually composed of members who have arrived in them recently, having left their original groups. They have less need to identify with other members of their culture.

In high-context cultures, school systems often follow standardized curricula and use textbooks and other materials adopted at the national level. Education systems in low-context cultures are more likely to be controlled by local communities and neighborhoods. Because members of low-context cultures share little in the way of background, they often have to fill in more information to communicate accurately, as Roman did with Bettina. This requires the kind of reader-centered writing taught in most writing classes in the United States. The writer has to try to anticipate what the reader knows and doesn't know, thinks and doesn't think, believes and doesn't believe. When it is not possible to be sure that the reader already has a piece of information, the writer is advised to supply it, just in case.

Consider the following example from a letter sent by an insurance company to a new customer:

> *Enclosed is the application on your new Ford Taurus. Please sign this at the bottom where indicated in yellow, and return the form to our office with a check for $60.17. A stamped return envelope is enclosed for your convenience.*

Why does the reader need such specific instructions? Every business does things differently, and every form looks different. In nations where business documents are standardized, everyone knows what to do with them, and instructions are unnecessary. The Americans going to the Czech program probably expected a letter similar to the following:

> *We have received your application for the Summer Institute. According to our records, you made the following requests:*
>
> - *Enrollment in the TESL program*
> - *Single, nonsmoking room in the Valentova Dormitory*
> - *No preference for suite mate.*
>
> *If you will not require transportation from the Prague airport to Pilsen, please tear off the strip below and return it to us. Indicate what day you will be arriving. If you will be arriving by train, indicate your estimated time of arrival.*

In high-context cultures, communication is often writer-centered. The reader is expected to work at extracting the meaning. The writer does not want to imply that the reader is unintelligent and therefore needs specific instructions; that would be insulting and might lead to conflict. American business letters, with their simple language and detailed information, often seem to members of high-context cultures to be condescending, designed for a person of low intelligence or knowledge.

Members of high-context cultures usually prefer

- Oral communications
- Cooperation rather than competition
- Group responsibility for decisions rather than individual responsibility
- Writer-centered communications.

People who live in low-context cultures generally prefer

- Written communications rather than oral
- More frequent communications
- More specific communications stating exactly what is going to happen, when, where, and how
- Reader-centered communications.

Analysis of the Case

What caused the discomfort of the American who had signed up for a language course in the Czech Republic? And why did the Czech officials not recognize the need for more information? Several differences between high- and low-context cultures were at work.

Oral versus Written Communication

As members of a low-context culture, the Americans expected more written communications and more specific information about exactly what to expect from the program. Think about your experience in choosing a college or university. You were probably inundated with information—catalogs, brochures, information sessions. You may have visited various schools before making your decision. This is necessary in the United States because institutes of higher education are different from one another. You have to decide between traditional liberal arts colleges, technical schools, and urban universities with extensive evening programs, for example. Two public universities in the same state may vary widely in the courses offered and required for a particular degree program. Choosing the school that will best meet your needs and wishes takes a great deal of research. You want to have the information in written form so you can compare the schools against each other.

In many high-context cultures, educational institutions are centrally run and very similar to each other. Since the members of the culture share similar values about what needs to be learned and how it should be taught, difference between schools may be merely a matter of location. The same is true of many other institutions in those cultures—people need less information because there is less choice.

The Czech officials may have preferred little or no written communication with the applicants simply because they were not used to having to provide much in the way of information to prospective students.

Individual versus Group or Central Control

In a low-context culture, businesses and other ventures rise and fall on the talents and persistence of individuals. In a high-context culture, however, the group (often the government) is responsible for the continuation of operations that the culture values. Without a steady stream of communication from the Czech university,

American applicants had reason to fear that the Summer Institute had been canceled, as is often the case in a system where bankruptcy is a fairly common consequence of poor planning, inadequate leadership, or simple economic fluctuations. In addition, the Americans were accustomed to institutions that required advance proof of the ability to pay before even registering participants for a class, since people in low-context cultures will cancel plans at the last minute if it meets their individual needs, even though it may inconvenience others.

It is also difficult in this situation to separate factors that are part of the traditional Czech culture from factors resulting from years of communist control. Unemployment and bankruptcy were not possible in the previous regime, as universities and industries were supported and run by the government. The standardization of all operations under this system, from wages and prices to living standards, made both individual striving and economic insecurity irrelevant. Czechs were used to stability in their institutions, which led to an inability to understand the insecurity the Americans were feeling.

Individualism versus Group-Centeredness

Members of low-context cultures compete with each other for resources, jobs, admission to schools, and so on. They are used to having to submit proof that they are among the most qualified or most worthy of acceptance. In more group-oriented high-context cultures, the emphasis is on providing goods and services to as many people as possible. The Czechs were willing to take as many applicants into the Summer Institute as applied (especially those whose currencies supported the program), while the Americans assumed that there was a risk of being rejected, either for lack of qualifications or lack of space.

Business Relationships

When people doing business with each other have a long history, sometimes dating back generations, they have little need for written agreements and contracts. They know their business partners and trust them. Czech applicants to the Summer Institute knew that the UWB had been there for many years and could be expected to live up to its obligations. The Americans had no such knowledge and little experience with a business agreement conducted on a "handshake" basis. The expectation in a low-context culture is that both parties to an agreement will sign off on it. In this case, the American applicants had signed off by sending in their application; they expected a reciprocal written acknowledgment of the joint agreement.

Shared Knowledge

One feature of a high-context culture is that people tend to stay put. They are born, grow up, attend school, and eventually work in the same communities. Therefore, there is little need for maps, written directions, or explanations of available services. Everyone learns this information from parents and others. When strangers are present, it may be difficult for high-context groups to know what the new-comers know and don't know. Rather than waste time on preparing information that may not be needed ahead of time, they will answer questions as they arise. Americans, who prefer to be independent, want written information they can refer to rather than relying on the availability of others to guide them.

Conclusion

The Summer Institute has continued in the years since this episode. The Czechs have gradually come to realize, to a certain degree, that Americans need and expect more information than they would normally give. Unfortunately, each year a new group of Americans apply to the program, bringing with them their low-context expectations, and each year there is some frustration on both sides. Furthermore, even when the nature of high-context cultures are explained to the American TEFL teachers, they admit that this theoretical knowledge does not reduce their anxiety. Cooperation between high- and low-context cultures depends on the ability of each side to attempt to understand and adapt to the other.

Questions for Discussion

1. If you were Helen Cornwall, how would you go about convincing the director to send out more information to Americans? Would you use oral or written modes of communication with the director? What arguments do you think might convince the director of the need for more information?

2. American managers working for Japanese-run companies are often surprised to find that they do not have individual offices, but are instead assigned desks in a large room with other managers, vice presidents, and other executives. They find that the noise of people talking and working around them distracts them. What do you know about high- and low-context cultures that might explain these different arrangements?

3. Americans working in Middle Eastern countries sometimes find that they must adjust the way they are used to conducting their business. They discover that meetings, even between people who work for the same company and see each other every day, usually start with a conversation about the health of people's families, the weather, and other "safe" topics. Tea is often served, and business is not discussed until the first cup is finished. What do you know about high-context cultures that might explain this?

4. A study of inquiry letters sent to universities revealed a pronounced difference between letters from American students and those from students in many other countries. American students write, "Please send me a catalog and application form," and include their address. Students from other countries frequently write long letters detailing not only their educational accomplishments, but also claims of good character and information about their families and hobbies. Is there anything in Figure 3.4 or the case study you have read that relates this behavior to the type of culture the students come from?

5. Some researchers have commented on the extensive use of cellular telephones in many high-context cultures. The preference for oral communication may be one of the factors in the popularity of this new communication tool. There also seems to be a generational difference in the United States—younger people seem to make greater use of the telephone than their parents. Do you think this is an indication that the culture of the United States is becoming more like high-context cultures? Looking at Figure 3.4, are there any other changes taking placing in U.S. culture or any other culture you are familiar with that indicate a change from high- to low-context or the opposite?

Writing Assignments

1. Write a two- to three-paragraph description of activities for students on your campus. This might be an article for the student newspaper. Then rewrite your piece for an audience from outside the campus community. Think about what assumptions you can make about the first audience versus the second. For example, you might write "Meetings of the Drama Club are often held in the Tiger Den." Students on the campus would know that the Tiger Den is a food court located in Jones Hall, which probably means that the members of the Drama Club eat during their meetings. Outsiders would need to be given that information so that they would know where to find the meeting and what to expect when they get there. Think about the ways in which a campus often resembles a high-context culture. What other characteristics of a high-context culture do you think are true of your campus?

2. Imagine that you work for a company that is negotiating with an organization in China to open a joint business venture. You are concerned because in your most recent encounter with the Chinese organization, you talked about starting contract negotiations, and their reply seemed to be, "Let's get started on our joint venture, and we'll work out a contract later." You know that written contracts do not carry the importance or legal consequences in China that they do in the United States. Write a letter to the head of the Chinese organization making a case for the need for a written contract.

3. Choose a product produced and distributed in the United States that has some text or graphics on the packaging. Food products are good choices for this exercise, including breakfast cereal, crackers, or cake mixes. Assume that you work for the company that produces this product and that you are starting to sell the product in the Czech Republic. What do you know about the Czech Republic from the case study, or about high-context cultures from Figure 3.4, that can help you sell this product? Redesign the package, writing new text and deciding on appropriate graphics. Write or tell how your new design will be effective with the target audience.

Additional Reading: Issues Relevant to the Case

Hall, C., & Thrush, E. Technical communications in Eastern Europe. (1992). *Proceedings of the 39th Annual Conference of the Society for Technical Communication*, p. 542.

Hall, E. T., & Hall, M. R. (1990). *Understanding cultural differences*. Yarmouth, MA: Intercultural Press.

Kim, D., Pan, Y. & Park, H. S. (1998). High- versus low-context culture: A comparison of Chinese, Korean, and American cultures. *Psychology and Marketing; 15*, 507–515.

Kozminski, A. K. & Cushman, D. P. (Eds). (1993). *Organizational communication and management: A global perspective.* Albany; NY: State University of New York Press.

Limaye, M. R. (1994). Facilitating research in multicultural business communication. *The Bulletin of the Association for Business Communication, 57,* 37–45.

Mikelonis, V. (1994, July 30). Rhetoric of transition in Central and Eastern Europe." *InterComm '94,* Ames, Iowa.

Ruch, W. V. (1989). *International handbook of corporate communication.* Jefferson, NC: McFarland.

Sebastian, B. (1996). Integrating local and corporate cultures. *Hrmagazine: On Human Resource Management; 41,* 114–120.

Shen, F. (1989). The classroom and the wider culture: Identity as a key to learning English composition." *College Composition and Communication; 40,* 459–466.

Tannen, D. (1994). *Talking from 9 to 5.* New York: Simon and Schuster.

Thrush, E. A. (1993). Bridging the gaps: Technical communications in the international and multicultural world. *Technical Communications Quarterly, 2*(3), 271–283.

Thrush, E. A. (1997). Multicultural issues in technical writing." In Katherine Staples & Cezar Ornatowski (Eds.). *Foundations for Teaching Technical Communication: Sources, Issues, and Curricula for an Emergent Discipline.* pp. 161–178. Norwood, NJ: Ablex Press.

Usage as an Interactive Strategy for International Team-Building

The Never-Ending Story

BOYD H. DAVIS
University of North Carolina at Charlotte

JEUTONNE BREWER
University of North Carolina at Greensboro

YE-LING CHANG
National Kaohsiung Normal University

Abstract: In this case, a technical communicator discovers that even the "little touches"—such as pronouns—are important in cross-cultural collaboration. Because his business is getting ready to train employees in different countries, the technical communicator must harmonize the training scripts to achieve consistency. He finds that, since different languages handle gender reference differently, translators and writers at each site will need to cooperate and share insights. The case asks readers to consider the difference between grammar and usage, and to discuss such questions as: How can technical communicators work with the notion of "face" in cross-cultural situations? What does a technical communicator need to know about English usage in general, and issues of nonsexist usage in particular, when establishing strategies for cooperation among international writers?

Note: To the best of our knowledge, there is no American pizza-restaurant chain in Asia or the United States precisely like the one we describe. However, the issue that Alex faces—harmonizing document design across cultures by paying attention to details that at first seem to be minute, even trivial—is not going to vanish. The information in and the wording of the faxes and e-mail messages in the case discussion are adapted from an interactive e-mail exchange among writers in Taiwan, Japan, and North Carolina developed and moderated by the authors in 1995.

Background for the Case

Pizza-for-Us is a franchised chain that started in Tucson a decade ago and spread rapidly to both coasts. While relatively young in the fast-food business, it's considered a solid investment on Wall Street, and buying a franchise is worth the high price. Management in the home office astutely profiles a variety of consumer habits in a particular area before selling a franchise. The home office closely monitors performance and quality and is adamant that the "special experience" at Pizza-for-Us restaurants must remain absolutely consistent.

While Pizza-for-Us will deliver pizza to consumers, its emphasis—and its high-profile advertising thrust—is on its family atmosphere. Each franchise site presents a cozy setting and a specific layout. There are no booths; instead, the restaurant has circular tables with a lazy Susan in the middle of each one. Family-sized, topping-rich pizzas are served on the roundtables. Customers share a pizza and rotate the lazy Susan to sample the variety of toppings on each eighth of the pizza. These toppings, like the decorative touches to the dining area, are regionally cued whenever possible: Pizza-for-Us keeps field managers busy charting regional demographics so it can move swiftly to target various niches. Service is fast, polite, and exceptionally well-rehearsed, with a longer-than-usual training period. Other restaurants eagerly recruit workers from Pizza-for-Us, from the people clearing the tables through the servers and on to the host or hostess.

For the last two years, field inspectors have noted that the restaurants in areas with large Asian populations consistently get repeat business; more patrons return to Pizza-for-Us restaurants than to other restaurants in the same price category. That has added to management's confidence; the chain is now ready to open franchises in Taipei, Tokyo, and Seoul, even though a number of other U.S. fast-food restaurants have already established a presence there. Negotiations have been successful; the local agreements are in place; construction is almost finished; and the training process for employees is about to start. So is Alex's problem.

Introducing Alex

Alex Calkins is a junior technical writer in the Publications Department at the Pizza-for-Us corporate headquarters in Tucson. His college internship was with the information services division of a software company, and he worked after graduation on a contract to develop manuals for a utility company, but this is his first real career position. Since he is new, his manager, Christa Johnston, has given him responsibility to develop only one part of the training materials for the waitstaff and has already cautioned him that at Pizza-for-Us, consistency in details is taken seriously.

"What you'll need to do for next week," she says, "is work on these training scripts. These don't have the special jargon that we'll teach the servers to use with the kitchen staff. You can look at that later. Right now, go over the way the host greets and seats the customers and how the servers highlight the menu and take orders. The writers at our new sites are busy translating the scripts. You'll handle their questions; some came this morning."

Later that day, Christa comes back to Alex with a thin manila folder. She's really in a hurry, he thinks. "You're going to have to do this by Friday," she says.

Alex's Problem

"Friday?" asks Alex. This is Monday, and the project so far seems pretty straightforward. "Oh, right," says Christa. "We think it would be a good idea if you brought your recommendations to staff meeting. We're going to try to streamline the whole training manual." She hustles down the hall. Back at his desk, Alex opens the folder. Clipped to the script are printouts of e-mail messages to Christa.

On top is one from Seoul. Mr. Lee wants advice on translating some of the sentences describing the menu and phrases for greetings. They don't match his expectations for correct English. The greetings seem a little informal to him. And what's behind the use of "s/he" in the script for the hostess: "S/he will be with you in just a moment to take your order." Is there some special reason for this usage?

Next is the printout of an e-mail message from Tokyo sent the same day. It's about a new issue—or is it? Mrs. Hatayama is concerned about the word *hostess*: Is this like a receptionist? She wants to offer a slightly different translation, since older Japanese might expect a cabaret hostess. And would he advise her on the use of *it* in phrases like "It's been great to serve you"? Japanese don't use an equivalent for this pronoun when *it* is a "filler," so can she change that a bit?

Alex pauses: *It* as a "filler"? He looks at Mr. Chen's e-mail from Taipei. Mr. Chen is concerned with the bulleted directions for the server. Those bullets could translate as commands. Could he soften the tone a bit to make sure the directions were requests? And is there a reason for using "he or she" to refer to the servers? What if they are all the same gender? Can't they just delete the pronoun in the English version, just like the Chinese? Customers will understand, and so will the staff.

Alex puts down the folder. He goes to see Lita.

Lita's Response

Lita Ganzer is in the training division, where she offers seminars on different aspects of communications. Alex had taken her short course on avoiding sexist usage and has signed up for the training series on cross-cultural communications—but it starts after Friday's meeting.

"You're right," says Lita. "This is a cross-cultural issue—in fact, there are several issues. The writers of our training scripts have been very careful to avoid what Americans consider sexist usage in English. Each of your translators is having problems with the script—that may be because of differences between their languages and English. But there's another issue here as well. I think there are probably some differences in cultural expectations. I'm looking at that in the seminar next month. Did you sign up for it?"

"My meeting is this Friday," said Alex.

"I have a meeting in a few minutes," said Lita. "But I'll lend you my first set of slides for that workshop. Take a look at them—you can open them on your computer—and see if they make sense to you. I could see you later, around 3:30, if you want to talk this through. I've got a strategy for team-building that you might want to use."

"I'll see you then and bring you some coffee," replies Alex. He takes the diskette from Lita and goes back to his desk.

Lita's Slides

Alex studies the slides (See Figure 4.1). How, he thinks, is he going to pull everyone together? He doesn't have any idea of what the writers in Taipei, Tokyo, or Seoul might think is culturally appropriate.

FIGURE 4.1   Involvement and Independent Strategies

Cross-cultural teamwork builds on cross-cultural communication. Use these insights taken from Scollon and Scollon (1995) to understand the communication situations illustrated in this case

When people communicate with each other, part of their message signals the degree to which they see themselves as being	• involved with each other • independent from each other
Communicators use various strategies to signal something about	• their own identity • their attitude toward the communication situation • how they want to preserve face in the situation
Involvement strategies signal alignment with the other person by claiming	• a common point of view • in-group membership *Example: All of us at PFU hope you'll join us in thinking this training process is the best we've ever developed. We keep your life in mind.*
Independent strategies signal some sort of distancing from the other person through an awareness of different	• points of view • group affiliations *Example: This notifies you of company policy about . . .*

Both strategies (involvement and independent) are "correct," but different groups and different cultures have different notions about which strategy is appropriate.

"That's actually going to be a strength," says Lita when he meets with her later that day. "You know that you don't know something, and you don't have any problem admitting it. That makes you ready to learn from other people. Neither you nor the other writers can be totally sure of what's appropriate in each culture or each language. You're going to have to think of a way for all four of you to be involved with each other in a common task, where each person has something unique to contribute. I have an idea for you."

"I'll take it," says Alex.

"Pronouns," said Lisa. "It's pretty obvious from the messages you shared with me that all of them are having some problems with how to translate the pronouns. English pronouns signal gender, which is why I went over pronouns in the non-sexist usage workshop. There are cultural expectations about gender roles, and pronouns can trigger those expectations or assumptions. Remember my examples about managers? They're certainly not all 'he's' and we don't want to suggest that they are."

"What about other languages?" asks Alex. "I speak Spanish, and it has gender."

"Well," said Lita, "I know that Mandarin doesn't. Here's your chance to find out about the others, and you can go from there to see what kinds of cultural associations are triggered. Here's why: All of your team members have unique information about language use and culturally cued expectations at their home site, just like you do. And all of you have access to different kinds of authority, like textbooks, grammar books, and dictionaries. These books prescribe correctness. Usage manuals, guidelines, or stylesheets let you know what's generally appropriate. If you can specify a focus, and position yourself and the other writers as equal experts, what you as writers report about your own practices will give you even more information."

"Do you mean," asks Alex, "if we all share information about how we write or what we have problems with, we can get a handle on cultural issues, too?"

"I like your use of 'we,' " smiles Lita. "I'll look at your plan if you want."

Alex goes back to his office to write a message. Later, he shows it to Lita, and after revising his phrasal verbs and colloquial expressions, he sends it to the other writers. He is already thinking of the writers as "our team."

Alex's E-mail: His Team-Building Strategy

On Tuesday morning, Alex logs on and finds messages waiting (See Figure 4.2). They're already deep in discussion: How can this be? He kicks himself mentally for forgetting the time difference. They're already through with Tuesday. They must have found the message first thing in the morning, and have gotten busy right away. He is lucky to be working with them, he thinks. He prints out the first set of messages and lays them out in chronological order. (See Figures 4.3, 4.4, and 4.5).

Quickly, Alex writes up the results of his own office survey, and sends it on. (See Figure 4.6).

The next morning, Alex finds another group of messages (See Figures 4.7, 4.8 and 4.9).

To: Mr. Chen, Taipei Office, Pizza-for-Us
            Mrs. Hatayama, Tokyo Office, Pizza-for-Us
            Mr. Lee, Seoul Office, Pizza-for-Us

From: Alexander Calkins, Tucson Office, Pizza-for-Us

Re: Training Scripts

Dear Colleagues,

Our manager, Christa Johnston, has asked me to work with you on the training scripts. All of us share a concern for quality and a concern that the language used in the training scripts will be appropriate. Your comments and questions are very useful, and I will take them to the Editing Team meeting on Friday to discuss how best to revise the training scripts so they can be suitable to each of your locations. I see that all of us have concerns about translating English pronouns. So that I can better understand these concerns, could you please e-mail me by Thursday evening (Tucson-time) some additional information in response to my questions for you about pronouns?

In English, as you know, pronouns signal gender, which can spill over into ideas about cultural issues such as jobs or even ways to greet people or refer to them. All of those issues are important if the training scripts are to be consistent and also appropriate. Here is a list of sentences, each of which might present a different kind of problem. Could you please choose several of these, and informally ask several people for their responses? (Would they be more likely to use "he" or "she"?) I would greatly appreciate your assistance.

1. The professor/The teacher won't dismiss our class early, will ___?

2. The chef/The cook was congratulated by the guests, wasn't ___?

3. Either Ian or Yoshi/Maria or Keisha will stay home, ___?

4. Germany/America/The U.S. supports the U.N., ___?

5. The interior decorator/lighting designer will finish soon, ___?

6. My dog/my cat/my parakeet will eat anything, ___?

7. Neither Yusuf nor Willem stayed at the office, ___?

FIGURE 4.2   Sharing Concerns

To: Alexander Calkins, Technical Writing Team

From: Mrs. Hatayama, Tokyo Office, Pizza-for-Us

Re: Pronouns

On #1: I got "does she" from one man and "does he" from the women and from one other man. This shows that the word /teacher/ gives us the image of he. Compared to this, /interior decorator/ seems to have the image of a "she." I thought it would be a "he," though. Also, what about using "they" when the subject looks singular? I hear this in the movies.

FIGURE 4.3   **Discussing Pronoun Usage**

To: Alexander Calkins, Technical Writing Team

From: Mr. Chen, Taipei Office, Pizza-for-Us

Re: Pronouns [in # 1 and #5]

Problems with #1 and #5. Mandarin has a very different system for pronouns. The "we" of speaker-hearer is indicated by a pronoun different from the pronoun for speaker-hearer-other person. This is very different for English. When we studied English, our professor said that learning the chart for pronouns wasn't enough, we had to look at situations for their use.

FIGURE 4.4   **More Discussion of Pronoun Usage**

To: Alexander Calkins, Technical Writing Team

From: Mr. Lee, Seoul Office, Pizza-for-Us

Re: #4, pronouns and countries

Our reference books say to use the singular, but the people in my office don't do that for either the U.S. or North America. Also, we have some British speakers on our staff, and when I asked them the questions, they inserted "Right?" instead of the pronoun. Is this acceptable? Also, is it conventional now to use "they" where my books say "he"?

FIGURE 4.5   **Pronouns and Countries**

To:	Mr. Chen, Taipei Office, Pizza-for-Us
	Mrs. Hatayama, Tokyo Office, Pizza-for-Us
	Mr. Lee, Seoul Office, Pizza-for-Us
From:	Alexander Calkins, Technical Writing Team
Re:	"They" for countries and groups of people

For the U.S., half of the people I asked use "it" and a fourth use "they." The others use "he" and "she". Using "they" is considered colloquial and sometimes, nonstandard. Many people use "they" in speech, but usually not in formal written texts, even though famous authors use it. This pronoun was a topic in our Nonsexist Usage workshop. I'm mailing you notes from that workshop so you can see some of our language constraints.

FIGURE 4.6　Pronouns Continue

To:	Alexander Calkins, Technical Writing Team
From:	Mr. Chen, Taipei Office, Pizza-for-Us
Re:	Animals

This could be important for ads and layout. People in my office say "it" for dogs and "she" for cats, sometimes for birds, when speaking English. Also, what about colors? Any gender associations there besides for babies' clothes?

FIGURE 4.7　Referring to Animals

To:	Alexander Calkins, Technical Writing Team
From:	Mrs. Hatayama, Tokyo Office, Pizza-for-Us
Re:	Colors and Animals

We have "he" for dogs and birds and "it" for cats. But we don't specify the pronoun unless we're talking in another language. Purple is imperial, white is for funerals, red is for festivals. I think we differ from American usage.

FIGURE 4.8　Colors and Animals

To: Alexander Calkins, Tucson Office, Pizza-for-Us

From: Mr. Lee, Seoul Office, Pizza-for-Us

Re: Changing the Subject

If you don't mind, I want to ask about servers and how they greet. When I was in Tokyo last spring, I went to an American hamburger restaurant. All the servers greeted me in a chorus. That's not in our training script, and it could make problems.

FIGURE 4.9   Servers and Greetings

Usage: The Never-Ending Story

Alex is a success at the meeting. He has something tangible to offer when the discussion of the training scripts begins, and he is able to suggest places where the script could have options for greetings and appropriate language, depending on the location of the franchise. With any luck, he thinks, he'll get tapped for a quality-control trip to those sites and meet his new colleagues face-to-face. He sends them e-mail with his sincere thanks and a copy of the changes in the script for their advice. By airmail, he sends each a special greeting card, enclosing a photograph of himself sitting in front of the monitor reading their messages. He buys Lita a double cappuccino and signs up for her next workshop on cross-cultural communications. Then Christa comes down the hall with a new problem: phrasal verbs.

Questions for Discussion

1. What are some of the issues of nonsexist usage that Lita might have covered in her staff workshop? Why do English-speaking writers need to focus on them? What do stylesheets and manuals for books and journals suggest?

2. What kinds of suggestions do you think Alex offers about the training scripts? Why do you think he made these suggestions?

3. *It* can cause several problems. An operating manual in English might use *it* in directions like these: "Put the key-card in the slot. Retrieve it when you hear the first tone. Replace it in the slot at the second tone." A Japanese writer can say "In the slot, at second tone, replace." There are other issues with translating pronouns that writers need to consider: What do you know, for example, about *you* in German, French, or Spanish? Every language brings its own set of problems: Why?

4. It's a good thing Alex has Lita to advise him. What if you don't have an adviser? Where can you get advice on questions about English usage? About different kinds of translations? About cross-cultural communications? What kinds of ongoing training are available in your area for professional writers? Do you know how to find a translator?

5. Christa forgot something; she didn't send a message introducing Alex to the writers at the other sites. How might this cause Alex to lose face? Hierarchies and relationships can be taken very seriously in many countries, and the other writers might not know Alex's position in the company. How can Alex rewrite his introductory e-mail to signal why he has been chosen to work with the other writers? Does he need to do this? Is there any way he can get Christa to do it?

6. Who are the audiences for the training scripts? How many purposes do the scripts play? What details give you this information?

7. At the end of this case, Christa brings Alex a new problem: phrasal verbs. What are they? Phrasal verbs usually embed a metaphor, and metaphors, like proverbs, are tricky to translate. Why? What other problems might arise for translators? English phrasal verbs can cause problems for writers in English, too: What kinds of dictionaries discuss them or give them usage labels? How can phrasal verbs change the tone of your document?

Writing Assignments

1. Conduct an online search, via the World Wide Web, of sites providing information about grammar and usage for pronouns, and about nonsexist or exclusionary language. Create a table comparing usage among countries or cultures.

2. Compare introductory technical writing texts on issues of cross-cultural communication. See, for example, Miles 1997. You might compare her focus on English as a Second Language with sections in Scollon and Scollon, 1995. For gender issues and "generic they," start with Meyers, 1993, and compare the findings with sections in introductory technical and professional writing texts.

3. Develop a similar project and your own survey using phrasal verbs as the focus. Examine the 1997 *Cambridge International Dictionary of Phrasal Verbs*.

Additional Reading: Issues Relevant to the Case

Note: Sentences used for collaborative research were taken from a survey developed initially in 1975 by Brewer and conducted with university and technical college students by Brewer and Davis for the twenty years prior to the international collaboration with Chang. Over that period of time, a number of changes in English colloquial usage and editorial guidelines took place. We recommend these sources for further study:

Battistella, E. (1997). Guidelines for nonsexist language. *SECOL Review, 21,* 104–125.
Meyers, M. (1993). Forms of they with singular noun phrase antecedents: Evidence from current educated English usage. *Word, 44,* 181–192.
Miles, L. (1997). Globalizing professional writing curricula: Positioning students and repositioning textbooks. *Technical Communication Quarterly, 6,* 179–200.
Scollon, R., & Scollon, S. W. (1995). *Intercultural communication.* Oxford: Basil Blackwell.

Chapter 5

Resolving Cultural Misunderstandings in Crisis Situations:

The Case of the Inexperienced Entrepreneurs

JAYNE A. MONEYSMITH
Kent State University Stark Campus

Abstract: This case presents a technical communicator who writes to a Korean business for the first time when his company is in the midst of a crisis. In his haste to make arrangements with a new supplier in time to fulfill an important contract, he accidentally offends the executives of the Korean business with his abruptness and with demands that they interpret as excessive. Due to the highly specialized nature of the product involved, the only way he can meet his production deadline is to overcome the reluctance of the Korean executives to deal with him. Some problems are rooted in the writer's inexperience: He is a technical expert who is inexperienced in both business and communication. However, he also fails to consider that differences in culture may necessitate different methods of communication. Several key issues are raised: What should a technical communicator know about Korean culture to develop and maintain effective working relationships? What is the best way to approach a Korean company with which you've never dealt before? How can the need to establish relations before transacting business be balanced with the need to come to closure in an emergency situation? How can problems caused by miscommunication be overcome? In addition to introducing students to concepts important in communicating with someone from a different culture, this case also serves as a review of the most important concepts in technical communication.

Note: All cultures are diverse. Characterizations of the way people in Korea, Japan, or the United States might react in a given situation are not intended to imply that all people living in a certain country are likely to react the same way. Rather, this case is designed to illustrate common sources of miscommunication that frequently occur in international and intercultural situations.

Background for the Case

NetRider is a small American start-up company that produces one product only: Network Computers (NCs), a new type of affordable computing device that costs much less than traditional personal computers (PCs) to buy and maintain. Unlike PCs, NCs provide users with access to the Internet and World Wide Web only; they do not supply applications such as word processing or programming capabilities. Rather than having a large hard disk and lots of RAM (memory), NCs have minimal RAM and no hard disk and instead use a network connection to store data.

NetRider is a fast-paced, cutting-edge, fly-by-the-seat-of-its-pants organization. Its prime objectives are low prices, impeccable quality, and fast service. Its preferred channels of communication are fax and e-mail; its motto is "Get it fast; get it now!" Most of its employees have a computer science background, essential for a high-tech company. None has any particular background in writing or communication.

How NetRider Got Started

A few years ago, when they were computer science graduate students at State University, a large, Midwestern university, Jackson Hart and two of his friends decided to start their own company. At first it was a hobby. Since they were always being called on to help friends and relatives set up their new modems and teach them to navigate the World Wide Web, they decided they might as well get paid for it. As their business became locally known, they diversified a bit, helping people upgrade and repair their own computers, customize software, and write simple programs. With this experience, plus their graduate-level education, the three friends soon could do virtually anything computer-related. They were doing so well that they brought in another friend, who was working on an MBA, to do their finances.

Gradually, through a series of coincidences, a new idea began to develop—to form a company to produce a new type of computer, called a Network Computer, or NC. Teaching people to access the Web highlighted for the friends how little of a PCs capacity most people use. Many of their clients used their computer only to surf the Web. This meant that they were paying a lot of money for capability they never used. In one of his graduate courses, Jackson wrote a paper on NCs and became fascinated with their potential to revolutionize the computer industry. When Jackson discovered that the university's business incubator, which helped new businesses by providing expertise and capital, was starting a grant program to help graduate students start their own small businesses, the partners decided to start a new business devoted solely to producing NCs.

It was a chance of a lifetime. They had the knowledge, the drive, and, thanks to the business incubator and their families, the money. The NC industry was just beginning, and they were right there on the ground floor. What initially seemed a dream quickly became a reality, and a new company, NetRider, was born.

The business incubator supplied the students with a small office for very low rent, helped them locate their first suppliers so they could get the components they needed, and helped them with marketing. By the time the partners finished their graduate degrees a few months later, they already had the business firmly established and were beginning to hire more people to help with production. The four original owners still made all the decisions and essentially ran the company. Since his vision and creativity were the driving forces of the company, Jackson Hart was unanimously voted president.

After making the first big sale to his own university, Jackson had another great idea. Higher education was a completely open market for NCs. Since technology is changing so fast, budget considerations often make it difficult for universities to continually upgrade their equipment. NCs are much more affordable than PCs and could easily be used in many areas of a university where full-service computers are unnecessary. Would it be possible to focus exclusively on the higher-education market? Jackson convinced his partners to give it a try.

Despite a clear market niche, NetRider still couldn't expand rapidly until it found a way to control costs. After consulting with marketing professors, Jackson and his partners decided to lower overhead by selling only through the Web, and to keep only an eleven-day inventory on hand. So far, they've been able to accomplish their objectives: low prices, impeccable quality, and fast service.

A Major Leap to Success

NetRider's sale of NCs to State University brought public attention to both the company and the university. State University was the first public institution to build student computer labs dedicated solely to NCs and to replace all the PCs in the library with NCs. NetRider's owners also caught the public's attention: Here they were, four young people just out of graduate school, well on their way to dazzling success.

Then, administrators at State University helped NetRider stage a major coup: the sale of three hundred NCs to State University's "sister university" overseas, the International Institute of Technology in Tokyo, Japan, an institution known worldwide for being on the cutting edge of technology. Most of the NCs would be used in International Tech's new multi-million dollar library complex.

Buying NCs instead of PCs would save the university hundreds of thousands of dollars over the coming years, while still allowing it to expand services. The university has enjoyed favorable publicity as a result of this purchase. It has altered courses in anticipation of the new NCs, and a huge ceremony has been planned for the opening of the library complex. Administrators at State University arranged for Jackson to meet personally with the Director of Computer Services—who is overseeing the acquisition process and is responsible for seeing that the NCs are installed on time—and the Director of the Library.

The story got picked up in several trade publications, the *New York Times*, and then, miracle of miracles, by the prestigious TV show, "Sixty Minutes." In the course of the interview, Ed Bradley asked Jackson if NetRider would be able to handle the great upsurge in orders that surely would follow the publicity it was receiving. Looking straight into the camera, Jackson said, "Absolutely, Mr. Bradley. We can handle any order, of any size, at any time. We come through. We deliver. Guaranteed."

The mood in the NetRider office the day after the "Sixty Minutes" segment aired was euphoric. Work on the NCs for International Institute of Technology would begin soon. A large order of microchips and a couple of other needed parts would be arriving any day now.

The Scenario

All of a sudden, though, it looks as if NetRider's stunning success might come crashing to a halt. Waiting for Jackson when he comes into the office soon after the "Sixty Minutes" airing is a fax from NetRider's supplier of microchips, Silicon Chips, saying that a fire in their plant will prevent them from fulfilling the order for chips needed for International Tech's NCs. It was a relatively small fire, but production has halted, and it is too early to determine when it might resume.

This is devastating news! NetRider needs the chips within a few days to ship the order to International Tech on time. Jackson not only does not have another supplier lined up, but he also realizes that since Silicon Chips custom-made the chips to specifications the two companies had designed together over a period of time, it is unlikely that another company can just step in and begin immediate production.

To assess the situation further, Jackson gets on the phone with his contact at Silicon, Ellen Rodriguez.

"I'm well aware of the bind you're in," Ellen says. "Look, our association has helped us as much as it has you. I've told you before that we've been wanting to expand for over a year now but have had trouble working out the finances. The International Tech order was a dream come true. We were even about to finalize a deal to set up a limited partnership with an overseas firm, International Chips. I don't know how the fire will affect that. We want to keep on working with you, but I need a couple of days at least to map out our strategy here."

"A couple of days!" Jackson shouts into the phone. "Ellen, I just don't have it! I need answers, and I need them now!"

"The fire was beyond my control," she responds icily, in a measured tone, "and though your concerns are important to us, they are not our only concerns. The insurance inspector hasn't even arrived yet."

Jackson realizes that he's gone too far. Time to retrench!

"I . . . I'm sorry, Ellen; I truly apologize. I know this is difficult for you. Still, you're going to need money even more now. If you can help us through this jam, it will help you in the long run, too. We're bound to get more orders—a lot more orders—if we can somehow deliver to International Tech on time!

"This is a really serious situation. International Tech has already gotten lots of news time on this thing—and so have we. If the NCs do not arrive on time, International Tech will have a public relations disaster, and NetRider is history.

"Call me back today, Ellen, no matter how late, just to touch base, OK?"

"I can't promise, Jackson," she says, "But if I can't, I'll definitely get back to you tomorrow."

Jackson and his partners talk late into the night, but they still do not have a definite plan when Ellen Rodriguez finally calls back, very early the next morning.

"OK, it's not definite yet," she says, "But I've been doing a lot of thinking and a lot of phoning, and I think that I may have a possible solution for you."

She then proposes that the company with which Silicon Chips is trying to form a partnership, International Chips in Seoul, Korea, be brought into the deal. Silicon will provide International Chips with the needed specifications for the chip, with the understanding that NetRider and Silicon will once again do business when Silicon gets on its feet.

Ellen explains that International Chips is a small, family-owned company that has only recently started doing business outside the Pacific Rim. However, the crisis in the Asian economy has led their president to believe that, to ensure long-term stability, they will need to either diversify their product line or expand their customer base outside of Asia. The company adheres to the traditional, formal values of Korean business. It moves cautiously but deliberately, making business decisions by cultivating personal relationships and exploring the reputation of potential customers.

"I've talked to my contacts in both marketing and production at International," Ellen says, "and they're amenable to entertaining a proposal. I've got to tell you, though, that I still think that your chances of meeting your original deadline are slim. International clearly could come through sooner than we could because we're going to have to get some new equipment in here. However, I don't know that they'll want to rush into anything. I've already faxed the specifications to the marketing manager so he can look them over, but the president will make the final decision. My experience tells me that they'd act more quickly if they already knew you. That's clearly impossible, but we might be able to get through some preliminaries very quickly. Could you wait until I can write you a formal letter of introduction? Then we could wait to see how that was received and proceed accordingly."

"Well, I appreciate the thought, but I really can't wait, Ellen. Tell you what; give me all the info I need to contact International directly, and I'll get right back to you if I need any help. And, thanks a lot, Ellen. I owe you, big time."

Ellen just doesn't understand how crucial time is here, Jackson thought. She's preoccupied with her own problems.

After quickly running through his options, Jackson decides to fire off a fax to International Chips (See Figure 5.1). That should get the ball rolling, he thinks. You've got to show people that you mean business.

NetRider   High-Tech Solutions for Higher Education

1111 East 24th Street   Cleveland, OH 44115

Lee Sang-Eung, President
International Chips
25-8ga Chongye-chon
Chong no-gu, Seoul
Korea

Dear Mr. Lee Sang-Eung:

Pursuant to your conversation earlier today with Ellen Rodriguez from Silicon Chips about their inability to accommodate an important order due to a fire in their factory, I'd like to propose formally that your firm produce and supply us with the microchips we need to build our NC computer, the NetRider. By now you should have received the specs from Silicon.

Since we need a supply fast to be able to fulfill our large order to International Tech, please respond ASAP so we can make arrangements. I'll be happy to provide any information that you need, even to the point of sending one of our production people over to oversee the manufacturing of the chips. I can't stress enough how important it is that we move on this, pronto!

Sincerely,

Jackson M. Hart, President

FIGURE 5.1   Letter from NetRider to International Chips

Jackson expects to receive a reply later that day, or the next day at the latest. What's the time difference, anyway, he wonders? When he doesn't, he sends another fax asking if the first has been received, and asking for an immediate answer. The next morning—a wait that seems like an eternity to Jackson—the fax shown in Figure 5.2 arrives in response.

Jackson is shocked. Was it possible that the writer didn't understand his faxes? He was asking for action, results. He couldn't wait to let International decide if it even wanted to do business. And he certainly didn't see how he could go to Seoul *now*, in the middle of a crisis. Don't these people understand plain English? What should he do now?

Han guk International Chips, Incorporated
25–8ga Chongye-chon
Chong no-gu, Seoul

The proposal you forwarded to us has been received, and we thank you for your interest in our products. And we already had an excellent conversation with Miss Rodriguez from Silicon Chips and regret very deeply the fire that has been the cause of so much misfortunes.

We look forward with anticipation to the prospect of developing a mutually beneficial relationship. Of course, we need your thoughts on quantity, delivery date, insurance conditions, etc. As soon as we get these informations mentioned I will discuss this project with our owners and we will be back to you after we have had an opportunity to discuss. We would be happy to give you our quotes in person should you be traveling to Seoul in near future.

With kind regards to you and your family,

Sincerely,

Lee Sang-Eung
President

FIGURE 5.2   Letter from International Chips to NetRider

Background for Analysis

Different cultural values lead to different communication practices, which in turn affect the way organizations transact business. A difference in values may be the underlying cause of the problems in this case.

People in many Asian cultures, including Korea, may have a different attitude about beginning a business relationship than most Americans. While Americans typically want to get right to the bottom line, Asians are more likely to want to get to know the people in the organization before they formalize a business arrangement. This may be particularly true of a small, family-owned firm like International Chips, which is still relatively new to the international market. Companies already established in the international arena are more likely to anticipate and be able to deal with American directness and hurry to strike agreements.

Koreans typically prefer to have direct contact with new business partners, meeting face-to-face if at all possible; speaking on the phone is a distant second alternative. Koreans want to have an opportunity to assess the reputation of a business and the reliability and capabilities of the people with whom they will be working. Unlike Americans, Koreans tend to value oral agreements more than written ones, and to make such agreements after they have had time to assess the situation.

Analysis of the Case

In firing off the fax to International Chips, the president of NetRider violated virtually all of the guidelines of international communication. The letter is too abrupt for a situation in which a business relationship has not yet been established. Its demanding tone, with no consideration for the reader's point of view, certainly would be considered rude. International Chips has not had time to think through the technical information provided by Silicon Chips, and they have had no prior communication at all with NetRider.

A fax is not the ideal way to establish the initial business contact. Direct contact, preferably in person, would typically be needed before most Korean companies would enter in to a new venture, especially a costly one that could be a one-time deal. Having Ellen Rodriguez do the initial groundwork was helpful, indeed vital to any chance of success, since she had already developed a relationship with International Chips. But Jackson did not listen to her advice. He would have saved time in the long run if he had let Ellen write a formal letter of introduction, and then called the president of International Chips personally.

Jackson's follow-up fax (see Figure 5.3) made the situation worse. Because of the time difference, the first fax—sent early in the morning from the Midwest—would not arrive in Seoul until late at night Seoul time, long after normal working hours; therefore, receiving a response the same day Jackson sent the fax was impossible. It's quite likely, then, that the first and second faxes were read about the same time.

It may also be perceived as an affront to offer to send an employee to negotiate who may be perceived as a lower-level worker (in the first fax Jackson, offered to send "one of our production people" to oversee production of the chips). Asian companies tend to value the type of authority and assurance that can come only from dealing with top executives. In this instance, when no previous contact has taken place, ascertaining the reputation of the company is vital.

Poor writing contributes to the situation as well. No specifics are given about deadlines or anything else, and though Ellen Rodriguez had sent the technical specifications of the chips and may have mentioned the original shipping dates, Ellen did not actually tell Jackson whether she gave such details. In any event, Jackson should not expect International Chips to say definitely that they will enter into an agreement without hearing specifics from NetRider itself. The fax also uses very informal language and slang such as "specs," which may be misinterpreted, and the tone is extremely demanding. The tone would be likely to offend even an American company with a philosophy similar to NetRider's. It goes beyond typical American directness by *demanding* that International Chips drop everything to

---

NetRider   High-Tech Solutions for Higher Education

1111 East 24th Street   Cleveland, OH 44115

Lee Sang-Eung, President International Chips
25-8ga Chongye-chon
Chong no-gu, Seoul
Korea

Dear Mr. Lee Sang-Eung:

I've waited all day for a response to my earlier fax. We need to know NOW
whether you'll be able to produce the chips we need to process our order from International Tech. This is a once in a lifetime opportunity, and it's vital that we meet
our deadline. Your failure to respond could result in the loss of huge profits for
both our company and yours, not to mention the public relations debacle it would
cause. If it's a matter of money, let me assure you that we are open to any reasonable offer. We just need to move on this.

Minutes count here. I'm standing by, waiting for your answer.

Sincerely,

Jackson M. Hart, President

FIGURE 5.3   Second Letter (Fax) from NetRider to International Chips

comply with NetRider's request. This approach violates the basic concept of "you-
attitude" crucial in any technical correspondence.

Every company, no matter how small, develops its own organizational culture. The fast-paced, risk-taking approach of NetRider, coupled with the owners' high level of technical expertise, have enabled the company to develop
cutting-edge technology and also to seize the opportunity for a lucrative contract. However, their fast success and relative inexperience have left them vulnerable: They had never given a thought to arranging for backup suppliers, or
the practical steps involved in handling a huge order fast. They have made the
mistake of thinking that as long as they continue to be technically innovative and
willing to take risks, they'll continue to be successful. But it may be their basic
lack of communication skills, and their total ignorance of the importance of such
skills, that is their undoing.

As a small company just beginning to deal with American businesses, International Chips is not likely to share NetRider's "get it fast, get it now" philosophy.

Rather than being motivated by the urgency of NetRider's situation, International Chips may take it a as a sign that NetRider may not be stable enough to be a reliable business partner. Considering the emergency situation and uncertainty of long-term payoff for the company, the president of International Chips may view his willingness to even hear the proposal as a very large favor to Silicon Chips, with whom he hopes to establish a partnership soon. In that event, NetRider's faxes would seem even more presumptuous and out of place.

Questions for Discussion

1. What specific parts of the letter from NetRider to International Chips might have been misinterpreted, or interpreted negatively, by a Korean reader (see Figure 6.1). What specific details seem to be a reflection of the writer's culture? Analyze the letter carefully, and discuss writing techniques that may make technical writing to international audiences more effective.

2. Analyze the fax from International Chips (see Figure 6.2). What clues in this response give an indication of how the writer perceived NetRider's fax?

3. One unresolved issue in this case is whether to contact the International Institute of Technology now to explain that their NC shipment might be late. Though one would not want to mistakenly conclude that all Asian cultures are identical or that all readers within a culture would react the same, is there anything that NetRider could learn from its experience in writing to International Chips that might make communicating with International Tech more effective? What similarities and differences do you see in the two situations? Reread the case problem to see how each organization is described.

4. Considering what you have learned about cultural differences between the United States and Korea, what could NetRider have done before faxing International Chips that would have increased its chances of success?

5. If you were an international communication consultant, how would you advise Jackson Hart of NetRider to proceed? What are the pros and cons of each course of action listed below?

   - Write to International Chips, trying once more to strike a deal.
   - Send an apology to International Chips.
   - Ask Ellen Rodriguez of Silicon Chips to talk to the president of International Chips on your behalf.
   - Make arrangements to go to Seoul immediately to meet with the owners of International Chips.
   - Look for another supplier.
   - Wait for Silicon Chips to resume production.
   - Contact the International Institute of Technology in Japan to tell them that their NCs are likely to be late.
   - Issue a press release advising the public—and the media—of the situation in an attempt to ward off unfavorable publicity.
   - Post an article on the NetRider Web site informing readers about the fire at Silicon Chips and how NetRider plans to proceed.

6. What general policies for communication with overseas clients might an organization establish to prevent the kind of cultural misunderstanding in which NetRider seems to be embroiled?

7. What factors in addition to cultural misunderstandings might make International Chips react cautiously to the offer from NetRider?

Writing Assignments

1. Assume the role of Jackson Hart, president of NetRider. Drawing on all the information above, write a diplomatic message to the president of International Chips in which you strive to ease any tensions or affront you unwittingly caused in your earlier communications. Your goal is to raise your company in the estimation of International Chips so that they still will be willing to do business with you. Feel free to add any details that do not violate the spirit of the situation as described in this case problem. To prepare yourself to write, study the letters in Figure 6.1 and Figure 6.2 carefully. Also consider the following questions:

   • What expectations of the Korean readers did the first letter from NetRider probably not fulfill? How can you increase the chances that the letter you are going to write now will do a better job? Consider content, organization, and tone of the message.
   • What reasons, specifically, do you think that International Chips may have for being reluctant to do business with NetRider?
   • What advantages could working with NetRider have for International Chips?
   • What specifics will need to be included about the work that you want International Chips to do (delivery schedules, insurance, number and types of chips, overseeing production, etc.)?
   • What concessions, if any, can you make to help negotiations go smoothly?
   • How will you propose to continue negotiations—through letters, faxes, telephone conversations, e-mail, personal visits?
   • So far, Jackson Hart has been thinking only about getting the chips on time. What else would you really need to be able to make a deal (e.g., price)?

2. As the president of NetRider, assume that after consulting with the other owners, you decide that it may be best to contact the International Institute of Technology to warn them that their order of NCs may be late. The address is

   International Institute of Technology
   Asahigaoka 4–2
   Hino Tokyo 191 JAPAN

   To prepare to write this letter, review the information in the case problem carefully to glean clues that will help you prepare the most effective message. Also consider the following questions:

   • How does the fact that Jackson Hart has already met the Director of Computer Services and the Director of the Library at International Tech affect the letter he needs to write? Compare the situation with International Chips, where no one even knew who Jackson was.
   • Think about the details about International Chips to determine how they will probably react to news of the delay. No one knows definitely how long the delay will be

yet. How will that affect what you write? Also, how will the fact that International Tech has received a great deal of publicity affect their reaction?

- To whom should you write: the Director of the Library, or the Director of Computer Services?
- What are the reasons, pro and con, for writing immediately instead of waiting until you have a definite delivery date?

Additional Reading: Issues Relevant to the Case

Abecasis-Phillips, J. A. S. (1994). *Doing business with the Japanese.* Lincolnwood, IL: NTC.

Carson, K. D. (1995). Enhancing communication and interactional effectiveness with Mexican-American trainees. *Business Communication Quarterly, 58(3),* 19–25.

Chu, C. N. (1991). *The Asian mind game.* New York: Scribner.

Connor, U. M., & Verckens, J. P. (1997). An international course in international business writing: Belgium, Finland, the United States. *Business Communication Quarterly, 60(4),* 63–74.

Gilsdorf, J. W. (1997). Metacommunication effects on international business negotiating in China. *Business Communication Quarterly, 60(2),* 20–37.

Haas, C., & Funk, J. L. (1989). "Shared information:" Some observations of communication in Japanese technical settings. *Technical Communication, 36(4),* 385.

Hall, E. T., & Hall, M. R. (1987). *Hidden differences: Doing business with the Japanese.* New York: Doubleday.

Harris, P. R., & Moran, R. T. (1996). *Managing cultural differences.* Houston: Gulf.

Hulbert, J. E. (1994). Overcoming intercultural communication barriers. *The Bulletin of the Association for Business Communication, 57(1),* 41–44.

Jameson, D. (1993). Using a simulation to teach intercultural communication in business communication courses. *The Bulletin of the Association for Business Communication, 56(1),* 3–9.

Jesswein, K. (1997). An introduction to international business on the Internet. *Multinational Business Review, 5(2),* 1–9.

Kitalong, K. S. (1997). Case studies in international technical communication. *Business Communication Quarterly, 60(4),* 132–134.

Leppert, P. A. (1996). *Doing business with Korea.* Fremont, CA: Jain.

Murray, M. E. (1994). Multicultural communication concepts in the business communication course. *The Bulletin of the Association for Business Communication, 57(1),* 40–41.

O'Rourke, J. S. (1993). Teaching intercultural business communication: Building a course from the ground up. *The Bulletin of the Association for Business Communication, 56(4),* 22–27.

Popham, P. (1987). *The insider's guide to Korea.* Edison, NJ: Hunter.

Ranney, F. J., & McNeilly, K. M. (1996). International business writing projects: Learning content through process. *Business Communication Quarterly, 59(1),* 9–26.

Sharp, H. M. (1995). Challenging students to respond to multicultural issues: The case-study approach. *The Bulletin of the Association for Business Communication, 58(2),* 28–31.

Smith, M. O., & Steward, J. F. (1995). Communication for a global economy. *Business Education Forum, 49(4),* 25–28.

Tovey, J. (1997). Addressing issues of cultural diversity in business communication. *Business Communication Quarterly, 60(1),* 19–30.

Weick, K. E. (1990). Organizing on a global scale: A research and teaching agenda. *Human Resource Management, 29(1),* 49–61.

Chapter 6

Translating User Manuals:
A Surgical Equipment Company's "Quick Cut"

BRUCE MAYLATH
University of Wisconsin at Stout

Abstract: When pressures build on a translation project's budget, time to deadline, and translation quality, is money, time, or quality likely to be sacrificed? This fictional but lifelike case looks at what can happen when such pressures build to the bursting point. Cordipatch, a manufacturer of synthetic heart patches, has contracted with LanguageCrossing, a translation company, to translate its manuals for surgeons. As the workload increases, as time to deadlines shortens, and as personnel shift, anxieties grow about the quality of the translated manuals, and thus the quality of the heart patch surgeries. An analysis follows of the factors influencing a translation's quality and concludes by showing how such factors can coalesce to ensure quality or scuttle it.

Note: This case study is imaginary. All names and products mentioned are fictitious. Any resemblance to any real-life counterparts is entirely coincidental.

Background for the Case

Mike is traveling abroad on a bicycle trip. He felt tired before he left, but now he feels faint. He's pretty sure the heavy sensation he feels around his heart is not a symptom of jet lag or homesickness.

The next thing he knows, he's in a local hospital. A doctor is gently slapping his face and telling him in somewhat broken English that the staff has discovered a perforation in his heart. The doctor, a surgeon, is preparing to perform an operation in which a synthetic heart patch will be attached at the point of the perforation to close it up permanently. The surgeon, who has performed this kind of operation only once before, will be relying on a manual written by the heart patch's manufacturer, Cordipatch, and translated on the company's behalf by a translation company named LanguageCrossings.

Just before the anesthesist places a mask over Mike's face, Mike sees the surgeon glancing at the manual and screwing up his face, as if to say, "What does *this* mean?" All of a sudden it occurs to Mike that the surgeon may be having the same problem with translated instructions that he had when he tried to adjust the brakes on his foreign-made bike by referring to instructions that were poorly translated into English. Growing drowsy now, he mumbles to the doctor, "Please don't mess up!"

This scene leads us to a pair of questions. First, how can technical communicators ensure that their documents in translation are accurate and usable—in other words, of high quality? The question is more than academic. The documents are manuals used by surgeons to attach synthetic heart patches onto human hearts. For patients, whether surgeons understand the translation is a matter of life and death. We might, then, follow the first question with a second: Will surgeons reading the translated manuals be able to attach the heart patches correctly?

Any difficulty the surgeon might have in interpreting the translated instructions goes back to what transpired between the manufacturing company, with its staff of designers, engineers, line workers, project managers, and technical communicators, and the translation company contractor, with its staff of project managers, translators, editors, reviewers, and document designers. The manufacturer of the heart patches has relied on a small translation company with "in-country" translators who live in the country where the translation will be used. Moreover, most of these translators are themselves surgeons.

However, because of a rapid increase in sales, and in numbers of new products—and thus the number of translation projects—the manufacturer is about to switch to another, larger translation company, which will take over management of the translation projects in addition to conducting the translations. This company employs translators who, while native speakers of the target languages, live in the United States and thus are not in daily contact with the languages and their inevitable changes over time. Moreover, few of them have medical training. As the move gradually takes place, the question of quality hovers over the company.

To understand how translations typically proceed, you need to know something about the personnel involved. Cordipatch, the company that designs and manufactures the synthetic heart patches, employs one or two project managers who line up the translation company and act as the liaison between the manufacturer and the translation company. Beth is a veteran project manager. She knows French and can proofread French and a little Spanish. Several months ago, she began training Jake, a novice project manager, to replace her. Jake can proofread a little Spanish. Because both Beth and Jake have had to split their time between managing translation projects and marketing projects, the company has just hired

Virginie, a brand new project manager from Canada and a native speaker of French, to handle translation projects full time.

LanguageCrossings, a small, local translation company, has handled nearly all of Cordipatch's technical translation projects to date. Martha, a veteran project manager, has handled Cordipatch's projects for years. However, because she is anticipating taking maternity leave, she has been training Katy, a novice project manager, to work with the company's network of translators, editors, and reviewers, in addition to acting as the liaison between LanguageCrossings and Cordipatch.

Added to the picture is SF-World, a large, San Francisco-based translation company to which Cordipatch is transferring its technical translation projects. For the last year and a half, SF-World has been translating Cordipatch's sales brochures.

Like most translation companies, LanguageCrossings uses a quality-control procedure to ensure the accuracy and reliability of its translations. The company has the client, in this case Cordipatch, submit an approved final copy of the document, in this case a heart patch manual written in English. A project manager at Cordipatch pulls together all the materials that the translation company will need. Cordipatch's project manager is then the point of communication for all dealings with the translation company. LanguageCrossings, in turn, assigns its own project manager to coordinate the manual's translation.

One of the first and most important duties of LanguageCrossings' project manager is to select translators, editors, and reviewers from its long list of in-country personnel (known in the business as "vendors"). The project managers make every effort to match the vendors' linguistic expertise and subject-area expertise to the type of project. Thus, for Cordipatch's manuals, many of the vendors are trained surgeons. The translators and editors are highly trained in rendering the meaning and style of a document's original language (the source language) into their own native language (the target language) and are familiar with the professional jargon used in their native country. The reviewer, on the other hand, is not well versed in the original language but is a member of the intended audience, in this case heart surgeons.

With a translation team in place, the project manager sends the document to the translator for initial translation and development of a glossary, to maintain consistent use of terms. Next, an editor (actually, a second translator assigned the job of editing) examines the initial changes and makes any changes he or she deems appropriate. From there the project manager sends the document to a reviewer, who makes sure that everything from style to grammar looks and sounds identical to the way the text would appear if written by a native surgeon in the target country.

The translation is then ready for formatting. The project manager forwards the text to a desktop publisher, who lays out the pages in a format that matches the conventions used by professionals in the target country. (Pages in Arabic and Hebrew, for instance, move from right to left.) Once formatted, the document returns to the initial translator, then the reviewer, for proofreading. Finally, the project manager proofreads and approves the document and delivers it to the client.

Depending on the document's size and complexity, the translation team may include more members, and the procedure may be repeated to ensure accuracy and reliability—in short, quality.

The Client Company and Translation Company

Multiple factors—some human, some logistical—can affect a document's quality. The humans involved are grouped under the client company and the translation company.

Client Company

- The project manager oversees the documents' development; hires the translation company; may recruit additional reviewers; and acts as liaison for the client company with the translation company.
- The technical writer prepares the original documents.
- The boss ultimately determines how much money and time are devoted to a translation project.
- The lawyer edits documents for their legal ramifications.
- The director of marketing may have influence over a translated document's design and composition.
- The designers and engineers develop the products that the translated documents accompany.

Of these, the boss is the most critical person determining a document's quality, because of the boss's ultimate decision-making power.

The Translation Company

- The project manager oversees the documents' development in translation; lines up a translation team of translators, editors, and reviewers; and acts as liaison for the client company with translation company.
- The boss makes ultimate decisions about which clients to accept and how much time and money to devote to each.
- The translator takes the source text and renders it in the target language.
- The editor checks the translator's work.
- The reviewer takes the role of a representative user, the person intended to read and use the documents, and critiques the documents' usability.

Of these, the translator is the most critical person determining a document's quality, because the translator makes the fundamental decisions about how the text will be rendered in the target language.

Logistical Factors

Logistical factors can also play a decisive role. While some, such as attitude or level of knowledge, may appear inseparable from the humans who hold them, these factors can be seen as entities apart from the persons involved as well. Attitude, for example, can change quickly and can be viewed as a logistical dynamic. Thus they are listed here. Logistical factors include

Money

- Budgets
- Economic downturns
- New spending priorities

Time

- Deadlines
- Holidays and vacations
- Unexpected interruptions
- Multinational calendars

Level of knowledge (of any person making decisions about the translation)

- Awareness of languages and language variation
- Awareness of translation procedures

Production and distribution technology

- Software platforms
- Telecommunications, including e-mail, FTP, and World Wide Web
- Fax machines
- Glossary technologies
- Prepress production, including document design and desktop publishing

Document version control

- Unclear or ambiguous original
- Multiple revisions
- Last-minute revisions
- Different translators, editors, or reviewers
- Preexisting, preapproved translations

Regulations

- ISO 9004–2
- EPA or FDA guidelines
- Customs and laws
- Labor and work councils
- Language legislation
- Labeling requirements

Length of communication chain

Attitude

- Spirit of cooperation
- Trust
- Can-do
- Win-win approach
- Sense of working toward a common goal

LanguageCrossings and Cordipatch

Let's go now to what has been happening at LanguageCrossings and its client, Cordipatch. Nearly always, client companies like Cordipatch are most concerned about three dimensions of translation projects:

1. Time
2. Quality
3. Cost

Generally, under pressure from management to bring the product to market, one of these rises to the fore and the other two suffer.

At Cordipatch, time is the chief dimension that drives their dealings with the personnel at LanguageCrossings. LanguageCrossings has been the sole provider of Cordipatch's technical translations for many years. Cordipatch's translations constitute a large share of LanguageCrossings' business. Beth says that because LanguageCrossings is smaller, "they're more responsive," giving quicker turn-arounds and more attention to Cordipatch's projects than did other firms she used several years earlier.

Both Beth and Jake put a high premium on a translation company's respon-siveness, and for good reason—their bosses have made it clear to them that under no circumstances can a translation be late. As Beth told Martha when the two began working together, "If we've got to get a product out the door, and we don't have a manual, well, shame on us. I mean, we can never let it get down to the manual being the deciding factor if a product goes out the door. So it's our responsibility to have the manual ready when the product's ready to ship." The reason for the crunch that Beth and Jake must contend with stems in large part from the production procedures Cordipatch employs for its manuals. When a manual starts on its path from conception to completion, the deadline is set so that it coincides with the release of the product for which the manual is intended.

Jake explains the process as he rehearses with Beth what the two of them will have to tell Virginie: "Sometimes the manuals are written by technical writers. More often, though, they're written by our product managers in-house."

"Right," says Beth. "And then there's the review stage."

"Yeah," Jake continues, "So next, the manual receives a review by the internal clinical, regulatory, and legal staffs. Each staff does its work independent of the others and takes the time it deems necessary. The staffs place a high premium on fine-tuning the original text in English, and as the staffs do their editing, the development of the manual is often slowed down."

"Exactly," interjects Beth. "But remember to tell her that the deadline for completion remains inalterable. Consequently, the translation period may get shortened by as much as two weeks, as the deadline for the product's release looms ahead of us."

The last month has proven especially tense. Beth remarks to Jake, "It seems like we're always rushing to get things done."

Ethical Considerations

The danger, of course, is that in the rush to complete projects, quality will suffer. More to the point, the quality of instructions for inserting heart patches is literally a matter of life and death. The project managers at LanguageCrossings are growing frustrated and nervous about Cordipatch's increasingly short deadlines. At its regular morning staff meeting, LanguageCrossings' project managers take up agenda item number one: dealing with Cordipatch. Katy exclaims what everyone at LanguageCrossings has been thinking: "This is a doctor putting a heart patch into a patient. You're not just advertising candy or something!"

Katy's concerns about the ethics of shortchanging quality for timely delivery at the expense of patients' lives are clear enough. Such expenses and violations of ethics are charged to manufacturers and their contractors, like LanguageCrossings, through liability assessment. A wrongful death or medical malpractice suit can cost millions of dollars. Martha lays out the situation for the rest of the project managers: "Look, folks, we're paying incredibly high premiums on our liability insurance, and it's because of this Cordipatch account. We're paying at least 25 percent more than we would be otherwise. It's getting closer and closer to the point that the liability premiums are eating up nearly all that we make in profit from the work with Cordipatch. And if we ever got sued for defective translation, it's questionable whether even the liability insurance would keep us in business."

A low, collective "Wow" is heard around the table. Katy says, "Gee, I didn't realize it was costing us that much."

"Sure," Martha continues. "Because of the dangers involved if translation quality falters, we're paying through the nose. So far, we've been able to swallow the extra cost, which is paid for in part by the extra charges Cordipatch incurs when it demands last-minute changes from us. However, with the increased number of projects and product releases demanding more translations in still more languages, I don't see how we can keep this up indefinitely."

Over the next week, the growing fear of error becomes palpable at LanguageCrossings. Just before the next staff meeting convenes, Martha mutters to Katy, "It's getting wild." Members of the LanguageCrossings staff begin to question whether keeping the Cordipatch account is worth the stress, the insurance premiums, and the growing fear of a potential lawsuit. The entire staff meeting is devoted to the concern about the Cordipatch projects.

Back at Cordipatch, Beth and Jake talk to Virginie about the translations of the heart patch manuals they've hired her to handle. Beth and Jake acknowledge that they put an extraordinary amount of pressure on the LanguageCrossings staff, to the point of demanding that major changes in a manual be done overnight. Beth tells Virginie, "We do push. We're very demanding clients when it comes to translations, and we realize that, but we're being beat up on this side by our bosses' marketing deadlines." The Cordipatch project managers feel comfortable with their demands, in part because LanguageCrossings has so often been accommodating.

"They've always turned things around for us very quickly, which we've appreciated," Beth tells Virginie.

Jake adds, "We've had to speed things up so often, and they're very good about it."

"They're right there," agrees Beth.

When Virginie asks if they know how LanguageCrossings accomplishes its speedy turnarounds, both Beth and Jake reply, after a moment's pause, "Well, no."

Beth confides, "As long as we get it, we're happy. Sometimes it's not been possible, and they let us know."

LanguageCrossings has been successful thus far for a number of reasons. First, it cultivates a network of more than fifteen hundred translators around the world. It has translators new to the company prove what they can do in specialized areas, like medicine, by starting off with small projects and working up to big ones. Second, it relies heavily on communication technology, like faxes, e-mail, file transfer protocol (FTP), and overnight air delivery, in combination with time differences. Thus, a request to have changes to the Bahasa language heart patch manual used in Indonesia made overnight can happen because as LanguageCrossings staff leave the office in the evening, they can e-mail the request to Suketo, the medical translator in Indonesia, who is just beginning his workday. He then e-mails the completed translation back as evening starts, just as the project managers at LanguageCrossings and Cordipatch are returning to their offices for their new morning. However, there may be only five translators of English-to-Bahasa medical documents in Indonesia, and only Suketo is trained as a surgeon. Hence, when translation projects of heart patch manuals multiply and their deadlines remain rigid, LanguageCrossings will either have to rely on a nonsurgeon unfamiliar with the surgical devices to translate or tell Cordipatch that it can't have all its projects done as soon as it would like. Lately, LanguageCrossings has had to do both, thus heightening the staff's anxiety.

Complicating matters further, new project managers are in charge at both companies. For years, Beth, representing Cordipatch, and Martha, representing LanguageCrossings, worked hand in glove to oversee the successful completion of the translation projects. Each had attained a high level of knowledge about translation procedures, language variation, heart patch manuals, and the idiosyncrasies of Cordipatch's culture and methods. Then, about the same time, Beth was promoted and began handing off projects to Jake, and Martha cut back her hours in anticipation of the delivery of a new baby and began passing on her projects to Katy. Both Jake and Katy are new to the work. Neither has had time to gain nearly the levels of knowledge that Beth and Jake have, just as the translation projects are growing more numerous and complex. After eight months, Jake, too, is promoted and replaced by Virginie, who is knowledgeable about languages and who, in Language Crossings' view, runs roughshod over the quality control procedures that prevent disaster. Fortunately, Beth and Martha are still on hand at each company. When the pressure cooker at each company appears ready to explode, the two of them are called in, talk to each other, and return the situation to a simmer.

So far, the project managers at Cordipatch have trusted the quality of the translations because of their confidence in the quality control procedures. First, they understand the thoroughness of LanguageCrossings' procedures. When they talk to LanguageCrossings' project managers, Beth and Jake acknowledge that the translators' medical expertise does much to eliminate potential problems of malpractice, poor patient care, and liability. They note that the surgeons who serve as LanguageCrossings' reviewers have even been known to flag errors in the instructions' medical procedures and report these back to Cordipatch. Second, in addition to the reviewers LanguageCrossings uses, Cordipatch employs its own reviewers to inspect its manuals. As at LanguageCrossings, Cordipatch's reviewers are always in the target country and are usually surgeons. Those who are not are often Cordipatch's own in-country sales personnel. The reviewers see the translation twice: once in its unformatted version, then after it is formatted. Sometimes they even review the document a third time.

"So far," Beth tells Virginie, "knock on wood, we haven't had any bad mistakes—nothing that would be procedurally incorrect. We've just had little things, like this word's misspelled or there should have been an accent on this or we don't technically say that quite that way. So we've been lucky. We haven't had any disasters so far in terms of anything that would be really incorrect or that would cause a problem for a surgeon."

Jake concurs, remarking that the reviewers are especially good about watching for anything that might affect the surgery itself or create a liability problem for Cordipatch. "It's their job," says Jake, "to make sure everything is correct."

However, much is changing at Cordipatch. The shifts in project managers have already led to increased concerns about whether the work will be done on time and error-free. Now Cordipatch is switching translation companies. The work that LanguageCrossings has been doing will now be taken over by SF-World. Cordipatch sees this as a necessary move. The explosive growth in its overseas business and the attendant multiplication of its translation projects have resulted in the overburdening of its project management staff. SF-World, a firm much larger than LanguageCrossings, has included in its bids an offer to handle the project management that Cordipatch itself has been doing. Cordipatch sees such outsourcing as its best option. SF-World will now oversee all Cordipatch's translations, with Virginie serving as Cordipatch's contact with SF-World.

Beth sees the new arrangement as a good solution, given her company's demands on her department. Drawing on her well-developed level of knowledge, she has interviewed numerous translation companies around the United States before settling on SF-World. Nevertheless, when she speaks to Jake of her satisfaction with her decision, a hint of trepidation enters her voice. "You know, Jake," she says, "for the last year and a half, we've had SF-World translate Cordipatch's marketing brochures for heart patches. Knowing SF-World is going to have an expanded role, we've sent them piles of materials on heart patches, including the manuals that LanguageCrossings translated earlier."

"That's right," says, Jake, in a reassuring tone. "SF-World tells me that they're compiling their own glossaries."

Beth hesitates. "I don't know. Here's what I keep mulling over: SF-World's translators live by-and-large in the San Francisco Bay area, not in-country like LanguageCrossings' do. I think they'll know the current culture and terms well enough, but I'm not sure. Then too, few if any of their translators are surgeons, although we know that some are gaining knowledge as medical translators. Most of all, though, I'm concerned about turnaround times."

"For sure," replies Jake, "but SF-World is more than large enough to handle the new project management role."

"Still," Beth ruminates, "its new portfolio with us will be just a fraction of its business. Will they have the same quick turnaround as LanguageCrossings? I know LanguageCrossings is expensive, but I think their service is what we really rely on, and I don't mind paying more if we're getting the kind of turnaround we're asking for and we're getting a quality product at the end. It takes a long time to build a good relationship with a translation company, and I know it's going to take a long time to develop the kind of relationship we want with SF-World, too."

As Cordipatch and SF-World move into their new arrangement, questions linger: Will SF-World's nonsurgeon translators render Cordipatch's manuals as well as LanguageCrossings' surgeon translators have? Will SF-World give the same scrutiny to translation projects as Cordipatch's project managers have? Will Cordipatch find SF-World's turnaround time acceptable? Will SF-World sacrifice quality for time? And hence, will surgeons reading manuals translated by SF-World be able to insert heart patches correctly and efficiently—without confusion and without loss of life?

Background for Analysis

Time will have to pass before there will be definitive answers to these questions. What is certain is that several of the factors listed above have the potential to affect the quality of Cordipatch's user manuals in translation. These include time; version control, especially last-minute revisions; attitude, especially trust; level of knowledge; and the client's boss—that is to say, upper management. Of these, the last is heightening the influence of all the others.

Time

It is easy enough to see the effect of time on the quality of user manuals in translation. The more rushed anyone handling the documents feels, the more likely that an inadvertent error will creep in or remain unnoticed. The old maxim "Haste makes waste" sums up well what happens in such a situation. The conditions under which Cordipatch and its translation contractors work—namely that staffs in every part of the company can slow down a document and impinge on the translation time, but the translation team cannot do likewise—appears untenable. In the long run, such conditions are an accident—and a liability suit—waiting to happen.

Document Version Control

In the case described, control over a document's versions is being affected by short deadlines. The resulting "crunch" leads to the Cordipatch staff's insertion of numerous last-minute changes in a text within a few days. Thus, within a week's time, a document that LanguageCrossings believed was completed on Day 1 gets "final" changes on Day 2, and again on Days 3, 4, and 5. Keeping track of which version is truly final, particularly as documents are raced by fax and e-mail around the globe, can be confusing, to say the least. Confusion always heightens the possibility of errors. In particular, all the computer cutting and pasting of editing changes can lead to the inadvertent erasure of text portions that are not to be changed.

Attitude

How members of translation teams view their work and each other can damage a document's quality when attitudes turn negative. To date, any effect that attitude might have on Cordipatch's translation projects has not been detectable. This has been in large part due to the long relationship between Cordipatch and LanguageCrossings. Viewing the relationship up close, one can see that the relationship is primarily trust and goodwill between Beth and Martha. However, when both of these players move out of their key roles at their respective companies and are replaced by newcomers who have not yet had time to establish trust, the relationship between Cordipatch and LanguageCrossings shows signs of strain. The relationship is mended at points of near rupture when Beth and Martha are called in and communicate with each other again. Whether the relationship could continue without Beth and Martha, or whether the new project managers can build up their own trust, is not clear. Indeed, with the transfer of the translation work to SF-World, the point is moot.

The factor of attitude is not, however. One can see in Beth's comments her uncertainty about whether the new relationship Cordipatch will have with SF-World will be as strong as its relationship with LanguageCrossings has been historically. Each party needs to trust that the other shares its concerns about time, quality, and cost, whether it be Cordipatch's tight deadlines, the manuals' usability to surgeons, or LanguageCrossings' insurance premiums. Attitude in this case encompasses not only trust but also the SF-World's project managers' view of the importance of the Cordipatch account. Beth acknowledges this factor when she points out that Cordipatch will be only a minor portfolio in SF-World's business. She wonders whether SF-World will recognize as well as LanguageCrossings has the critical nature that time plays in Cordipatch's translation projects. If SF-World does not, Cordipatch's Virginie will not trust SF-World's personnel. If her attitude toward SF-World becomes condescending, will SF-World's project managers skimp on quality control merely to "give her what she wants" on time? If trust dissolves, which company will be the first to break the relationship? More to the point, what catastrophe will catalyze the rupture?

Level of Knowledge

Of all the logistical factors that could affect translation quality, level of knowledge plays the most critical role. If the new project managers have not yet gained sufficient knowledge of translation procedures—particularly their role in them—the more likely the translation process will go haywire and translation quality will drop. Likewise, if the translators and editors lack sufficient knowledge of the products whose manuals they are translating, their renditions of the manuals in the target languages are more likely to be inaccurate, less reliable, or confusing. Nevertheless, for all the gaps in knowledge that appear to be opening among members of the translation team, the gaping chasms in knowledge are seen most visibly in upper management.

The Client's Boss

Ultimately, all the logistical factors are controlled by the people involved. Beth, Jake, and Virginie's bosses exhibit a dangerous lack of knowledge about what happens during translation, as manifested by their decision to allow all players except the translation team time to render a high-quality manual.

The problem is that the Cordipatch project managers' bosses have only the vaguest ties to any cultures or languages outside their own. Like many Americans, they believe that a knowledge of English—particularly their own American English—is sufficient to run a global operation. Their attitude about their own level of knowledge—in this case of languages and translation—manifests what psychologists term *cognitive dissidence*. They acknowledge that their company must rapidly expand its overseas business, and they acknowledge that the language that surgeons use in operating rooms in these new markets is most often not English. Thus, they willingly approve spending large sums of money on the translation of manuals. Despite this level of knowledge, however, they do not consciously acknowledge that their ignorance of other languages and cultures affects their ability to make wise decisions for these new overseas markets. Most immediately, their low level of knowledge affects their decision about how much time to allow to achieve a high-quality translation that helps save lives.

Cordipatch's most recent annual report reveals the contradiction. In a section called "Around Hearts, Around the World" it says:

Demand for heart patches from clients outside North America has never been greater. We at Cordipatch have made as a major goal the extension of our presence so that Cordipatch can make the most of the opportunities that worldwide business markets offer.

Later in the report, in a section on "Financial Condition," the Chief Executive Officer (CEO) and Chief Financial Officer (CFO) write:

Management reviews and modifies the system of internal controls to improve its effectiveness. The control system's effectiveness is guaranteed by the selection, retention, and training of high-potential employees, an organizational structure that divides responsibilities efficiently, and a strong budgeting system that controls costs.

One wonders whether management can plausibly review and modify its internal controls for translation quality with the same effectiveness it achieves in its ledger sheet quality. While management can review the company's documents to know if their numbers add up, it is doubtful that it has the knowledge necessary to know if the words in its translations add up to first-rate medical documents.

During the same time Cordipatch and LanguageCrossings were replacing their project managers, *Chief Executive* magazine reported that only 10 percent of CEOs of U.S. Fortune 500 firms "were fluent in a language other than English" ("Say It in English"). Although Cordipatch's executives are clearly attempting to ensure an effective control system "by the selection, retention, and training of high-potential employees" in their hiring of Virginie, their mandate to squeeze out translation in whatever time remains before product release, however short, indicates that they are not making the same well-informed decisions that trained, well-qualified personnel would make. It seems odd that management would allow its lawyers to slow down a document to get its legal language exactly right but not allow translators ample time to get the target languages exactly right, when the liability stakes in both cases are exceedingly high. This is, after all, a matter of heart patches, not candy, as Katy remarked.

It does indeed seem odd, until one considers what translator Igor Vesler points out about American clients. After delineating how clients' low levels of knowledge about languages and translation procedures have led to frighteningly high costs, both monetary and human, he writes:

Why do so many clients have such an irrational (to put it mildly) attitude toward translation? Of course, there may be any number of reasons, but I believe that one of the most important is the paradox involved when U.S. clients commission a translation from English into a foreign language. In this situation the client is generally not the consumer of the final product, and is therefore unable to evaluate the quality of the product that he has paid for.

> *What does the U.S. client see when he receives a finished translation into Russian? He sees a text written in a weird alphabet (once a client, showing off his erudition, referred to it as the "Acrylic" alphabet) mixed with Arabic numerals. He may be able to guess at some of the names, but all the rest is a "black hole" to him. So when he sees that it is neatly done, and the format looks the same as the original—he assumes that everything is in order. Only later, when the Russians he is dealing with start to ask questions which reveal their lack of understanding of what the "translation" is supposed to say, does the client begin to be dimly aware that he has ended up with a wooden nickel. He's in the situation of a man who has just purchased a car in which everything seems to be in its proper place—the seats, the steering wheel, the engine, however, the only problem is—it doesn't run. Ultimately, this translation may cost him a lot more than a car. (Vesler, 1997, 22–23)*

Clearly, it is not realistic for management to thoroughly learn every language into which the company's documents are translated. It should be just as clear, however, that it is not realistic for management never to learn anything about these languages or about the process by which the company's working language is translated. Learning just one language thoroughly provides an understanding of how complex and time-consuming the rendering of meaning from any language to another truly is.

Furthermore, management can quickly learn some of the lessons that project managers, who likewise cannot master all the languages for the projects they oversee, pick up about the languages with which they deal. For instance, it takes only a few minutes to show how changing one noun to plural in English can entail a long chain of changes to noun, adjective, and verb endings in a German sentence carrying the same meaning. As an example, we can look at the following sentence in English:

> *The Belgian firm Ateliers des Constructions Electriques in Charleroi has now developed a simple device, which automatically separates worthless gangue from natural diamonds.*

One can render the sentence in German as follows:

> *Die belgische Firma Ateliers des Constructions Electriques in Charleroi hat jetzt eine einfache Vorrichtung entwickelt, die vollautomatisch natürliche Diamanten von wertlosem Begleitgesten sondert.*

If one now takes the English sentence and substitutes the word mechanism for device, the German sentence must change in the following ways, highlighted with roman type:

> *Die belgische Firma Ateliers des Constructions Electriques in Charleroi hat jetzt* ein einfaches Mechanismus *entwickelt,* das *vollautomatisch natürliche Diamanten von wertlosem Begleitgesten sondert.*

Thus, a one-word change in the English sentence results in changes to four words in the German sentence.

Another example involves language technology. It behooves every manager of a global organization to learn that many languages, particularly in Asia, require "double-byte" entry (using two or more keystrokes instead of one) on a computer keyboard to form the ideograms or diacritical marks. Just knowing this detail helps decision-makers come to terms with the greater complexity and time involved in translation of such languages.

Many members of U.S. upper management have been loath and perhaps too arrogant to raise their levels of knowledge about language and translation. Some U.S. companies, such as Coca-Cola and Ford, have in recent years overcome this problem by placing foreign-born executives in key roles, including CEO. Such moves should serve as a shrill alarm to Americans who still aspire to management at any level: If you expect to direct your company in the global marketplace, begin now to raise your knowledge of languages and translation. If you don't, the next surgical "quick cut" may come not to your manuals' translation time but to your own promotion.

Questions for Discussion

1. What would you do about the situation described in the scenario if you were in Katy's position as a project manager at LanguageCrossings? What would you do if you were a project manager at Cordipatch?

2. Some translation companies, like LanguageCrossings, tout their network of in-country translators, based in the locales where the translated documents will be used, as a benefit to customers. Other translation companies, like SF-World, pitch their staff of in-house translators as an advantage to customers, because of the staff's ability to work together easily and speedily in the same location. Which arrangement do you view as more beneficial and for which sorts of projects and documents?

3. Which languages do you know well enough that you can evaluate the usability and effectiveness of, say, simple instructions for adjusting the brakes of a bicycle? What steps can you take to achieve competency in other languages?

4. Why do you think so many Americans are reluctant to learn and use languages besides English? Why do you think Americans who use English in public but who learned a language besides English at home sometimes try to hide the fact that they know two languages?

5. The world has seen many lingua francas, languages used to facilitate communication between persons who speak different languages. In ancient times, both Greek and Latin were used as lingua francas. During the Age of Discovery, especially in the sixteenth century, Portuguese was used by traders in many parts of the world. By the twentieth century, the spread of the British Empire and American influence made English the lingua franca of business, science, and the Internet. Some documents, like airplane engine manuals, are not translated but are instead written in simplified, controlled English (in

which terms are strictly defined) to maintain consistency and precision. Still, most firms find that their customers prefer reading documents in their native languages. Which documents do you think ought to be translated, and which might be transmitted in a lingua franca, such as English or French?

6. Many translation companies report that, while the largest segment of their work is for documentation heading in and out of the United States, the fastest growing segment of their business is for documentation staying within the United States. Part of the growth is a result of the North American Free Trade Agreement. Go to any store in the United States, and you'll see many package labels in English, French, and Spanish for the joint U.S., Canadian, and Mexican market. The labels are just as useful for French speakers in Maine, northern New York, and Louisiana, and for Spanish speakers in Florida, Texas, and California as they are for French Canadians and Mexicans. More striking, perhaps, is the increase in translations into Navajo, Chinese, Somali, Hmong, and other languages for communities within the United States. In what ways will the emphases on niche marketing, multiculturalism, and reaching populations in their native languages affect the way American firms conduct business both at home and abroad? In what respects is the situation today different from 1900, when quite a few documents were translated into German, Swedish, Yiddish, Italian, and other languages for immigrant groups settling in the United States?

Writing Assignments

1. Prepare a set of instructions for translation. You will not be doing the translation yourself. Rather, you'll be making the English text easier for a translator to use. Start with a set of instructions that you or someone else has already written. Then make the text as clear, simple, consistent, and translatable as you can by adhering to the following guidelines:

   - Identify words that may cause difficulty. Determine whether they are both precise and familiar. Define specialized terms in an accompanying glossary.
   - Identify and eliminate idioms by substituting words with straightforward meanings.
   - Make sure all terms are used consistently in meaning throughout the text.
   - Eliminate humor (which is often untranslatable).
   - Edit sentences to make them relatively short independent clauses.
   - Leave room on the page for simultaneous translation or at the end of the instructions for consecutive translation, where other languages will appear. Many languages take 30 percent more space than does English to say the same message.
   - Find out as much as you can about cultural and rhetorical differences and adapt the text. For instance, Americans like a summary introduction, but Japanese readers often want a long introduction of theoretical principles before getting into steps involved. Germans like lots of detail and background information.

   Note: Instructors who would like a fuller explanation of this assignment can find it in Maylath, 1997.

2. Take the role of the boss at LanguageCrossings, and write a memo to the boss at Cordipatch, explaining diplomatically (you want to keep Cordipatch's business) your concerns about rushing the translations of manuals for heart patch surgeries.

Additional Reading: Issues Relevant to the Case

Andrews, D. C. (Ed.). (1996). *International dimensions of technical communication.* Arlington, VA: Society for Technical Communication.

Flint, P., Van Slyke, M. L., Staerke-Meyerring, D., & Thompson, A. (1999). Going online: Helping technical communicators help translators. *Technical Communication, 46,* 238–248.

Hager, P., & Scheiber, H. J. (Eds.). (2000). *Managing global communication in science and technology.* New York: Wiley.

Hoft, N. L. (1995). *International technical communication: How to export information about high technology.* New York: Wiley.

Lovitt, C. R., & Goswami, D. (Eds.). (1999). *Exploring the rhetoric of international professional communication: An agenda for teachers and researchers.* Amityville, NY: Baywood.

Maylath, B. (1997). Writing globally: Teaching the technical writing student to prepare documents for translation. *Journal of Business and Technical Communication, 11,* 339–352.

Say it in English. (1997, March 24). *Minneapolis Star Tribune,* p. D1.

Seguinot, C. (1994). Technical writing and translation: Changing with the times. *Journal of Technical Writing and Communication, 24,* 285–292.

Vesler, I. (1997, March). Translation quality: The price tag. *The ATA Chronicle,* pp. 22–23.

Chapter *7*

Adapting to South American Communication Patterns:
Odyssey's Proposal to Remedy Inconsistent Car Sales

BARRY. L. THATCHER
Ohio University

Abstract: This case explores some rhetorical and cultural patterns of South American audiences. Andrew Gordon, a U.S. citizen, is the director of sales and manufacturing for the Odyssey car company in the northern region of South America. In Ecuador, Odyssey is experiencing irregular sales because of a car taxation law. Andrew's objective is to help in the revision of the tax law so that the sales of his vehicles, especially the Landrunner, can be more consistent. Andrew has a number of questions about the audiences and rhetorical adaptations he might consider: What mix of oral and written discourse will best achieve his purposes? What audience-author relations does he need to develop in order to be effective? How will Andrew explain the unfairness of the current law using strategies that Ecuadorian audiences will understand? And how will Andrew demonstrate sensitivity to a U.S. author requesting changes in Ecuadorian laws? This case guides Andrew through these and many other decisions as he tries to ethically and respectfully adapt his rhetorical approaches to be more effective for his South American audiences.

   Note: Odyssey, Andrew Gordon, and Emilia Montúfar are fictitious, although they are modeled after actual situations. However, the rest of the people involved are real, including the president of Ecuador, Jamil Mahuad; Heinz Moeller, the president of Congress; and José Luque, author of the Transit Commission's letter.

Background for the Case

Andrew Gordon directs the Northern South American market of the Odyssey Automobile Corporation. This market includes Venezuela, Colombia, Ecuador, Peru, and Bolivia. Gordon's home office is in the United States, but he communicates regularly with the directors of each country, and he travels semiannually to the region. Odyssey is well established in this part of Latin America. In fact, Odyssey has been in Ecuador for more than forty years and has been assembling the Japanese-made *Landrunner* (a sport-utility vehicle, or SUV) in Ecuador, under the Odyssey name, for more than fifteen years. Because of its longstanding history and good relations with Ecuador, Odyssey has achieved the greatest penetration in the Ecuadorian market. Although Ecuador is relatively small, with a population of just over 11 million, Odyssey wants to maintain, if not improve, its market share. Andrew Gordon coordinates the exportation of U.S.-made vehicles to this part of Latin America and oversees the assembly of Landrunners in the Quito, Ecuador, plant.

Recently, the director of the Ecuadorian market, Emilia Montúfar, notified Andrew about a problem with the assessment and payment of automobile taxes in Ecuador. The new president of Ecuador, Jamil Mahuad, has begun to enforce much more consistently the gathering of property taxes on automobiles, and this stricter enforcement has resulted in very inconsistent sales for Odyssey, which directly affects the assembly quotas on the Landrunner. The problem with the law is that automobile owners are required to pay a full year's assessment of property taxes on a new vehicle regardless of when the vehicle was acquired. Thus, an owner who buys a Landrunner on December 31 will pay the same tax as the person who bought it 364 days earlier, on January 1. Both owners will have to pay taxes again on the vehicle in the next year.

The Scenario

The tax law has effectively decreased sales of all new cars in the latter months of the year, creating problems with assembly and storage of Landrunners at the Quito plant. Logically, if a person plans on buying a car near the end of the year, that person will probably wait until the first month of the following year to avoid paying the property tax for that year. A person thinking about buying a new Landrunner worth $30,000 can save $2500 on property tax by waiting until the first month of the next year. This leads to decreased sales near the end of the year. For example, the following figures for 1997 show the number of Landrunners assembled and sold in the cities of Guayaquil, Quito, Cuenca, and Machala:

January	295	May	180	September	121
February	195	June	177	October	87
March	188	July	180	November	31
April	187	August	160	December	22

The same inconsistency is true for the sales of other Odyssey autos, but it is particularly important for the Landrunner. The Landrunner assembly plant does not have sufficient storage, so it is paying large sums of money to rent a storage facility and transport the Landrunners there in preparation for the dramatically increased sales at the beginning of the year. However, this storage facility cannot store enough cars for the first-of-the-year rush. Further, Odyssey has to keep extra workers at the assembly plant to assemble the Landrunners for the months of greatest sale; but according to Ecuadorian law, Odyssey cannot lay off or fire those workers just because sales slip at the end of the year. Thus, the assembly plant operates with full personnel in December but assembles fewer vehicles than in January. Also, Odyssey has to rent the storage facility for the whole year but really only uses it at the end of the year. The effects on the Odyssey sales staff are similar, but not as dramatic. They are paid partly on commission, so they earn much less during the latter part of the year.

Preliminary Groundwork

After some discussion, Andrew Gordon assigns Emilia Montúfar to investigate further and look for ways to have the law revised. Montúfar reports that other automobile dealerships have not seemed as concerned as Odyssey. However, some government officials, most particularly the Transit Commissions of the provinces in Ecuador, have specifically addressed the inconsistency in the tax law. The Transit Commissions are caught in the middle because they are required to verify the payment of property taxes when the vehicle's owner registers the vehicle annually at their offices. But so many people avoid paying the property taxes when they purchase a car at the end of the year that the Transit Commission gets stuck deciding whether to punish owners for what they feel is an inconsistent law. In fact, the Transit Commission of the Guayas Province has published a letter in Guayaquil's largest newspaper, *El Universo,* addressing this very issue and calling on President Mahuad to reform the law. Emilia translated the letter to English and sent it to Andrew. The translation of the letter is presented in Figure 7.1.

According to Emilia, this letter provides important historical background on the issue, demonstrating the complexity of the issues and institutions involved. After reading Emilia's translation of the letter, however, Andrew is confused. He finds the letter unclear and hard to follow. Andrew is used to working with legal prose, but this letter seems to have problems. After discussing the letter's translation, Emilia states: "Oh, that's right; when I translated the letter, I wasn't thinking about reworking the writing to be more acceptable to U.S. readers. I did just a translation of the words." Andrew then assigns Emilia to make the translation of the letter understandable to him and his bosses back in the United States. Fortunately, for Andrew and Odyssey, Emilia is an excellent resource on cultural issues. She was born in Venezuela but educated in the United States, and she has a B.S. and a MBA from prominent U.S. universities. She is an accountant by trade, not a communicator, but she is bilingual and bicultural. Emilia sends Andrew her

TRANSIT COMMISSION OF THE GUAYAS PROVINCE

TO THE PUBLIC

In response to the publication made by the Bureau of Industrial Development on April 15, 1997, the Transit Commission of the Guayas Province unanimously resolved to publish a clarification and/or answer through the means of communication about the assessments and negotiations that this body adopted against the methods of **REGISTRATION** and **TAXATION** of new and imported cars. That in a terse and clear way it was determined that this Directorate which began to function since August of 1992 has been against those procedures that have been utilized for more than twenty years and began to carry out negotiations so that this system did not continue, as is evident in the deliberative nature of the resolution adopted by this organization in an ordinary session on February 15, 1997, in which it was unanimously resolved to solicit the most distinguished Constitutional President of the Republic, Jamil Mahuad, to reform by executive decree, according to the Art. 78, Letter A) of the Constitution, the Art. 14 of the General Rule of Tax Law of Motorized Vehicles of Land Transportation, published in the Official Register N. 127 on February 13, 1989, in the sense of which: "The owners of new vehicles will pay the tax within 30 days from the date of acquisition, according to that which is established in the Art. 8 Law 004 and the Art. 52 of the political constitution of the state, that is, paying the annual portion determined from the first day of the month following the month of acquisition of the new vehicle, until the 31 of December of that year, or giving up ownership of the vehicle, this last applicable in the case of residents or naturalized persons that are not dedicated to the selling of automotive vehicles."

What is needed is to respect the proportionality that the constitution mandates without having an answer for the moment to the legal requirements from the Ministry of Finances that was sent in a correspondence dated February 9, 1997. In light of that we are doing the respective consultations to the Attorney General and Inspector General of the government to avoid possible future clarifications, since the civil servants of this Ministry in multiple occasions have verbally indicated to our civil servants to levy taxes for the complete year, notwithstanding the date in which the vehicle was registered.

Clarifying that the Transit Commission of the Guayas Province does not receive not even five percent (5%) of the total value that the owner of the vehicle pays.

The problem first presented itself to our institution from the moment we were converted to an agency for withholding monies which corresponds to the Treasurer and we hope the Finance Ministry will receive tax payments through the province administrators and that as requirement for registering the vehicle, the owner will have to present the receipt for having fulfilled the payment of this obligation to the Treasurer.

José Plaza Luque
President
Transit Commission of the Guayas Province

FIGURE 7.1   Emilia's Translation of actual letter to the public, found in *El Universo.*

TRANSIT COMMISSION OF THE GUAYAS PROVINCE

TO THE PUBLIC

The Transit Commission of the Guayas Province proposes to reform the terms and administration of new car registration and taxation.

The terms of taxation are unfair. The Attorney and Inspector General have insisted that taxes be to be levied for the whole year, notwithstanding the date in which the car was registered. As a result, one car owner pays the same tax for a car acquired on December 31 that another owner pays for the same vehicle that he acquired on January 1st of the same year. Because of this inequity, we resolved to solicit President Jamil Mahuad to reform the terms of taxation.

To be more fair to the owners, we suggest changing the terms to a monthly basis, or as follows: "The owners of new vehicles will pay the tax within 30 days from the date of acquisition, according to that which is established in the Art. 8 Law 004 and the Art. 52 of the political constitution of the state, that is, paying the annual portion determined from the first day of the month following the month of acquisition of the new vehicle, until the 31 of December of that year, or giving up ownership of the vehicle, this last applicable in the case of residents or naturalized persons that are not dedicated to the selling of automotive vehicles."

In addition to these terms, the methods of charging and withholding taxes need clarification. The Attorney and Inspector General want our Commission to administer the collection of taxes, but they have not explained to us the legal guidelines. Thus, we suggest that the Finance Ministry receive tax payments through the provincial administrators.

José Plaza Luque
President
Transit Commission of the Guayas Province

FIGURE 7.2 Emilia's Cultural Translation of Original Transit Commission Letter.

cultural revision of the Transit Commission's letter (Figure 7.2), in which she tried to rewrite the letter the way a U.S. writer would.

After reading the revised letter, Andrew decides that it would be more cost-effective to work toward changing the taxation law rather than to develop better storage for the Landrunner assembly plant. Both Andrew and Emilia began brainstorming about strategies for having the law revised.

History of Odyssey and Ecuador

Odyssey has developed good relations with Ecuador. In fact, when Odyssey began assembling Landrunners in Ecuador in 1983, the Ecuadorian government rearranged the import laws to create Free Zones (Zonas Francas), which eliminated duties on materials imported for the assembly of badly needed Ecuadorian products. Odyssey's Landrunner assembly plant employs several hundred Ecuadorian employees and provides Landrunners at substantial savings for Ecuadorian consumers. Odyssey has a history of treating employees well and of dealing fairly with the Ecuadorian government.

Jamil Mahuad's government is focused on modernizing import duties, tax laws, and many other government regulations. Traditionally, Ecuador has supported U.S. policy in Latin America, and perhaps because of its size, it also tends to rely on the United States economically. Ecuador is a democratic republic, with a unicameral National Congress. For close to twenty years, it has had a democratically elected president and Congress. Because members of Congress range from archconservative to leftist, Congress is famous for raucous debates.

Changing the tax law requires a proposal from either the president or from one of the prominent members of Congress. If the proposal receives a majority vote in Congress, it is sent to the president for signature. Andrew has established good relations with the president of the Congress, Heinz Moeller. Since Mahuad's government is relatively new, Andrew has not been able to establish formal connections, although both Odyssey and Mahuad are interested in doing so. Emilia Montúfar has contacted Heinz Moeller about the issue, and Heinz Moeller requested that Andrew draft a proposal to change the laws. Moeller will circulate the proposal to other automobile dealerships to see if they would also support it. If he feels he has enough support, he will introduce the content of the proposal to the National Congress and ask for a sustaining vote.

Communication Scenario

Andrew decides to create a proposal to revise the tax law. He has various possible audiences for this proposal: the president of Ecuador, Jamil Mahuad; the president of the National Congress, Heinz Moeller; the other automobile dealerships (with or without the intervention of Heinz Moeller); and other public audiences, such as a letter to the public, based on the Transit Commission's letter.

Background for Analysis

Andrew needs to adapt his writing to the cultural and communication norms of his Latin American audience. This does not mean that he should adopt or mimic Latin American writing strategies. Rather, he should envision his own purpose for writing and maintain his basic approach but adapt his writing to his audience, a strategy common to good writers. The degree of adaptation will be based on the flexibility and self-awareness of Andrew himself: How clearly can Andrew understand the ways his own culture has reinforced his personal writing strategies? How easily can he feel comfortable using writing strategies based on another culture? How well does he understand how those strategies will influence his audience? And how well do these other writing strategies fit him personally and professionally? Some theorists have argued that charity, or goodwill and good intentions, seem to become increasingly important in intercultural communication where normal communication patterns seem to break down (Benjamin, 1989). It appears that communicators from other cultures are more likely to look beyond some cultural differences when good intentions are perceived in others. Clearly, Andrew's honest and effective adaptation of his own writing strategies for his Ecuadorian audiences will demonstrate goodwill; an artificial adaptation or no adaptation at all will most likely communicate ill-will.

Although as a whole, the United States and Latin America seem to demonstrate major differences in writing strategies, Andrew should not assume that everyone in the culture writes a particular way. Writing strategies are preferences of usage based on history and culture; and many writers vary a great deal from their predominant cultural heritage, based on their own history and background. As Andrew will become increasingly aware, Emilia is bicultural and does not fit neatly into either Latin American or U.S. cultural patterns. However, despite the great need to be aware of the many variations in other cultural patterns, Andrew should not fall into the other trap of cultural ethnocentrism—of assuming that his culture is the most natural way and the lens by which all other cultures are evaluated (Stewart & Bennett, 1991). Understanding the cultural and communicative heritage of his Latin American audience is Andrew's first step in becoming an effective intercultural communicator. His next step is to determine the local differences of his audiences based on their own unique personal histories and backgrounds. This is very important in Latin America.

Orality, Writing, & Drama

As Andrew approaches writing the proposal, he should question whether a Latin American audience assumes the same purposes and roles for writing as an audience in the United States. In Ecuador, as in much of Latin America, oral communication tends to predominate because of cultural, economic, social, and communicative traditions. In this part of Latin America, the Incas and other indigenous tribes had not developed substantial writing systems at the time of the Spanish conquest. Their communications were either mostly oral or used the Quipu, which was a system of beads much like the abacus, which was used to relay simple messages (see Abbott, 1996). Also, a lack of publishing houses, the poor quality of translated materials, and the relatively greater cost of printed materials has made orality the primary medium in Ecuador. Because much of the Spanish conquest of the Andean region of Latin America was realized under the guise of official written documents (from Spain and the Catholic Church), many Mestizos and Indians are wary of written communications and much more reliant on face-to-face oral communication (Cornejo-Polar, 1994). Ecuador also has an interesting legend about orality: One president of Ecuador, who held office during the 1970s, remarked that his thumb was tired of signing all the documents one day. The press investigated whether the president could actually write, or if he used a thumbprint as his signature. The issue of whether he could write was never resolved, but nobody doubted his effectiveness and intelligence. He simply did not appear to need written communication skills.

Understanding this oral history in Latin America is critical. If Andrew approaches this writing situation with U.S. assumptions about the roles of writing, he might fail. The United States has a much stronger tradition of relying on writing to mediate interactions between people and institutions, the U.S. Constitution being one famous example. Thus, it is more common for a U.S. communicator to rely on what's written as a guide for organizational, personal, and legal behavior than for an Ecuadorian communicator to do so. Ecuadorians might be suspicious of or resist written communication, especially if it sounds official, if they don't know the author, or if they don't know the context. Consequently, as Andrew approaches writing the proposal, he might consider the amount of resistance to writing and whether some initial oral investigation of the audiences, the issues, and the taxation context would facilitate better reception of his written communication.

Despite the oral tradition, writing has an important place in Latin America. In Andean Latin America, oral communication influences the patterns of written communication a great deal. During Spanish colonialization, indigenous populations used oral and community-based dramas to resist the Spanish reverence of governmental and evangelical writing (Cornejo-Polar, 1994). These dramas often integrated official written communications with ironic and mocking twists, demonstrating how the power of the community could appropriate these documents for their own purposes. As a consequence, written communications that address new policies and laws are often dramatic, involving people, places, and situations. The Transit Commission's letter exemplifies this strategy; it sounds almost like a script for a play.

The critical question for Andrew is how to adapt his proposal to the assumptions about writing that he will probably see in Ecuador. Perhaps the best approach is to dramatize the issue, from Odyssey's perspective, in order to make his point about revising the tax law.

High and Low Context

Just as a drama or play relies on stage props, costumes, actors' interactions, and background to add meaning to the spoken words, so do communications in Latin America tend to rely on the context—the stage of the communication—to make the point. Thus, based on the oral and dramatic traditions, written communications in Ecuador tend to invoke the contextual information right into the text. Andrew notices that the Transit Commission's letter is full of stage-like markers: dates, people involved, circumstances, prior dialogue, and issues. This strategy is what some researchers have called *high-context* communication (Hall, 1976). The high-context strategy is probably what made the Transit Commission's letter difficult for Andrew to understand. The point is stated indirectly—politeness strategies in high-context cultures such as Ecuador tend to be based on articulating the main point by articulating the relations among people, issues, and the stage on which they happen. U.S. communicators tend to be lower context—that is, a U.S.

writer makes the meaning literally clear in the text itself without relying too much on the context. Writing for U.S. audiences is less like writing a script for a play and more like developing policies—like the Constitution—that are supposed to be mostly stageless, understood and applied regardless of context. The letter that Emilia wrote, following U.S. communicative patterns, is more direct.

One difficult adjustment for U.S. writers working in higher-context cultures is that when both author and audience know the stage or context, the communication can be indirect and subtle, yet powerful and precise. On the other hand, when the context is uncertain, the communication tends to be loaded with contextual markers. Thus, in high-context cultures, the degree of contextual detail needed in the communication, based on prior knowledge, varies much more than in lower-context cultures such as the United States. The Transit Commission's letter was loaded with contextual markers because it was published in a daily newspaper, a context that was so general that the author could not assume that the audience understood much about the stage. Emilia explains that from her perspective, U.S. writers "have a more homogenized sense of audience and context—they seem to envision a real basic scenario that can be applied to many other scenarios. Latin writers, on the other hand, seem much more sensitive to place and the audience and how much information in that place will the audience need." She cautions Andrew about this point, for Andrew will need to tailor the contextual information and the directness of his proposal based precisely on the amount of knowledge the audience has about the context of taxation issues. If the context is unknown, Andrew will have to set the stage. If it is known, setting the stage will feel redundant to the readers and possibly offend them.

Another important part of high-context communication is its relationship to history, especially the history of the relationships among authors and audiences. Andrew might need to develop greater skills in interpreting how Odyssey's relationships, history, and context have influenced and can influence the ongoing dialogue about the tax law. Andrew notices that the Transit Commission's letter is extremely cautious about the relations of the people involved, the stage on which the tax law takes place, and the point the author tries to make.

Individual and Collective

Andrew has noted that many Latin Americans are closely tied to their families and social classes, or what some people label as the *in-group*. This in-group exerts powerful influences on the behavior of many Latin Americans, and thus most countries in Latin America are defined as the most collective in the world (Hofstede, 1984; Trompenaars, 1994). In-groups are also stratified and explicitly marked throughout society. For example, one of Andrew's best friends in Ecuador, the chancellor of a private university, has remarked that there are sixteen different social levels in Ecuador, with most being easily identifiable by last name. Jokingly, Andrew's friend explains that "I don't know where to place you in these sixteen societal levels. Sometimes I place you near the top because of your productivity; but other times, I place you near the bottom because of your table manners." One of Andrew's most difficult adjustments is understanding the levels of social hierarchy in Ecuador, so as not to equate two unequal groups as equal. Further, understanding the behavior of the in-group provides significant insight into the possible behavior of a member of that group.

This almost absolute acceptance of inequality can rub some U.S. personnel the wrong way, for aren't all people equal? People who work hard and look out for themselves can succeed. These maxims, of course, are based on an individualistic society that seemingly denies social influence on everyday behavior and focuses on measurable individual achievement. Just as researchers argue that Latin American countries are the most collective, they consistently maintain that the United States is by far the most individualistic (Hofstede, 1984; Trompenaars, 1994). The individual seems defined by measurable achievements and economic status. Andrew's chancellor friend, who has a Ph.D. from a U.S. university, explains that he feels that social stratification in the United States is vague and tends to be economically based, whereas the social stratification in Ecuador is overt and based on a complex mixture of economics, race, history, and culture.

This difference in individual and collective cultures means that Andrew's personal achievements and willpower will probably mean less to the Latin American audience than they would to a U.S. audience. Andrew's ability to carry his point—his persuasive power—is based more on his in-group or social standing. And if Andrew's social standing is not high enough, he will need to find somebody in Ecuadorian society whose standing is high enough to make his point. This "leveraging" is actually a common strategy in much of Latin American society, and it is known as the *palanca* (Albert, 1996). *Palanca* is translated as a lever or control stick, but it really means getting the people from the right social position to articulate the preferred applications of policies. What this means for Andrew is that either he needs to make sure that his title and position are powerful enough or he needs to get somebody in a higher position to make that statement for him. If Andrew carefully analyzes the Transit Commission's letter, for example, he will notice the careful use of leveraging: The Commission attempts to persuade the right people to make the points for them.

As Andrew analyzes the situation with Emilia, he realizes that she is not in a position to make the argument. Especially because she is from Venezuela, not Ecuador, and because she is not situated in the right Ecuadorian social class, she does not have the social power to make the point. Emilia does, however, know Heinz Moeller, the president of the Ecuadorian Congress. And although Emilia and Heinz Moeller are unequal in terms of social power, Heinz Moeller might listen to Andrew—the director of sales and marketing for Northern South America. Andrew, however, probably will not find a voice with Jamil Mahuad, the president of Ecuador. If Andrew address the proposal to him, he will need to find a *palanca* to do so. Can Andrew get one of the powerful people at Odyssey to sign the proposal? Or can Andrew get Heinz Moeller to sign it or at least become the *palanca* to push the proposal through to the president? Historically, the president of the Ecuadorian Congress is at odds with the president of the country, and this seems to be true for Moeller and Mahuad.

Universal and Particular

The difference in individual and collective cultures is also linked to value systems and applications of laws. Individualistic cultures tend to rely on universal values, such as freedom, justice, and equality, which ostensibly need to be applied to all, regardless of social situation. The idea of a level playing field is important to many in the United States. On the other hand, collective cultures tend to have particularist values; the applications of laws are based on the social standing of the persons involved. There is a popular saying in Ecuador: "la ley es para el poncho" (the law is for the *poncho*—i.e, Indian). This means that those who are in a social position above the Indian are held to different standards and applications of the law. In other words, there might be sixteen types of applications of the same law for the sixteen social levels in Ecuador. The playing field is inherently structured.

This difference becomes readily apparent when analyzing the persuasive strategies of the two version of the Transit Commission's letter. The original letter never argues explicitly that the law is unfair. Emilia, however, understanding the U.S. predisposition to equality and fairness, uses these universal values as a persuasive strategy in her second translation. The idea that a law is unfair tends to be important to U.S. audiences (Stewart & Bennett, 1991), while specific applications to certain groups is the persuasive approach in the Transit Commission's letter.

Thus, when developing persuasive strategies for the proposal, Andrew might consider particularist rather than universalist approaches. That is, he should focus on how the law affects the different groups of people involved with it. Andrew also might be careful about using such words as equality, equal application, and fairness.

Problem Solving and Time

One important difference between U.S. and Latin American cultures seems to be rooted in perceptions of problem solving and time. When Andrew first began his job as director of this South American market, he seized the opportunity to make a difference by laying out clearly the most pressing problems and organizing current strategies to overcome these problems for the future. His approach represents what many researchers label as the predominant logic of the United States— "null logic," or thinking that is structured to avoid future problems (Stewart & Bennett, 1991). This approach seemed so natural for Andrew that he was surprised when it turned out to be less effective for his Latin American personnel. When Andrew asked Emilia about the ineffectiveness of the approach, she wryly explained that "many North Americans tend to see life as a problem to be solved. Thus, they structure their whole existence around avoiding future problems, and in so doing, they miss out on a lot of the positive experiences of the present." This characterization did not seem fair or logical to Andrew. On his first trip to Ecuador, Andrew took a trip to climb Cayambe, one of Ecuador's most beautiful volcanoes. After traveling for ten miles on a winding road, Andrew and Emilia come to a sign right before a bridge that said "bridge is out." Andrew asked, "Why was that sign not posted at the entrance to this ten-mile road, warning the travelers of future problems?" Emilia said that it was somewhat typical, for trying to avoid future problems was not a predominant tendency there. Although it is not true of all Ecuadorians, Emilia explained, "Latins seem to have a greater capacity to enjoy the trip through the Ecuadorian countryside with less worry about whether they achieved their future objectives."

This difference in thinking about the future also means time frames tend to be structured differently. Some researchers have argued that Latin American times frames are *polychronic*: characterized by flux, simultaneity, multiple tasks managed at the same time, and apparent disorganization, focusing on the importance of place and involvement of people rather than adherence to schedules. On the other hand, U.S. time frames are characterized as *monochronic*; they are linked linear structures of cause and effect with an organized flow of events (Condon, 1985; Hall, 1976, 1981). Monochronic time "seals off one or two people from the group and intensifies relationships with one other person, or at most, two or three people . . . [and] it alienates people from the context and experience of social relations" (Hall, 1976, pp. 19–20).

When analyzing the two versions of the Transit Commissions letter, Andrew notices a difference in the time frames and future. The original letter has a complex, polychronic time frame, in which relationships, people, and events are orchestrated in complex ways. Emilia's second translation tends to be monochronic, an organized, linear flow. Additionally, the second version has a more negative tone, indicating that a problem really exists, that it needs to be solved, and that the letter can solve it. Additionally, the two versions tend to invoke different feelings about the future. Andrew thinks about which letter is more oriented toward the future, and why. Which letter portrays the issue of taxation in tones of a problem to be solved? Which letter sets up specific procedures for avoiding the problem? Which is more negative, harsher?

When approaching the taxation issue, Andrew might consider using more Ecuadorian strategies and avoiding the "life is a problem to be solved" approach. Andrew probably needs to be careful about his negative tone and his projection toward the future.

Cause and Effect

This difference in time and problem solving corresponds to differences in cause and effect. Emilia explained it this way: "The Latin American equivalent of 'I dropped the ball' is *Se me cayó la pelota*, which, literally translated, means 'the ball fell from me myself.'" The Spanish language tends to mask the agency behind the cause of something, whereas the structure of English tends to highlight the person or thing responsible. This difference also reinforces the polychronic and monochronic time frames. As Andrew rereads the original translation of the Transit Commission's letter, he still cannot thoroughly understand the cause and effect there. Some researchers explain that this complex, social cause and effect is especially difficult for U.S. personnel who are used to an "agented" cause and effect in which the person or thing responsible for the situation is clearly identified as "causing" the problem (Stewart & Bennett, 1991). It seems more understandable in the revised translation, perhaps because the cause—the unfair tax law—has caused the effects—problems in gathering taxes.

If Andrew is still puzzling over the original translation, he is probably not unique. Many scholars have argued that understanding cause and effect is perhaps the greatest problem for U.S. personnel working in Latin America. Castañeda (1995), a Mexican theorist, argues that cause and effect in Mexico is so complex and so deeply rooted in social and historical frames that North Americans rarely can grasp it. Albert (1996) explains that even when U.S. personnel have years of experience working in Latin America, they should still consult local Latin Americans for help in understanding cause and effect.

This difference has important ramifications for Andrew's proposal. How can he effectively explain the causes of Odyssey's inconsistency in sales of cars? What types of new policies will achieve the desired effects? That is, how can Andrew be sure that his solution will have the desired effects? Andrew does not have the time to research the policy-making process in Ecuador. He might, however, use the same strategies that the Transit Commission uses—that is, dramatizing the context and issues to explain the cause and effect, and leaving the interpretation and analysis of cause and effect to the Ecuadorian audiences, who understand the context much better than Andrew.

Whirlpool Approach to Latin America

According to one prominent scholar, people from the United States have traditionally used the Whirlpool approach to try to "fix" things in Latin America (Pastor, 1992). When the United States is interested in an issue in a Latin American country, the United States tends to get involved suddenly, and usually violently, churning and spinning the issues with vigor and intensity. However, when the issue dies down, the United States leaves as suddenly as it came, ignoring the country until the next prominent issue or whirlpool. From Emilia's perspective, this tendency has been true for Venezuela as well as Ecuador, especially during the oil crises in the 1970s. Thus, Ecuadorian audiences might at first be skeptical of Odyssey's interest in the tax law, especially if Andrew begins with the furor of a whirlpool. Perhaps Andrew's best bet is to emphasize longstanding relationships and Odyssey's interest in the long-term welfare of the country.

Logically, Andrew also needs to be careful about how he express Odyssey's interest in changing the tax laws, because associated with this whirlpool idea is the idea that many North Americans think the rest of the world sees the world just as the United States does. This "cultural ethnocentrism" (Stewart & Bennett, 1991) is not only associated with the United States; other countries also feel that their view is natural and best. But Latin America is perhaps particularly sensitive to this issue, given the very dominant cultural, historical, and economic influence of the United States (Kras, 1989). Since Ecuador is a small country, about the size of

Nevada, many of its inhabitants have traveled to other countries, especially to the United States, Europe, and the rest of Latin America. There is also a large foreign component in many of the businesses in Quito and Guayaquil, the major cities of Ecuador. Thus, many of the government and industrial officials with whom Andrew works have extensive knowledge and experience of other cultures and countries. Andrew's Ecuadorian counterparts are probably culturally and socially sophisticated.

Because Odyssey has been in Ecuador for a long time and has established deeply rooted relationships, Andrew has a good tradition to work from, but he needs to consider carefully his approaches to the proposal. How can he be sensitive to the U.S. patterns of domination that could appear? How can he be sensitive to the whirlpool pattern of sudden and intense involvement and just as sudden abandonment? How can Andrew develop these sensitivities into his writing as well as the negotiations that happen before and after his writing?

Questions for Discussion

1. What are the different assumptions about the uses of writing and orality in the United States and Latin America? How will Andrew decide how much orality to use to explain the policies? How can he design the best oral and written interactions for this situation?

2. How is the history of the communicators and of the subject of communication important for the document's purpose? How will Andrew verify that his Ecuadorian audiences understand his purpose for the written proposal?

3. How does the Ecuadorian definition of the audience and its relationship to Andrew influence the way Andrew will approach his audiences? What should Andrew consider when thinking about his audience?

4. How does the high context and preference for orality influence the audience's informational needs? How much contextual information is appropriate for this informational need?

5. What changes might Andrew make in the organizational or structural patterns of the original document (the Spanish to English translation of the letter)? How might Andrew accommodate the Latin American preference for drama and polychronic structures while maintaining the original sense of the policies?

6. How will Andrew explain the unfairness of the current law using particularist rather than univeralist strategies? How can he know if these strategies are effective?

7. What problem-solving strategies would best suit Andrew's audiences? How will Andrew develop the strategies and ensure their reliability? How will Andrew ensure that U.S. conceptions of cause and effect are understood by his Ecuadorian audiences?

8. How will Andrew demonstrate sensitivity to the fact that he is a U.S. author requesting changes in Ecuadorian laws? How can he ensure long-term involvement and concern for the Ecuadorian people?

Writing Assignments

1. Write a persuasive proposal to Heinz Moeller, the president of the Ecuadorian Congress, requesting him to distribute the proposal to other automobile makers and dealers as a way of generating local support for changing the law.

2. Write a letter to Jamil Mahuad, the president of Ecuador, requesting him to begin working on legislation to change the tax law. The letter should be signed by the president of Odyssey. Plan a series of pre- and post-letter meetings in which Andrew can meet with representatives of Mahuad's government to set up the best approaches. (For this information, you might want to consult the Web. Ecuador has an official government Website as well as many private sites.)

3. Write a letter to the public that will appear in Ecuador's daily newspapers, much like the Transit Commission's letter. In this letter, propose a course of action that will solve the problem.

Additional Resources: Issues Relevant to the Case

Abbott, D. P. (1996). *Rhetoric in the new world: Rhetorical theory and practice in colonial Spanish America*. Columbia: University of South Carolina Press.

Albert, R. D. (1996). A framework and model for understanding Latin American and Latino/Hispanic cultural patterns. In D. Landis & R. S. Bhagat (Eds.), *Handbook of intercultural training*, (2nd ed., pp. 327–348). Thousand Oaks, CA: Sage.

Benjamin, A. (1989). *Translation and the nature of philosophy: A new theory of words*. London: Routledge.

Castañeda, J. G. (1995). *The Mexican shock: Its meaning for the U.S.* New York: New Press.

Condon, J. C. (1985). *Communicating with the Mexicans.* Yarmouth, ME: Intercultural Press.

Cornejo-Polar, Antonio. (1994). *Escribir en el aire: Ensayo sobre la heterogeneidad socio-cultural en las literaturas andinas*. Lima, Peru: Editorial Horizonte.

Hall, E. T. (1976). *Beyond culture*. New York: Doubleday.

Hall, E. T. (1981). *The silent language*. New York: Doubleday.

Hofstede, G. (1984). *Culture's consequences: International differences in work-related values*. Thousand Oaks, CA: Sage.

Hoft, N. (1995). *International technical communication*. New York: Wiley.

Kras, E. (1989). *Management in two cultures*. Yarmouth, ME: Intercultural Press.

Pastor, R. A. (1992). *Whirlpool: U.S. foreign policy toward Latin America and the Caribbean*. Princeton, NJ: Princeton University Press.

Stewart, E. C., & Bennett, M. J. (1991). *American cultural patterns: A cross-cultural perspective*. (rev. ed.). Yarmouth, ME: Intercultural Press.

Trompenaars, F. (1994). *Riding the waves of culture: Understanding the diversity in global business*. Burr Ridge, IL: Irwin.

Varner, I., & Beamer, L. (1995). *Intercultural communication: The global workplace*. Chicago: Irwin.

Chapter 8

Cultural Issues in
Corporate Hierarchies:
Keeping Your Distance Isn't That Simple

ROGER BAUMGARTE   PHILIPPE BLANCHARD
Winthrop University   *Rio de Janeiro*

Abstract: Gerald, the main character in this case study, is a thirty-year-old working for a large multinational company in Cleveland. He is chosen for an assignment to a newly acquired subsidiary in a Latin American country. There he finds that his subordinates and colleagues respond to him and their work responsibilities in ways that often seem paradoxical and perplexing. In most respects, they are motivated to work hard and pull together to achieve the goals of the company. In other respects, they seem to be irresponsible and uncooperative, and various strategies he pursues to improve the situation only serve to make matters worse. Gerald's experiences and challenges will be analyzed with reference to the cultural dimension of power-distance (Hofstede, 1991). How one perceives and exercises authority can differ markedly over cultures. Understanding this critical dimension is crucial to effective communication strategies and management practices that cross cultural boundaries.

Note: This case is based on the research of Geert Hofstede (1991). It is intended to introduce the reader to one of the four dimensions he developed to characterize a large number of cultures around the world. The details of the case are entirely fictional. The cultural norms depicted herein are not intended to stereotype Latin American countries, since the cultures of these countries are quite diverse. Rather, the specifics of this case represent slightly exaggerated versions of norms that can be found in a variety of cultures around the world, blended together to form a composite to exemplify Hofstede's dimension called "power distance." It is hoped that the reader will gain some insights into the practical implications of this dimension in an industrial context.

Background for the Case

Gerald was ecstatic. He was feeling the power of his new position already, and the plane hadn't even taken off. Just sitting in business class gave him a sense of exhilaration. Here he was, thirty years old, on his way to Seraleugo to be head of communications in the newly acquired subsidiary of Catalytic Devices, Inc. CDI is a multinational corporation based in Cleveland that manufactures catalytic converters for nearly a third of the world's automobiles. To provide for a smoother and cheaper supply of the basic components for producing these devices, CDI had just acquired a large plant in Seraleugo, where critical raw materials could be found in abundance. Although the plant in Seraleugo had supplied CDI with an essential component for many years, recent quality control and delivery problems forced CDI to take action to ameliorate the situation. The acquisition contract between CDI and the plant in Seraleugo called for three employees of the Cleveland office to serve as the transition team as CDI took control of plant operations.

For Gerald, this promotion, his third in five years at CDI, was unexpected. Ever since the acquisition was made public, rumors had circulated about who would get the foreign assignments. Having no strong attachment to Cleveland, Gerald was open for new adventures, but he knew it was unrealistic to wish for this one. The three people from the central office going to Seraleugo would, of course, be assigned at the highest levels of management. One of them would serve as the CEO at the plant. The other two positions had vaguely written job descriptions. Undoubtedly, since these two appointments would represent the only other personnel from the United States at the plant for the first year, they would probably have a wide range of responsibilities, many of which would be outside of his training and experience. He applied on a whim, thinking that if he hadn't promoted himself aggressively right from the start, he would still be working in the "cattle pens," his term for cubicles he endured during his first years at CDI.

The first interview went well, and his optimism grew when he was invited back for a second. The company considered his fluency in Spanish to be a tremendous asset. It also helped that a document he wrote recently had gotten a great deal of attention from those making the critical decisions. It was a public relations piece written to address media reactions to a product defect and recall that CDI had experienced some months earlier. A large segment of his report found its way into the final document that was eventually released to the public. This delicately worded act of contrition, complete with firm intentions to make amends, was credited with avoiding lawsuits and maintaining the good image of CDI, not to mention calming the nerves of anxious shareholders. The fact that the company had just named Curtis, the VP who happened to be in charge of damage control for that incident, as the CEO in Seraleugo was a coincidence that also improved Gerald's chances. Gerald got the job largely on the basis of Curtis's insistence that he had the essential problem-solving and diplomatic skills to assist in the transfer of control in Seraleugo.

After only two months of debriefings by the acquisitions team, brushing up on his Spanish, and arranging for the transfer of his household effects, Gerald and his two colleagues were on their way to Latin America. Leaving the familiar was challenging, but not nearly as challenging as it was for his two colleagues, both of whom would be bringing families to Seraleugo shortly after their arrival. The long hours of preparation had left the new management team on a first-name basis: Gerald, the head of communications; Curtis, who was fifty-seven, the CEO, and Andy, fifty-two, the new plant manager.

First and Second Impressions

The first days in Seraluego were a whirlwind of introductions, orientations, meetings, banquets, and tours of the region. Because of his superior level of Spanish, Gerald often found himself serving as interpreter for the other two, especially for Andy, who seemed to have difficulty understanding the locals. Seraleugo was in a rather isolated region of the country, although there were some posh resort areas a half-hour away. Gerald was unconcerned about the lack of social life. He was completely dedicated to making the most of this new opportunity. The team's strategy was to take control immediately and to rectify production and quality-control problems as quickly as possible.

Gerald was assigned to work out of the human resources office alongside Mr. Diaz, the director of the department. The office of human resources was charged with a wide range of responsibilities, from hiring, to payroll, to supervising the plant cafeteria. Most of Gerald's job responsibilities involved writing technical documents that required him to gather information from the heads of other departments. He had two local communications specialists working directly for him, Rosa and Jésus, both young and seemingly eager to please. Jésus had proficient skills in English and was able to compose appropriate reports based on the data that were supplied to him. While Jésus's grammar was nearly perfect, Gerald would occasionally modify some of his phrasing to reflect more common English usage. Rosa wrote only in Spanish and was charged with the bulk of the documentation to be done in Spanish.

Gerald was also assigned a private secretary, Carmen, who did little other than answer his phone, take messages, and serve as a gatekeeper in his outer office. Carmen had adequate conversational skills in English, but her secretarial skills did not extend beyond that of receptionist. To meet the growing needs of his small department, Gerald needed a secretary with more appropriate skills. He, therefore, had Carmen assigned to Andy, since she could help him with the Spanish language. Gerald hoped to recruit a competent replacement but, unfortunately, that took several months to achieve.

Gerald was pleased with Rosa and Jésus, at least initially. He felt that he enjoyed very productive working relationships with each of them. They often confided in him about personal and family matters. Based on their many stories, he became well acquainted with their entire families, even first and second cousins, though he never actually met any of them. Often though, he thought that the stories went on too long and took time away from critical work that needed to be accomplished. Recently Jésus spent an entire hour telling Gerald about a cousin's fiancé, the wedding they were planning, and their financial difficulties.

Finally, Gerald said, "Well, I am sure that your cousin and his bride will be able to work things out. Now we need to get back to this week's reports. How is that inventory monitoring form you were constructing coming along?"

Jésus responded a bit nervously, "Oh, sir, I am so sorry for wasting your time with my trivial family matters. Please forgive my rudeness. I will get the inventory form finished before I leave today."

"No need to apologize, Jésus. I appreciate the work you do. And thanks for getting the form finished today. I need to have it for my meeting tomorrow."

"I won't leave until it is finished," Jésus assured him.

Although Jésus and Rosa were always willing to talk about their families, they seemed unwilling to open up about matters that were of the keenest interest to Gerald. For example, he tried to seek their opinions about some confusing aspects of the managerial structure of the organization. He asked, "On paper, Mr. Gomez is responsible for all of the maintenance of plant machinery. Yet, when I met with him about formulating a performance appraisal, he seemed to know so little about the specific responsibilities of his workers. Who really runs the show in maintenance anyway?"

Jésus and Rosa looked at each other with some confusion. Finally, Rosa asserted, "Mr. Gomez is very well respected by his workers."

"He was the head of maintenance when my father worked here, and that was many years ago," Jésus added quickly.

Sensing their evasiveness, Gerald continued, "But most of the crew on maintenance seem to take their orders from Mr. Gutierez, isn't that true?"

"Oh, Mr. Gomez is the uncle of Mr. Gutierez," Rosa responded timidly.

"Mr. Gomez has much more responsibility. Mr. Gutierez is only a team boss in production, in the initial processing department," added Jésus.

Gerald persisted. "But since most of the heavy equipment is in that department, doesn't Mr. Gutierez supervise most of the maintenance done on those machines?"

"Those machines are frequently breaking down and require a lot of regular maintenance," Jésus responded.

"Things have gone much better over there since Mr. Gutierez has been in charge," Rosa asserted.

The evasive responses would continue indefinitely. Gerald knew that they had worked there long enough to be aware of what he was asking. He concluded that Jésus and Rosa simply didn't trust him enough to confide their own opinions on such matters. They seemed cooperative in most other respects. When he asked for specific documents or information, they readily supplied them. Their frequent unwillingness to offer a candid assessment or opinion on work-related issues was frustrating and somewhat disappointing to him. He hoped that the situation would improve over time.

Gerald got similar reactions about his attempts to write documents in Spanish. While his Spanish was good in both written and oral forms, he knew that it was not faultless, and he thought it important for a native speaker of Spanish to review his work. Since his arrival, he had tried to solicit comments and feedback from each of them on various documents he had written in Spanish, without much success.

They would typically assert, "Your writing is that of a native, quite professional," or "How did you learn to write such sophisticated Spanish? Your writing needs no correction."

As much as he appreciated their flattering remarks, he was certain they were overlooking serious problems in his writing. Even when he planted specific grammatical faults in the texts he wrote, they did not remark on them. He knew that they were being less than candid with him.

To their credit, once they were focused on their jobs, they worked quite assiduously. They seemed highly motivated to do their jobs well, and he seldom had difficulty meeting deadlines. However, in addition to their tendency to talk endlessly about personal matters and not provide him with useful feedback, there were other aspects of their work habits that began to worry him.

For one, their achievement motivation tapered off dramatically when he wasn't there to supervise them. In fact, on days when he was tied up in meetings with Curtis and Andy or visitors from the central office, he had the impression that very little was accomplished. While he was there, work seemed to progress at a reasonable pace, and both of them appeared to be enthusiastically devoted to their tasks. In fact, they sometimes seemed a bit overeager to please him and seek his approval. Frequently, they interrupted his work asking for instructions about trivial aspects of their assignments. They seemed incapable of completing even routine documents without his approval, even though he clearly indicated that they could take care of these matters on their own. At one point, he constructed a list of routine documents that did not require his signature. This strategy backfired badly since the documents occasionally did not reach their destinations, and it was eventually determined that they had never left his office. To sum it up, he felt that they were irresponsible. They worked effectively when closely supervised, but seemed to take no initiative or responsibility to do the work on their own.

For example, Curtis had called for an early deadline on a Spanish-language document being composed in Gerald's office. Rosa had been working on it and making adequate progress.

Given the change in deadline, Gerald asked Rosa, "When would be the earliest you could finish this document?"

"When do you want me to finish it?"

"Well, Curtis needs it as soon as possible."

"I will get right on it then."

"But Curtis wants to know now when it will be finished."

"When does he want it?" Rosa repeated.

Gerald, feeling the pressure, but also wanting to be reasonable, responded, "You are in the best position to judge how long it will take. When do you think you can you get it out?"

Trying to hide her frustration, Rosa finally suggested timidly, "Tomorrow?"

Gerald knew enough about the task to realize that expecting the finished document tomorrow was quite unrealistic. "Take until Thursday at noon, Rosa. That will give you three full days to complete it."

"That would be fine, sir," she said.

Even though she worked late both nights and came to him on numerous occasions seeking clarification about a variety of points, the document wasn't completed until Friday morning. Gerald appreciated her efforts, but was disappointed with her inability to estimate the time requirements of the task and take responsibility for her work. He made several other attempts to delegate responsibility, without much success. He felt that he had to micromanage nearly all of the work that was being done in his department.

At one point, their unwillingness to take responsibility for the work nearly caused him a major embarrassment. He had completely forgotten about a critical, although routine, document. Both Rosa and Jésus were aware of his oversight, but neither said anything about it. Neither took the initiative to see that the work got done. If it hadn't been for an oblique reference to the document that Andy had made in an unrelated meeting, Gerald would have completely forgotten the assignment. Luckily, no harm was done.

Working with Rosa and Jésus was a paradox. They seemed obsessed with seeking his approval for trivial matters, but they would not bring more serious problems, ones with far-reaching consequences, to his attention. He needed to check everything and follow up on all assignments to ensure that he would not be embarrassed by their lapses.

Attempts at Solutions

Gerald wasn't alone. The issue of getting local staff members to take more responsibility for their work came up nearly every time he, Curtis, and Andy were together outside of earshot of the locals.

Curtis argued, "Even the department heads need constant supervision, I can't turn my back for a moment."

"It's a constant struggle keeping Jésus and Rosa on task," Gerald added. "All they want to do is tell stories about various family members."

"You have to admit though," Andy countered "they aren't lazy. Productivity has increased steadily every month we have been here. Although we have a way to go, we are in much better shape than we had predicted six months ago."

"Yes, but, we need to have an effective way to motivate them without constantly peering over their shoulders," Curtis persisted.

"I just wish I could get them to work as hard when I am not around as they do when I am in the office," Gerald agreed.

"We will soon be in a position to offer financial incentives for our best employees," Curtis asserted.

"Yes, but that would require an effective system for appraising job performance, something that has been sorely lacking," Andy added. "It continually amazes me how this place has functioned without any such procedures, no records kept in personnel files, not even an informal system for appraising job performance."

"You're right. That needs to be our first step before introducing financial incentives," Curtis concluded.

The absence of documentation of work performance became an issue early on, when Curtis fired one of the staff members in the accounting office who was, in effect, incompetent. Apparently, he had been hired because of a family connection, and it was clear that he did not have the skills appropriate to the position. Not being able to find any other position in the office that suited him, they had to let him go.

Unfortunately, the man's brother-in-law was a lawyer, and he filed a complaint with the local judiciary. The company had to hire local lawyers, and the resulting legal morass had been dragging on for months. The lack of documentation had left the company in a vulnerable position, and it appeared they might actually lose the lawsuit, even though the worker in question had no qualifications as an accountant. Thus, in addition making an incentive program possible, there were other reasons the company needed an effective appraisal system.

After a long discussion, it fell to Gerald to formulate the system, devise the appraisal forms, and write an appropriate document for department heads explaining how the appraisals would be conducted. Initially, the task seemed straightforward. Appraisal systems that existed at CDI plants in the United States could be modified to fit Seraleugo. Gerald simply needed to work with the department heads to derive the specific criteria to be used on the appraisal forms for each department. This is where real difficulties began to arise. Despite the fact that the U.S. team had an organizational chart representing the chain of command throughout the plant, actual responsibilities for everyday operations reflected a complex, sometimes covert hierarchy that was nearly impossible to decipher.

Even in the human resources office where he worked, every document seemed to carry a variety of signatures, always including, of course, that of Mr. Diaz, the director. Despite the fact that Gerald was assigned to this office to monitor its activities, he seldom saw Mr. Diaz. On three occasions, he tried to arrange meetings, but each time he had to wait almost an hour to be admitted into his office. The meetings were short by local standards and characterized by tensions and problems in communication. While both Gerald and Mr. Diaz used the politest forms of address in Spanish, their interactions seemed cold and unproductive. Gerald was frustrated by Mr. Diaz's tendency to condescend and appear annoyed by his persistent questions.

The director's manner was in sharp contrast to what Gerald had experienced during his first days in Saraleugo, when Mr. Diaz played a major role in the welcoming festivities for the U.S. team. Gerald wondered what he had done to offend

Mr. Diaz. At any rate, Gerald could not understand his lack of cooperation, since Mr. Diaz could, if necessary, be replaced by someone chosen by the U.S. team. Interestingly, when Gerald saw Mr. Diaz speaking with Andy one time, Mr. Diaz seemed much friendlier and more cooperative. Gerald was sure that it was something he had said or done, but he had no idea what it could have been.

Similar problems became evident when Gerald tried to approach the other directors and heads of departments. Writing this job appraisal proposal became a genuine annoyance, since all of his attempts to gather critical information from the relevant people in the hierarchy were consistently frustrated. He began to interpret his problems as stemming from their resistance to the U.S. takeover. Yet in many respects, morale among both management and plant workers was high. The quality-control and delivery problems were being brought under control, and the customer base had been broadened thanks to CDI's contacts in the United States and abroad. Improved sales and overall cashflow allowed the plant to meet all payrolls on time, something that had been a problem before the acquisition. Most employees, outwardly at least, seemed pleased with the improvements resulting from the acquisition and eager to learn from the U.S. team. But Gerald seemed unable to reap the benefits of all this goodwill, especially when it came to dealing with the directors and department heads. For a while, he tried asserting himself more forcefully; then he would vacillate and think that what was needed was a greater degree of diplomacy. He just wasn't sure what the problem was.

One strategy that occurred to him was to implement an appraisal system in his own small department. In this fashion, he hoped to learn from his experiences and have a model to convince others of the advantages of a formal job appraisal system. He also thought it would be one more way to communicate to Rosa and Jésus both his approval of their overall level of productivity as well as his dissatisfaction with their constant need for supervision. He devised an appraisal form that contained ten dimensions on which their performance was to be evaluated, from "exceeds expectations" to "unsatisfactory." The rating scales were followed by a paragraph or two reflecting what Gerald saw as their major strengths and weaknesses. Rosa and Jésus would receive these appraisals as part of individual interviews designed to provide feedback on their work performance.

The actual interviews were conducted on the six-month anniversary of his arrival. Attempting to be sensitive and diplomatic, Gerald was careful to point out both their strengths and weaknesses. He praised each one regarding specific projects and tasks that were well done and, at the same time, admonished them to address areas of weakness, many of which concerned taking more individual responsibility. He was pleased with the meetings, although he was disappointed that Rosa and Jésus offered so few comments or reactions to his appraisals of their performance. However, the real disappointment came in the weeks that followed, when it became obvious that none of their behaviors had changed and, in fact, morale seemed to be deteriorating. His relationship with them, which at the beginning could have been characterized as warm and eager, became increasingly cold. He worried that he had been too harsh.

Other Challenges

Simultaneously, Curtis had also asked Gerald to work with the human resources department to clean up the plant's hiring practices. Seraleugo was located in an economically depressed area of the country, and there was no shortage of job applicants. However, it seemed that the plant had the habit of hiring relatives of current employees, rather than screening applicants based on the appropriateness of their job skills. The lawsuit brought by the fired accountant had taught them a difficult lesson. Something needed to be done to address this problem.

While the tendency toward nepotism created few problems among the non-salaried laborers in the plant, the mismatch between job skills and the responsibilities of the various key positions was much more noticeable in management. It was clear that hiring of relatives resulted in a bloated and inefficient managerial bureaucracy with many complexities in the chain of command that made it difficult to determine who answered to whom. Dealing with this issue was also complicated by the fact that Gerald had such a poor working relationship with Mr. Diaz, the director of human resources. In an early meeting that included Curtis, Mr. Diaz, and his staff, Gerald gave a short presentation on the use of job descriptions and objective criteria for selecting among job applicants. As a result of this meeting, Gerald had the green light to work with Mr. Diaz's staff to formulate appropriate job descriptions, which would stipulate more objective criteria for hiring decisions.

For Gerald, working with Mr. Diaz's staff was similar to working with his own staff. Everyone seemed cooperative. They learned the concepts quickly and were able to write selection criteria and passable job descriptions with little difficulty. However, three months after implementing the new policy, nothing had changed in their hiring practices. All the recent additions to the workforce had family ties to individuals in positions of responsibility. In fact, the difficulties Gerald was facing in his attempts to devise and implement job performance appraisals seemed to parallel the problem of nepotism in the hiring practices. The local norm seemed to be that hiring and promotion were more a function of personal connections than of qualifications.

On the other hand, all three members of the U.S. team seemed genuinely impressed with how well people in the office and in the plant seemed to get along. Nearly all of the department heads were related either by blood or by marriage, and each seemed to care about the others' welfare. The company clearly benefited from these cooperative relationships.

This benefit was most obvious in the early months, when the company was going through radical changes to improve productivity and quality control. These changes were required not only to meet the needs of the CDI production facilities in the United States, but also to respond to the increased customer base throughout the world. Since the acquisition, the demand for CDI products had increased nearly 50 percent. To manage such a major increase in productivity and to implement critical improvements in systems to ensure quality while undergoing major structural reorganization required a high degree of cooperation. Everyone genuinely pulled together to weather the changes. Many key decisions were implemented overnight. It was all puzzling to the U.S. team; in some respects the locals at Seraluego seemed infinitely adaptable, while in others, they seemed totally resistant to change. All things considered, Gerald, Andy, and Curtis doubted whether such major changes could have been weathered as effectively in a U.S. context as they were in Seraluego.

One last issue was an endless source of concern for the U.S. team. Bribery seemed to be a way of life for locals and everyone with whom they did business. The most obvious example involved the head of procurements. He was having lunch with one or another supplier nearly three times a week, frequently at an exclusive and expensive resort thirty miles away. It was not unusual for these lunches to last for four hours.

Curtis had been invited on these outings in his first weeks in Seraluego, and he was impressed by the lavish meals and the value of the gifts he was given. Most were of a personal nature, such as bottles of expensive liquor or an exquisite set of earrings for his wife. He saw them as bribes, but he also realized that they seemed to be the accepted way of doing business with local suppliers. The lunches made him extremely uncomfortable, and he declined future invitations. He worried that the tight relationship between his procurement officer and key suppliers was based more on loyalty than on getting the best price. In addition, he had learned in his predeparture training in Cleveland that such bribes were strictly illegal by U.S. law, even when they involved U.S. companies abroad. So he knew better than to ask his superiors in Cleveland about how to deal with the situation. On the other hand, bribery seemed to be just another part of the everyday challenge of doing business in this country. He was in a quandary about how to deal with this issue.

Background for Analysis

Gerald and his colleagues were facing a number of challenges, which all revolved around the hierarchical nature of the culture surrounding the Seraleugo plant. While there are a number of issues at work in this case, the focus of the analysis will be on Hofstede's (1991) dimension called *power distance* (PDI). PDI is one of four typologies Hofstede employed to characterize cultures around the world. The other three are individualism/collectivism, high and low uncertainty avoidance, and masculinity/femininity. PDI is defined as the extent to which people in any organization expect and accept that power will be distributed unequally. It directly reflects how people think about hierarchies and status differences.

Cultures scoring low on PDI, such as Denmark, Australia, Canada, and the United States, tend to suppress or deny differences in social status. These cultures tend to espouse the value of social equality even when differences in power and status are clearly evident. In the case of the United States, the value placed on equality is stated explicitly in the Declaration of Independence: "all men are created equal." When presidential candidates campaign among farmers in Ohio, they wear plaid shirts and jeans, just "to be one of the guys." People in the United States, even individuals with large differences in status, are comfortable using first names. Parents encourage their children to make many of their own decisions—about what clothes to wear, what to eat for breakfast, and so on. Children are often involved in family decisions. Students are frequently encouraged to think on their own, to develop their own opinions and express them as exercises in "critical thinking."

The opposite end of this dimension is high or large PDI. It is characterized by the expectation and acceptance of large differences in power and status. Countries scoring highest on PDI are Malaysia, most Central and South American nations, and many West African and Arab nations. Hierarchies in these cultures are considered a normal aspect of everyday life. Some people have higher status, some lower, and it is important to know precisely where one fits in the hierarchy. There is comfort and security in knowing one's place. There are important rules governing social interactions with individuals of different statuses, regarding the language to be used, the forms of address, even the content of what gets expressed. As long as an individual follows these social norms, the person can generally be assured of polite treatment from others. Some of the key differences between low and high PDI are outlined in Figure 8.1.

Gerald found himself in a high PDI culture, which contributed to many of the difficulties he experienced. First of all, his age was a problem. Gerald probably should not have been selected for the position. High PDI cultures tend to respect age much more than low PDI cultures, and it would be very difficult for older individuals who are well-established in the hierarchy to be obligated to cater to the demands of a young person. They would find it demeaning, embarrassing, and irritating to honor his many requests for what they viewed as sensitive and privileged information.

Things would have been simpler for Gerald if he had been given a less-ambiguous job title. Being the "head of communications" working "next to Mr. Diaz, the director of human resources" confused those around him in terms of his authority. He further undermined his own authority by getting rid of his secretary. High PDI cultures adhere to the norm that powerful people should look powerful, and not having a personal secretary put him in the category of the less-powerful. From a PDI perspective, to accomplish the tasks he was assigned, Gerald needed to assert his importance. Lacking the appearance of power seriously handicapped his effectiveness. He had less of a problem working with Rosa and Jésus, since they were young and he was clearly their boss. Problems became more evident in his attempts to work with the other department heads. As the department heads saw it, Gerald was an impertinent young upstart coming into their realms of authority, asking a multitude of demeaning questions, trying to specify how to evaluate and promote their own employees. Had he been older, in a clear position of authority, he would probably have received a much warmer reception.

In high PDI cultures, the relationship between boss and subordinate is different from that in low PDI cultures. Bosses are expected to be authorities, to have all of the information they need to be good bosses. They typically do not consult with

Figure 8.1   Key Differences in Low-Power and High-Power Distance Societies

Beliefs and Behaviors in Low-Power Distance Cultures	Beliefs and Behaviors in High-Power Distance Cultures
Inequalities among people should be minimized	Inequalities among people are both expected and desired
There should be, and there is to some extent, interdependence between less-powerful and more-powerful people	Less-powerful people should be dependent on the more powerful; in practice, less-powerful people are polarized between dependence and rebellion
Parents treat children as near-equals	Parents teach children obedience
Teachers expect initiative from students in class	Teachers are expected to take all initiative in class
Decentralization of power in organizations	Centralization of power in organizations
Superiors may consult subordinates	Subordinates expect to be told what to do
The ideal boss is a resourceful democrat	The ideal boss is a benevolent autocrat or paternalistic dictator
All should have equal rights	The powerful have privileges
Power is based on formal position, expertise, and ability to give rewards	Power is based on family or friends, charisma, and ability to use force

Note: Adopted from Hofstede, G. (1991). *Cultures and organizations: Software of the mind.* New York: McGraw Hill.

subordinates; rather, their job is to tell subordinates what to do. They are expected to have clear ideas about the requirements of each task that is assigned and to be willing and able to give appropriate direction and guidance to ensure that the tasks are carried out appropriately. All initiatives are the province of the boss; subordinates are not expected to take the initiative—indeed, they are actively discouraged from taking it, especially if it might make the boss look bad or incompetent.

The boss is also expected to be paternalistic, to feel some personal responsibility toward subordinates. It is not unusual for bosses in high PDI cultures to be actively involved in the personal lives of subordinates, introducing single employees, for example, to potential marriage partners, being an honored guest at their marriage, and even giving marital advice to the couple should problems arise in their relationship.

As for the employees, they are expected to work hard and be loyal to their boss. Good employees do not disagree, criticize, or talk disrespectfully to the boss. They tend to see themselves somewhat as obedient children who do what is expected of them. Of course, like all children, they are sometimes less compliant, even unruly, when parents aren't around. Bosses will often have a tolerant attitude about such lapses, although, of course, this tolerance has its limits.

Bosses can demonstrate displeasure to a wayward employee by showing him or her less attention and personal involvement. Such treatment clearly communicates to the employee the error of his or her ways. Formal job appraisals are not needed. Providing a good example is key to success in high PDI cultures. When a boss is committed and does the very best for the company and its employees, or at least appears to do so, a virtuous circle can be initiated throughout the company as employees tend to follow suit. On the other hand, if the boss is seen as opportunistic and uncaring about employees, these employees, even though they appear to be compliant and industrious, may in fact undermine productivity and, like their boss, be interested only in personal profit.

When job appraisal systems do exist in high PDI cultures, they tend to function differently than in low PDI cultures. They tend to be less formal, and written feedback tends not to be the norm. An employee would meet with a superior, often someone who is well above his or her own immediate supervisor, and the superior would generally take a paternalistic approach to providing feedback to the subordinate. The superior typically knows a great deal about the subordinate, his or her family, and other personal factors. The appraisal could resemble the advice one would receive from a caring grandparent. High PDI cultures also tend not to mix messages of praise and admonition, as did Gerald in attempting to talk about his employees' strengths and weaknesses. It is more likely that such feedback would be one-sided, either praising or admonishing, but not both at the same time.

Nepotism in hiring and promotion is considered to be common sense in a high PDI culture, not an evil to be avoided. Why would one want to hire complete strangers? What reason would they have to work hard and be loyal and productive? In some respects, showing preferences to friends and relatives has advantages. Everyone tends to be more committed to the organization, and employers tend to be more humane in their concern for employees. When the organization is profitable, the system can work well. Furthermore, as in this case, the loyalty and deference shown by subordinates allows for the quick and efficient implementation of decisions made by superiors. There is less need to convince subordinates of the advantages of a change in policy that comes from clear authority figures. It is the boss's job to make such decisions and the employee's role to carry them out.

Gift-giving, which can spill over into outright bribery, is more common in high PDI cultures. It is important to realize that at its roots, giving a gift is a gesture of goodwill, reflecting the desire to promote a good relationship. Cultures differ markedly on this issue, and some groups are unable to have any contact with outsiders without an initial exchange of gifts. Gifts may also represent deference to people of high rank and, therefore, can become elaborate or expensive. They fit with the norm that important people should look important and be shown appropriate deference. Refusing gifts can be interpreted negatively, since, by proxy, one is also refusing the person bearing the gift. However, what constitutes a gift and what constitutes a bribe is a complex and delicate matter. Typically, people within a culture are rather clear about the difference, while this distinction can be perplexing to those outside the culture. Nevertheless, the habit of bribing business contacts can flourish more readily in a climate where gift-giving is the norm, and it can pose serious problems for international corporations doing business in high PDI cultures.

Analysis of the Case

Note: To some degree, this case provides an overly simplistic depiction of normative behaviors and practices in a high PDI culture. In addition to simplification, key characteristics have been blended together from a variety of high PDI cultures to highlight the general implications. High PDI in France, for example, differs in important ways from high PDI in Mexico. Do not overgeneralize the cultural differences assumed under the rubric of high-power and low-power distance. While there are empirically demonstrable differences among cultures along this dimension, in everyday interactions, such differences are manifest in varied and perhaps less exaggerated forms than what has been depicted in this case.

Although there is little Gerald can do about his age, there are a number of strategies that would improve his effectiveness in this high PDI context. First of all, he should have an appropriate position of authority, commensurate with his diverse job responsibilities. It would greatly facilitate his work to have a clear and unambiguous job title. His office arrangement should reflect his authority. It would be more appropriate for him to be more closely aligned with other authority figures, such as Curtis or Andy, or at least with Mr. Diaz. In any event, he should not have eliminated his secretary, without another one already in place. He was probably perceived by the locals as a low-level functionary brought along by the two leaders from the United States because of his abilities in Spanish. They may have viewed him as a translator. This perception may have been reinforced by the fact that Andy acquired Gerald's former secretary, and Gerald had to function for some time without adequate support.

In many ways Gerald's behavior was inappropriate for someone of authority. His tendency to vacillate between forceful and diplomatic strategies made him appear weak and uncertain. To genuinely assume a position of authority in a high PDI culture, Gerald not only needed to have the trappings of power, he also needed to be clear in his own mind about what he wanted to accomplish, and then use his authority to get it done. Gerald did not have sufficient authority or persuasive power to convince the locals of the benefits of job descriptions and performance appraisals.

In addition, Gerald's interpersonal behaviors were unbecoming to an authority figure in a high PDI culture. One of the key ingredients in this cultural approach to leadership is paternalism. His difficulties with Rosa and Jésus stemmed largely from their perception that he was callous, insensitive, and focused only on work. They have been culturally socialized to think that a good employee is one who pleases the boss by doing precisely what the boss requests—that is, to work hard on assigned tasks to gain the boss's approval. They would never consider it appropriate to correct their superiors or to give their own opinions on delicate matters. In exchange for this loyalty, they expected Gerald to care about them and to care for them. Instead, he appeared cold and uncaring. In the exchange about the deadline, Rosa was playing out her cultural script to please her boss. Gerald, by asking inappropriate questions and proposing an unrealistic deadline, appeared immature and incompetent.

A subordinate would prefer to feel a sense of pride about a boss, but Rosa and Jésus found little to be proud about with Gerald. To them, he vacillated impulsively and unpredictably between praising them and criticizing them, and ultimately he cared little for anyone other than himself and his personal agenda. He never asked questions about their families or seemed at all concerned about their personal lives. It became increasingly difficult for them to respect him, to feel a sense of loyalty, or to be motivated to please him.

With respect to the use of job descriptions to hire qualified personnel and performance appraisals to reward competence and effort, devising appropriate strategies can be complicated. This same assessment can be made about the practice of using bribes to gain advantages in the marketplace. Whenever an enterprise of any sort—be it religious, educational, or entrepreneurial—interacts with a different culture, there must be compromises if cross-cultural relationships are to be mutually satisfying and productive. In this case, there are advantages to nepotism to ensure a workforce that is committed and congenial, and bribes can facilitate relationships and increase the chances of making a sale. However, businesses function most effectively when talent and effort are rewarded, and sales are based on quality and value rather than favoritism. These are fundamental principles of the free-enterprise system. While they are ideals that are only approximated in reality, most international corporations try to do more than pay lip service to them. This is probably less a function of moral scruples than of a bottom-line mentality. It is a simple fact that, in the long run, rewarding talent, effort, quality, and value is seen as more profitable than nepotism and the practice of accepting bribes.

So how should CDI deal with such practices as nepotism and bribery? Curtis and his colleagues should be clear in their policies about dealing with these issues and then use their authority to enforce them. Guidelines should be clear and fair. In the case of nepotism, it is probably undesirable to suppress all nepotism, given the strong cultural norms reflected in the practice and its clear advantages for the welfare of the company. On the other hand, given the high degree of competition in today's global markets, it is critical to attract and nurture genuinely qualified personnel. Thus, strict guidelines must be implemented requiring that job candidates have appropriate qualifications to be hired. In some cases, this may require training people who hold important positions to bring their skills in line with the needs of the organization.

In the case of bribery, outright bribery should be forbidden, and gifts should be discouraged. However, since it is unlikely and perhaps undesirable to suppress all gift-giving, it is probably more appropriate to monitor it, keeping careful records of all gifts given and received. When gifts are received, they should be entered routinely into the accounting procedures. These data can be compared to business transactions to ensure that deals are not being inappropriately influenced.

Gifts carrying a company logo, such as pens, calendars, and the like can be accepted without maintaining records, since these are more a matter of advertising than bribes. Gifts of a personal nature, such as expensive bottles of alcohol or personal jewelry, should be turned over to the company and could eventually be distributed to personnel as part of a Christmas bonus, for example. This principle of accountability applies to giving bribes as well. Should it be necessary to bribe a government official, for example, to facilitate some process such as acquiring a clearance on imported goods, a consultant or a lawyer typically acts as an intermediary and bills the company in a legal fashion.

Regardless of the circumstances, it is critical for authorities to be clear about the rules, and they should follow these rules themselves as well. If the employees see their superiors setting an example of fairness and frugality, they will typically be willing to follow suit. This would especially be the case if employers were "good bosses," that is, successful, a descriptor that could apply to Curtis and his colleagues at CDI. In high PDI cultures, subordinates are generally willing to learn from authorities who are seen as powerful and successful.

It is important to note that the lessons in this case have gone in both directions. Curtis and his colleagues should be learning the values of loyalty and taking care of their charges in ways that extend beyond what would be considered normal in their native cultures. An effective and productive synergy can develop when cultures learn to blend their strengths in a cooperative fashion, each learning and growing because of their exposure to the other. Such lessons have far-reaching consequences, beyond immediate professional needs, and can potentially change self-perception in fundamental ways. This is the most important benefit of living, working, and playing with people who are different from ourselves.

Questions for Discussion

1. In what ways was working in a high PDI culture advantageous to Gerald and his colleagues? What were the disadvantages? What aspects would you like and dislike about living in a high PDI culture?

2. Applying what you have learned about functioning effectively in a high PDI culture, how might Gerald have more productively handled the exchange he had with Rosa about the deadline for her writing project?

3. How would Rosa and Jésus define their ideal boss? In what ways would Gerald have to change to live up to their ideal? From the standpoint of being an effective boss, that is, encouraging competent and effective performance from subordinates, do you think it would be appropriate for Gerald to become more like their ideal boss? Or would he be better off just being himself, and allowing Rosa and Jésus to adjust to his style? Give arguments for each point of view.

4. Gerald was nearly embarrassed by overlooking a specific writing task for which he was responsible. Neither Jésus nor Rosa pointed out his mistake. Based on what you have learned about high PDI cultures, discuss how he might direct Jésus and Rosa to take the initiative to avoid such oversights in the future.

5. Should it be legal for U.S. businesses working abroad to use bribery in order to function competitively in today's marketplace? Are U.S. restrictions unreasonable? In the long run, to be most competitive, what strategies should international businesses cultivate with respect to bribery?

6. An astute reader may have detected an implied value judgment in this case, that cultures with low PDI are somehow superior to those with high PDI. The characters who were from the low PDI culture, the team from the United States, were the "good guys" who were in charge, who purchased an inadequately managed factory, solved many of its problems, and tried to rid the system of nepotism and bribery. It is important to avoid such judgments. Discuss what the challenges might be if the tables were reversed, if members of a high PDI culture such as France were to acquire a manufacturing plant in the United States, a low PDI culture. Where would the cultural clashes lie, and how might they be addressed from a high PDI perspective?

Writing Assignment

Interview an exchange student, or anyone, from a high PDI culture—such as a country in Central or South American, Malaysia, West Africa, or an Arab country. Ask open-ended questions that would elicit perceptions of differences between the United States and the home culture. Where appropriate, note how responses might be conceptualized along the PDI dimension. Compare your results in the context of a class discussion. Ask:

- What do you miss most about your home culture?
- What do you like most and least about living in the United States?
- How is the behavior of students and teachers different from what you experienced at home?
- How are children raised differently?

Additional Readings: Issues Relevant to the Case

Ferraro, G. P. (1998). *The cultural dimensions of international business* (Third Ed.). Upper Saddle River, NJ: Prentice Hall.

Fisher, G. (1980). *International negotiation: A cross-cultural perspective.* Yarmouth, ME: Intercultural Press.

Gudykunst, W. B., Ting-Toomey, S., & Nishida, T. (1996). *Communication in personal relationships across cultures.* Thousand Oaks, CA: Sage.

Hofstede, G. (1991). *Cultures and organizations: Software of the mind.* New York: McGraw Hill.

Smith, P. B., & Bond, M. H. (1999). *Social psychology across cultures.* Boston: Allyn & Bacon.

Chapter 9

A Venture between American Academe and Corporate Malasia:
The CyberUniversity Blues

THOMAS F. LANNIN
CyberInstitute Inc.

Abstract: A Malaysian consultant and economics professor contacts a young American professor, notifying him that he has a very wealthy client interested in making a reality of the professor's cyberuniversity idea. The American professor contacts a close associate, an expert on Malaysian business customs and language, for advice and ends up partnering with him and the Malaysian consultant. Together, they build a project plan, which the client approves and starts to fund immediately after it is presented in Kuala Lumpur. The three-man team continues designing and constructing the project. They build a faculty and curriculum, research other on-line distance-learning programs, develop a technology base in Kuala Lumpur, and meet with administrators of American universities to obtain letters of agreement. Unfortunately, the two major players on the Malaysian end, the client and the consultant-professor, are unable to carry out tasks necessary to completing a crucial phase. The client also changes his mind about the quality of the two universities interested in beta testing the project and serving as the first providers of on-line certificates and degrees. Shortly before implementation, the client develops cold feet and cancels the project. In the end, the American professor has learned a valuable lesson about cross-cultural communication issues, especially how difficult it is to create a global service from scratch.

Note: This case is a disguised version of an actual attempt by an American consultant-professor to develop a virtual university in Malaysia.

Background for the Case

In the winter of 1996, a young Malaysian computer science student at a university in North Carolina hired an American technical communications consultant, Dr. Cormac McInnish, to write a proposal for the Malaysian Institute of Microelectronic Systems (MIMOS). Seeing himself as a future entrepreneur, and a rich one at that, the student wanted to convince MIMOS to use his integrated software to provide JARING—Malaysia's Internet—customers with better services, including on-line shopping, local and global news, and university preparatory classes.

Cormac was more interested in the on-line educational aspects of the plan rather than the purely commercial features. Developing a virtual university from scratch posed an awesome challenge. The young Malaysian, who had a two-year degree from a private technical college in Kuala Lumpur, was highly competent in computer science. Cormac convinced himself that even if the proposal failed at least he would learn a great deal about both Malaysia and information technology.

After several months of working together on the fifteen-page proposal, which included original illustrations and research, the two men submitted the document to MIMOS through the young man's father, a retired major in the Malaysian Air Force. The young man told Cormac that the government thought highly of the project and would do everything it could to help them implement their concept, including providing immediate accreditation in Malaysia, once solid financial backing was established.

The estimated startup costs were between $100,000 and $200,000 (U.S. dollars), which the client assured Cormac would not be a problem since the client's rich uncle was the backer. He told Cormac that he contacted his uncle frequently about budget expenses. At one point, he even drove to Mississippi for a business meeting with his uncle. Cormac never met the uncle.

Much to Cormac's chagrin, mysterious meetings, secondhand information, and verbal promises became part of the communication process. Finally, Cormac insisted on a written agreement before he finished creating the cyberuniversity, the main phase of the proposed project. After spelling out his fees to the young client, he heard nothing. Cormac soon discovered the Malaysian student had left the country, dropping out of the university without a degree.

The Next Stage of the Project

In November 1996, roughly six months later, Cormac received a phone call from a friend, Dr. William Grove Smith, a professor of journalism at the University of Georgia.

"Cormac, it's Bill. How'd you like to revive that cyberuniversity project you were working on?"

"Are you serious? Of course I would."

"I have a Malaysian buddy, a guy I've known since my days teaching at the University Sains Penang. He represents a wealthy client interested in developing an on-line university."

"Really?" Cormac felt the rush of excitement that comes from starting another project. "What type does he want? Something modeled after us or the British?"

"I'd think us, even though the Malaysians prefer to send their kids to England or Australia. Less crime and their systems are almost identical. Anyway, we need to impress on this client why our curricula and models are better."

"Exactly. So tell me more about your friend. Can I trust him? After getting burned by this kid, I'm a little leery about doing business with any Malaysians. By the way, what's his name?"

"Dr. Haji Said. He's a full-blooded Malay, not Chinese. I think that student you dealt with came from a Chinese family, didn't he?"

"Yeah. Why?"

"There are big cultural differences between the two. The Malays are very well connected to each other, and Haji's client is Malay. Anyway, if anyone can help us, it's Haji. He's a successful business and technology consultant in an incredibly competitive market. And he's a great guy."

"Still, I want to get something in writing from both him and his client. I want a nondisclosure agreement."

"Sure. Tell him your requirements as a consultant, and see what you can work out. All I ask is a finder's fee. Here, let me give you his e-mail address."

They finished their conversation, and Cormac drafted a proposal that afternoon and e-mailed it to Dr. Haji. A few days later, Dr. Haji responded, saying that Cormac, Bill, and he would partner as consultants, and he would act as the group's official spokesman during any talks with Mr. Kelana, the wealthy client. He would also be paid separately by his client, and only after the cyberuniversity went on line.

By the end of January, after two months of contract negotiation, the three men had hammered out a mutual agreement, and the client signed for the first of three phases.

According to the proposal, Phase One would involve Cormac's flying to Kuala Lumpur. The most important features of this phase were to

- Meet the client and understand his initial needs and requirements
- Give a computerized slide presentation on the overall design of the cyberuniversity, including administration, faculty, courses, tuition and fees, technical support, on-line library, and other important information
- Establish the main "campus" in Kuala Lumpur, which meant having a physical address, something the government required
- Develop and coordinate a staff of at least five people, including two programmers, a secretary, a receptionist, and an advertising and marketing person
- Determine what hardware and software was needed.

Background for Analysis

Before he could proceed, Cormac knew he had to learn more about Malaysia. He had visited the country twice, but had never been to Kuala Lumpur, and he knew little of its history. One thing he knew from experience was to learn as much about a client's culture as possible; appearing ignorant or uninterested could kill a business deal.

Peninsular Malaysia achieved independence from Great Britain in 1957. In 1963, Sarawak, Sabah, and Singapore joined Malaya to form Malaysia. Singapore separated from the union two years later; it has a 77 percent Chinese majority. Presently, Malaysia has three primary ethnic groups: Malays, Chinese, and Indians. Indians have lived there for centuries as merchants and traders. The immigrant Chinese population expanded greatly in the mid-1850s when new tin mines were established on the peninsula. Soon, the Chinese minority, which remains at about 30 percent of the population, controlled about 80 percent of the economy.

In 1971, after a period of violent social unrest, this economic pattern changed. During the administration of Tun Abdul Razak, the government implemented a nationalistic economic policy to reduce poverty and rectify the adverse economic conditions under which most Malays suffered. They restricted non-Malay investment in companies to a minority 49 percent interest and increased the Malays' share of the nation's wealth as well as their employment in professions non-Malays had once dominated. Today, *bumiputra* (native) Malays receive priority over Chinese and Indians in attending the University of Malaya and in promotion to mid-level to high-level government positions.

Despite official statements declaring how multicultural and diverse Malaysia has become, a former Malaysian head of public schools whom Cormac had met on a plane told him that class and ethnic tensions lie beneath the surface. For one thing, Muslims are supposed to lead a pure lifestyle devoid of alcohol, tobacco, gambling, and infidelity, and to devote themselves to helping the poor and respecting others. Most Malays are Shiite Muslim, the exceptions being those living in Sabah, who are usually Christian or animist. Malaysian city-dwellers consider themselves fairly cosmopolitan and tolerant, but Shiite Malays from the northeast are more conservative, in general, and fundamentalist Islamic leaders frequently ask the people to ignore government laws and policies they believe will corrupt the faith.

In effect, Malays publicly accept Buddhist, Christian, and Hindu religious observations, personal habits, and professional practices, but privately many are insulted by or resentful of them. For example, virtually no Muslim Malay woman would be seen wearing a miniskirt in public or staring at a man, and Muslim Malay men rarely wear shorts and are very discreet about watching women. Young Chinese and Hindu women express their independence or love of Western styles by wearing miniskirts and sleeveless blouses. Many Chinese men wear shorts and T-shirts, smoke, spit on sidewalks, and gamble at Mah-Jong well into the night. Like the Malays, the Indians are more modest and subdued in appearance and public expression. The Chinese and Indians, nevertheless, seem genuinely grateful that a government whose official religion is Islam is so tolerant of differences.

Nowadays, much depends on a person's status in society. Even though a downturn in the Asian economy created much uncertainty, especially in the stock market, the new wealth helped topple many established social barriers. Chinese, Indian, and Malays can be seen dining together in fashionable restaurants, making key decisions at business meetings, and talking casually on street corners. Indian professionals hold significant positions in government, law, and medicine, and their education and facility with English are usually superior to most Chinese and Malays. In fact the language that helps cement the country together is English, a legacy of colonialism.

One of the things Cormac discovered in his research is that introverted students who rarely or never speak out in traditional classroom settings become more extroverted and participatory in on-line chatrooms. Given the conservative and noninteractive environment of the typical Asian classroom, an on-line format would enable students who had never talked to each other or their professors to communicate regularly via e-mail and in scheduled office chatrooms. It seemed an excellent way to unify people of diverse ethnic and cultural backgrounds who normally would be afraid to address issues openly if they thought their identities would introduce prejudice into the discussion.

Overview of Phase One

During spring break in 1997, Cormac flew to Kuala Lumpur. Even in the middle of the night, the tropical heat and humidity engulfed him as soon as he left the protection of the airport terminal. Broad leaf evergreens lined many of the roads, and billboards advertising Motorola, Malaysia Telecom, and other high-tech companies dotted the landscape.

The next morning, Dr. Haji met Cormac at his hotel, the Concorde, which is situated on the busiest street in the city, Jalan Ampang.

"This is a very exciting project," Dr. Haji noted, nodding his head and looking out the hotel's huge windows. The Malay was confident, almost nonchalant. "Mr. Kelana was excited with your proposal. It's a hot subject now, this on-line education. He has the money and the connections to make it happen. Keep in mind that the real money will be made in the implementation phase, not these preliminary ones. We need to hook him, to make him sign on for the other phases. So you need to start thinking less like an English teacher and more like a business consultant. That's why he's paying you the big bucks, right?"

Bill had told him a little about Dr. Haji, how he'd had been educated at Stony Brook, Cornell, and the University of Kiel, England, where he took a doctorate in economics. The professor, it seemed, had become quite Americanized. At one point, he pulled out his cellular phone. "Let me call Tam," he said, referring to the client by his first name. Mr. Kelana, it turned out, was a country club friend as well as a client. "I'll arrange the first meeting at his headquarters, which is just down the street at the Wisma Bangsar. It's thirty stories high. A beautiful building that's won awards for design. And he owns it."

An hour or so later, Dr. Haji 's driver pulled up in a new Mercedes.

"You mean we're going to drive there?" Cormac asked, pointing at it. "But the building's right there."

"Of course."

"Doesn't that seem kind of wasteful?"

Dr. Haji gave a kind of half frown, half smile. "It's too hot to walk. Besides, I don't want to ruin this new suit I just bought."

Feeling guilty, Cormac got in the back seat and looked out at Malaysian pedestrians, many of them women wearing modest scarves and colorful full-length batik dresses, walking slowly in the smoggy heat of Kuala Lumpur. The street was filled with luxury cars with businessmen in the back seats.

Taking an elevator to the twenty-ninth floor, Cormac felt butterflies in his stomach. What if the guy doesn't like my PowerPoint presentation? What if he asks technical questions I can't answer? What if he thinks the curriculum is incompatible with what Malaysians want, or it's too difficult to implement?

After the formal introductions, Cormac followed Mr. Kelana, Dr. Haji, and two staff members into a small conference room equipped with a computer, a twenty-one-inch monitor, and a brand new computer slide projector. Cormac took a deep breath and began his talk. The presentation lasted about an hour, and when he finished, the first thing Mr. Kelana asked was, "When can you begin Phases Two and Three?"

"As soon as I get back to the States."

"Then we have a deal."

Overview of Phase Two

Phase Two, it was agreed, would require Cormac to do most of the work, and Phase Three would require an equal share from Bill and Dr. Haji, with Dr. Haji acting as an intermediary between Mr. Kelana and the Ministry of Education, whose approval was mandatory. In Phase Two, Bill and Cormac had to decide which two American colleges might offer the most innovative, quality-oriented long-distance learning programs for a price affordable to the average Malaysian college student. It was imperative to narrow down criteria and locate the best two institutions within this phase's two-month time frame.

The major goals were as follows:

- Report on faculty selection
- Define and approve curriculum
- Establish quality control standards
- Create Web pages, market the joint-degree program; include faculty résumés
- Create frequently asked questions (FAQs)
- Establish teaching philosophy, departments, and other vital information

- Create database that houses all future records, including registration informa-
  tion, faculty profiles, and other essential data, at Wisma Bangsar headquarters
- Complete a faculty manual
- Draft a course catalog
- Deliver two memoranda of understanding (MoUs).

Fortunately, half of these tasks were already completed. The most difficult was
to get the two memoranda of understanding from qualified universities.

On March 14, Cormac met Dr. Haji at the Shangri-La Hotel, thinking that they
were going to discuss plans for Phase Two. Dr. Haji seemed distracted, and not too
long after they had started talking, he pulled out a memo. "This is for you. Tam
and I discussed these already, and these are some additional projects we'd like you
to handle for us."

With a combination of fear and excitement, Cormac scanned the memo.
Among the nine projects were plans for him to

- Incorporate a company in Charlotte and in Kuala Lumpur that would project
  an image for their various interests
- Make presentations on the Multimedia Super Corridor project to companies
  in North Carolina's Research Triangle
- Call on Charlotte-area campuses to see which were interested in offering virtual MBAs via videoconferencing
- Get American MBA students to visit Asia's financial capitals; the new company would make all the arrangements
- Organize educational fairs to promote colleges and represent them in Malaysia
  at nominal fees.

He couldn't believe it. "Wait a minute, Haji. I'm a little confused. Aren't we
supposed to be focusing on the main business of developing a cyberuniversity?
What's all this stuff?"

"Yes, of course. All of these will come as a result of your doing business here
now. The cyberuniversity comes first. We just thought you could help set these
up for us and share in the profits. Here, let me show you how much you can make
on each."

Dr. Haji spent the next thirty minutes charting out profit margins and
percentages.

This was a totally new direction, and Cormac wasn't happy about it. Not wanting to offend, he agreed in principle to help out with the ventures, without telling
Dr. Haji that he needed to talk things over with Bill.

While Bangsar staff worked on naming the virtual university, Cormac returned to the United States to fulfill the goals of Phase II. After several names were
rejected by the Ministry of Education, or stolen by competitors forming their own
private nonvirtual campuses, Bangsar submitted Asia Network Technological College (ANTC) and received approval. Bangsar's graphic artists designed a school
logo featuring a red ant.

When Cormac received news of the campus name, he called Bill. "Have you seen what they've come up with?"

Bill laughed. "Yeah, and it doesn't surprise me. From an Asian perspective it's pretty smart marketing. To them, an ant represents hard work, endurance, sacrifice, community. All those traits emblematic of Asian culture. "

Phase II Research

Bill and Cormac spent the next month researching traditional and nontraditional education; collecting, organizing, and documenting data; e-mailing messages to Dr. Haji and various communications experts and academic officials; and visiting universities to examine administration, faculty, staff, and technological facilities. They knew that in order to receive full approval to grant certificates in a joint-degree program from the Ministry of Education (which Malaysians refer to as a "twinning programme," based on the British system), a signed memorandum of understanding between Bangsar/The CyberFactory and two American colleges or universities was vital. This was the hardest task. Many colleges seemed too expensive for middle-class Malaysians, technologically handicapped, or bogged down in bureaucracy. Bill and Cormac finally chose a state university in New York and a small private college in North Carolina because the first had videoconferencing technology in place and the second was eager to increase revenue by teaching courses on-line. The New York school's multimedia classrooms were very well-equipped: students from eight different campuses throughout upstate New York could see, hear, and interact with the professor and fellow students. As it turned out, it was exactly what Mr. Kelana wanted, and he authorized a team to build a comparable multimedia classroom environment on the sixteenth floor of the Wisma Bangsar. At least that's what he told Bill and Cormac.

Overview of Goals for Phase III

Dr. Haji and Cormac had coauthored a detailed, bulleted list the day before the American professor left Malaysia in March 1997. Dr. Haji was confident that Mr. Kelana's staff would supply the necessary support and resources to enable the American consultants to carry out Phase III. In his heightened state of enthusiasm, Cormac thought anything was possible. The crucial task was making sure that Bangsar set up a videoconferencing facility allowing for beta-tested broadcasts between Malaysia and the United States.

Reporting Findings to Malaysian Client

In late May and early June of 1997, Cormac was again in Kuala Lumpur to report on the achievements for Phase II, hoping to immediately begin work on Phase III. The day after arriving, he met with Amal, the young managing director, who was Mr. Kelana's nephew. Amal was responsible for arranging plane and hotel reservations, sending funds for incorporating an office in Charlotte, and scheduling meetings. He was also supposed to be in charge of having Bangsar do its part in implementing the goals of Phase III. These duties were in addition to his main job, overseeing Bangsar's Global Café worldwide operations.

The first thing Cormac learned was that instead of reserving a floor of the Wisma Bangsar for ANTC's fixed classroom—another government requirement—Bangsar was looking to purchase a three-story building in a less expensive, more accessible part of the city. Thus it would be impossible to complete an important section of the agreement because it would take weeks to find the right property and perhaps more than a month to staff it.

As it turned out, Mr. Kelana truly had decided to buy a new building, calling it CyberFactory—Asia. Yet he had told neither Cormac nor Bill, only Dr. Haji. In effect, he had violated part of the agreement, apparently believing that this field was evolving so rapidly that sudden changes in strategy were *de rigueur*. Unfortunately, his nephew Amal was overly hesitant, nervous, and distractible. Rarely did he make a decision without his uncle's approval. Because his uncle was so busy attending to his dozen or more different companies, interaction between him and the Americans was often awkward and confusing. It was hardly the efficient business style Cormac was expecting, and he was becoming more and more frustrated with the intercultural communication process.

Things began to go from bad to worse. Cormac had hired a clinical psychologist and expert on testing to prepare interview questions and practice SAT exams. When the psychologist arrived in Kuala Lumpur, she discovered that Dr. Haji had been so busy with his other entrepreneurial ventures that he had neglected to line up a single Malaysian student for an interview, testing, or focus group. These were crucial marketing requirements, yet he shrugged aside his negligence by dismissing the importance of interviewing students.

In essence, very little got accomplished during Phase III. Mr. Kelana was preoccupied with other ventures, tied up in meetings, or traveling out of the country to oversee his other businesses.

At the end of May, after the academic year was over, Bill arrived in Malaysia. When he discovered how behind schedule the project was, he became quite worried. From that point on, he and Cormac spent ten to twelve hours a day trying to complete Phase III without Bangsar's help. At one point they met with Microsoft's Malaysia representatives to see how that company could help with long-distance communications. It turned out that Microsoft was eager to help if Bangsar provided the necessary capital and infrastructure.

On June 6, after two cancelled meetings, Bill and Cormac presented an overview of achievements during Phases II and III to Mr. Kelana. Shortly after the presentation began, Mr. Kelana interrupted them.

"I'm sorry, stop for a minute. I must tell you that my head is telling me one thing about this project, and my stomach another. My head says that this is good and will work, and my stomach says the time is not right. That we should wait. Here I must trust my stomach, my instinct. I'm very sorry, but I must back out because this no longer looks profitable to me for the first year."

Cormac felt the flush of anger and panic suffuse his face. His two years of work were washing down the drain. Kelana seemed oblivious to the way he was contradicting himself. In Phase I he stated that he wanted to give back something to his country for the opportunities it had given him, that making a profit in the first year wasn't important. While Bill, the better diplomat and Malaysia veteran, nodded and agreed with Mr. Kelana, Cormac sat in an enraged, baffled silence. After agreeing to pay Bill and Cormac consulting fees according to an agreed-on schedule, Mr. Kelana ended the meeting, stating that he would be interested in renewing this effort at a future date, depending on how profitable it would look for him.

Meeting Aftermath

Back in their hotel suite, Bill and Cormac reviewed Mr. Kelana's reasons for backing out of this project:

1. Competition from KUB Malaysia to build a virtual university in the Multimedia Super Center may hurt enrollment and therefore profitability. The government had given official approval to this project on May 19, 1997.
2. JARING, the main Internet server in Malaysia, had proven to be unreliable, thus acting as a barrier to good on-line communication between Malaysian students and American professors.
3. The new physical plant and the technical support and marketing people would not be in place until mid-August of 1997.
4. Neither U.S. university had a reputation or distinctive image in Malaysia; a convincing marketing campaign would involve too much time and effort. There were also concerns over whether the private college could deliver a solid on-line program.
5. Bangsar would probably not turn a profit until the end of the second year.

Still in a state of moderate shock, Bill and Cormac drafted a response to Mr. Kelana and faxed it to him that night. The response stated:

1. The proposed KUB Malaysia virtual university in the Multimedia Super Corridor involves an expenditure of RM250 million (approximately $66 million), making it more a traditional campus than a virtual one. The degrees issued will be from Malaysian, not foreign, institutions, producing a project far different from the one currently involving Bangsar.
2. Telecom Malaysia and other telecommunications companies are entering the server–provider market. The increased competition should promote a higher quality of service and greater accessibility that will offset JARING's inefficiency.
3. If the new physical plant, server, and personnel are established in mid-August of 1997, the main effect will be that alpha testing and beta testing will push back the start date several months if full videoconferencing and integrated voice e-mail and other sophisticated Internet technologies are used. Rather than classes beginning in September, a more realistic time would be early January 1998.

4. One of Bangsar's functions, as stated in the original proposal, was to create a Web site for colleges and faculty involved in this project.
5. The point at which the enterprise becomes profitable depends on which option Bangsar chooses. If full videoconferencing capabilities are established at a Bangsar site in Malaysia and only a minimum of students enroll, it will be very difficult to make a profit. On the other hand, if a combination of long-distance learning multimedia is used and the marketing campaign has a modicum of success, Bangsar can realize a modest profit by the beginning of the second year. Everything depends on enrollment; initial investment in equipment, personnel, and operations; and the agreement Bangsar can reach with participating institutions.

A month after returning to the United States, Bill and Cormac were still attempting to get Mr. Kelana to honor his business agreement. In spite of repeated e-mail messages and phone calls, neither he nor Amal responded.

Two months later, Bill called Dr. Haji, who told him that Mr. Kelana did not think the work during Phases II and III justified the consulting fees. Flustered, Bill responded that he would be happy to assemble a final report to justify the fees, even though Mr. Kelana had signed an agreement and no such report was required.

Responses to Client's Request for Justification of Fees

After the client refused to pay for the work completed during Phases II and III, Bill and Cormac submitted a 270-page final report, including proposals, letters, agreements, and research material, to Mr. Kelana.

"If he doesn't go for this detailed catalogue of accomplishments and accompanying evidence," said Bill, "then I don't know what else we can do to convince him. There's more than enough here to justify our fees."

"And they're right in line with those for international educational consulting."

"The big question is, will we get paid?"

"When we left Kuala Lumpur, I would have said, 'Sure.' Now your guess is as good as mine."

Analysis of the Case

As it turned out, neither Cormac nor Bill ever received his full consulting fees. Recovering the fees would have proven too costly and time-consuming to be worth the effort, and they ultimately chalked up the venture to experience.

Establishing trust with clients from one's own country is difficult enough, but when one conducts international business, learning as much as one can about that country's corporate culture is not always enough. There can be many roadblocks along the way.

One of the biggest factors that inhibited clear communication and under-standing between the Malaysians and Americans was a matter of style. Because of their work schedules and the long distance between countries, it was impossible for the Americans to attend several key decision-making meetings with Dr. Haji and Mr. Kelana, such as the contract negotiations for Phase I, which Dr. Haji hammered out privately.

Cormac thought it important to get another opinion about how things received approval in Malaysia, so he contacted a woman he had met on the plane, a former head of public schools. She told him that Malays are considered the diplomats and gentlemen of Asia, but that insincerity always lies close to the surface. She added that Prime Minister Mahathir's policy is "Do as I say, not as I do," a reflection of broad practices. In effect, a nod or a smile can mean the opposite of what the receiver perceives.

Another Malaysian cultural trait is the notion that one should not argue or dis-agree with another person directly. Invariably, if Mr. Kelana disagreed with the Americans' suggestions or plans, they heard about it from Dr. Haji or Amal.

Amal, in particular, typified the subordinate's deference to authority. On the one hand, he held a very good job and high salary by virtue of being a relative. On the other hand, he was expected to work extraordinarily long hours and be slavishly loyal. He internalized his dissent, refusing to let his uncle know his true feelings.

Another characteristic of Malay culture is a propensity toward understate-ment. Typically, Malays downplay a potentially serious situation or joke about its consequences. This tendency can be humorously diverting, but it is invariably frustrating. For example, almost every time Cormac raised the subject of payment for work completed, Dr. Haji would assure him that Mr. Kelana was an honest client and would pay him "shortly," or at least before he returned to the States. Dr. Haji never assuaged the American's anxiety in this and related matters, and he often deliberately evaded or ignored crucial aspects of the agreement, empha-sizing the ones that would benefit him if the project ended before Phase IV. His dismissive attitude created tension and friction. Bill and Cormac acted politely by burying their apprehensions in a frenzy of work.

The unstated reason behind Mr. Kelana's hesitancy to continue the project was that he foresaw what was happening to the Asian stock market. Trained as an in-vestment banker, he knew that to avoid being ruined he had to rethink his invest-ments, including any new ventures, before the forthcoming depression. Two weeks after the consultants left Kuala Lumpur, the bottom started to fall out of Southeast Asia's stock markets.

In addition, Mr. Kelana's and Dr. Haji's interest in generating successful ven-tures further complicated goals. Their entrepreneurial quest for first-year rev-enues clogged their long-term vision and sidetracked everyone from completing the final phases.

Both Mr. Kelana and Dr. Haji raised legitimate concerns about the mar-ketability of the U.S. colleges in Malaysia, despite the fact that obscure and rela-tively unknown colleges from the United Kingdom and Australia had established campuses successfully in Kuala Lumpur, some of them within the last few years.

What was so hard for the client to understand was that $5,000 a year would not buy Malaysian students the equivalent of an Ivy League degree. The job would have been much easier were the market rich and/or very high-achieving Malays rather than middle-class Malays who could not get into the top hundred U.S. colleges.

Despite the initial faith placed in the client, Bill and Cormac believe that he violated their trust by not valuing or compensating them properly for work completed in Phases II and III. They had delivered a final report illustrating how they had surpassed the signed agreement for those phases and had completed the work in good faith. The client apparently had no intention of paying them once he decided the project would prove more difficult to implement than he originally thought.

The two Americans learned much about creating a distance learning program during this venture, but they also learned to be extremely cautious when dealing with foreign investors. Their recommendation to others would be to insist that clients make a large financial commitment up front rather than simply promising to do so while paying only for travel expenses. As most corporate attorneys will confess, international agreements are very hard to enforce, especially when the client has financial and political clout dwarfing the consultant's.

Trying to develop the first virtual campus in Asia while using the resources of traditional American campuses and a foreign corporation requires vision, creativity, flexibility, and sensitivity to the political, economic, and social changes affecting a developing nation. It involves a good amount of risk, and it requires considerable trust, precise communication, and honest debate between people separated by twelve time zones and two highly different cultures.

Questions for Discussion

1. What are the benefits and drawbacks of the collaborative work between (a) Cormac and the young Malaysian student, (b) Cormac, Dr. Haji, and Bill, and (c) Cormac, Bill, and Mr. Kelana? List your answers in two columns: Benefits and Drawbacks.

2. Who would benifit the most from reading this case study? Why?

3. In what ways could Cormac have better prepared himself for the cultural hurdles he faced in Kuala Lumpur? Should he have depended more or less on Bill's expertise in handling Dr. Haji? Respectively, how responsible is each person—Cormac, Bill, Dr. Haji, and Mr, Kelana—for the failure of this venture?

4. From what you gather from this study, what are some of the main cultural differences in communication style between Malaysian and American professionals?

5. Would you have challenged Dr. Haji about driving to the Wisma Bangsar as Cormac did, or would you have said nothing, given the context? Why?

6. How valid were Mr. Kelana's reasons for ending work on the cyberuniversity project? Which were the best reasons? Which were the weakest? Within the framework of cross-cultural communications, how well-constructed was Cormac and Bill's response to the client?

7. What kinds of biases are evident here, and how do they impede clear communication between cultures? Is it a cultural bias to impose English as the principal language of business communication in Malaysia, or does it simply make good business communication sense?

Writing Assignments

1. Find the Web sites of four on-line universities, two of which are not U.S. or Canadian. Write a brief analysis of the effectiveness of each cybercampus's on-line marketing campaign, asking such questions as

   - Who is the primary audience for the various degree programs?
   - What is the style and tone of the language used to convey information about the cybercampus? Is it clear? Well-defined? Sincere? Vague? Full of platitudes? Artificial? And so on.
   - How credible does the university seem? Would you want to get an on-line degree from any of the on-line campuses whose sites you investigated? What standards or criteria did you use to reach your conclusion?
   - What, if any, are the differences in the marketing and communication language between the North American on-line campuses and the non-American on-line campuses?

2. Assume that you are a student living abroad who needs to acquire two more classes (electives) before you can graduate with a bachelor's degree. You live in a metropolitan area and have access to classes at a university, but you would need to be fluent in the native language to attend. You are competent in that country's language, but not expert. You possess excellent on-line communication skills and know your way around the Internet. Will you increase your fluency in that country's language so that you can take traditional classes that will allow you to complete your degree? Or will you enroll in an on-line course for about the same or a lower cost? After establishing a brief overview of the geographical and cultural setting, provide at least three good reasons to support your decision.

Additional Resources: Issues Relevant to the Case

Asian, C. (1997, April). Learning in cyberspace. *World Executive's Digest*, 2, 30–35.

Cover story today: Distance education. (1996, March). *Academic Leader*, 3–4.

Cubitt, G., & Moore, W. (1995). *This is Malaysia*. London: New Holland.

Cushman, R. (1996, Nov.). From a distance. *Lingua Franca*, 53–63.

Dorgan, M. (1997, July 27). Malaysia: High-tech utopia? *San Jose Mercury News*.

Ibrahim, A. (1996). *The Asian Renaissance*. Singapore and Kuala Lumpur: Times Books International.

Leavitt, M. (1996, Winter). Virtual "U." *Multiversity*, 12–15.

Ng, A. (Ed.). (1997). *Malaysian higher education: A concise guide*. Selangor Darul Ehsan: Impact Communications.

Chapter 10

Human Error, Communication Failures, and the Sinking of the M/S Estonia

Recipe for Disaster

ELIZABETH M. LYNN
Kettering University

Abstract: The *Estonia* case identifies a wide range of factors that raise questions about a technical communicator's responsibilities. This analysis of the tragedy suggests that, in a crisis involving public safety, loss of life might be reduced by better communication planning for crises. As of the year 2000, for example, most passenger ships still identify deck levels only by name, rather than by number, which can confuse passengers seeking a lifeboat in an emergency. Does the technical communicator have a moral or ethical responsibility for advising superiors of potential risks that may be more apparent to a communication expert than to a technical expert? In particular, this case raises many questions about the scope of responsibility the technical communicator has when public safety is at stake in a multilingual environment. Does the technical writer's job end when safety or operating instructions are provided in a single language? When should safety plans address public communication needs?

Note: As the world embraces increasingly higher levels of technology, the hope that technology can protect humanity from fatal errors has evolved into an increased realization of the role that human error and communication failure play in causing major

*disasters. In recent years, as communication scholars have analyzed technological disas-
ters, some communication patterns have been identified that appear to contribute to, or es-
calate, tragic circumstances. This case has been written to add to that body of knowledge
by analyzing the communication circumstances in the 1994 sinking of the* Estonia, *a luxury passenger ferry, in which more than nine hundred people died. To the extent that these
communication patterns repeat themselves in other tragic incidents, it may be possible to
begin formulating risk-reduction guidelines to incorporate into the education of senior-
level managers.*

Background of the Case

The twentieth century saw major changes in the cruise industry. Four of the
changes are described in this section: changes in ship ownership, changes in
staffing, changes in ship registry and safety standards, and rapid growth. Each of
these changes played a part in the sinking of the *Estonia* and may well lead to similar tragedies at sea.

Changed Patterns in Ship Ownership

At the start of the twentieth century, large shipping fleets throughout the world
were typically owned by powerful families. The owner knew all of his ship captains on a personal basis and monitored the staffing of key crew members. A good
captain could count on lifetime employment with a single family of shipowners.
Since a ship's captain was personally known to the owner and trusted by him, the
captain had wide economic discretion in operating the ship, such as spending extra
days at sea to avoid a major storm. In addition, the captain and crew members usually spoke the same language with the same level of fluency.

Today, however, this family ownership model has all but vanished. As heads
of families died off, heirs sold their interests to corporate groups. Ships now tend
to be owned by large corporations and managed by other companies, which bid
on contracts. Typically, the lowest bidder wins the award, so costs must be tightly
controlled to ensure profitability. Since the managing company selects the captain,
ship owners have little or no personal relationship with him.

Changed Patterns in Staffing

Today, the captain is not only responsible for navigation, safety, and technical operations; he must also operate the ship in a cost-effective manner and—as in other
corporations—must justify budget deviations. Job security has significantly diminished as the corporation's economic interests have risen in priority. As a consequence of these economic factors, today's ship captains have the authority to
delay a voyage, but feel great economic pressure from other captains, owners, and
the management company to stick to a schedule—which can mean heading into a
storm rather than around it.

Technological advances—improved radar, weather satellites, GPS systems, improved ship-to-shore communications equipment—give the captains more precise information than ever before on the weather conditions into which they are heading. But, at the same time, captains, crew, and passengers have become increasingly dependent on that equipment to operate properly in all weather conditions. In short, the level of risk is diminished only as long as the technological equipment functions and the crew is sufficiently trained to operate it correctly.

Ship captains and officers typically are college graduates with extensive experience at sea. Selective numbers are given the opportunity for further study at the World Maritime University, a branch of the United Nations. Most ships' officers come from Greece, Italy, Japan, Norway, the United Kingdom, and the United States. They are an elite, highly-trained group.

Crew staffing, however, is an altogether different story; and passenger safety today is at risk due both to reduced numbers of able-bodied seamen on cruise ships and to their linguistic limitations. Currently, a typical ocean-going passenger liner carries approximately 1300 passengers and 700 crew members. Most crew members are not professional seafarers but are rather entertainment staff—the hotel staff, the catering staff, and the performers.[1] Fewer than 100 are likely to be professional seafarers who are available to assist passengers or to carry out orders in the event of an emergency.

Simple math yields a ratio of one hundred thirty passengers to one professional seafarer. Alarmingly, that ratio can grow to one thousand passengers to one able-bodied professional seaman—a ratio that currently is common on cruise ships in the Northern European routes. Such statistics also presume that all able-bodied seaman are available to assist passengers during an emergency—a clear fallacy, since as many as one-third could be sleeping off-shift, and others would be assigned to specific technical tasks.

Passenger safety in emergency conditions is also being jeopardized by the diminishing numbers of professional seafarers who speak the language of the ship's captain, the language of the passengers, or emergency-level English. Shipping companies have discovered the benefits of hiring seafarers from third world countries who will work for low wages with no retirement or medical benefits. Consequently, unlike the officers' native countries, most seafaring crew members today come from China, India, the Philippines, Russia, South Korea, and Eastern Europe. Significantly, while many of these crew members are multilingual, most have had little or no exposure to English as a second language.

---

[1]Typically, professionally trained seafarers have attended one of 503 maritime training institutes worldwide. In addition, the International Maritime Organization (IMO), an agency of the United Nations, provides education through its World Maritime University (WMU). Based in Malmo, Sweden, the WMU is staffed by visiting faculty from maritime institutes throughout the world. WMU staff members also provide short specialized courses to fourteen branches located in Algeria, Egypt, Argentina, Bangladesh, Brazil, Chile, the People's Republic of China, Cote d'Ivoire, Ghana, India, Malaysia, Mexico, Morocco, and Pakistan.

In sum, then, shifts that have occurred in both ownership and staffing of cruise ships are forecasting new risks to passenger safety at sea. As Dr. Kit Porter has shown in a study for the World Maritime University, crew size and language commonality are directly related to the likelihood of serious accidents occurring. Porter points out: "When crew sizes were larger, fewer tasks depended on one person. There were more people hearing instructions and more possibilities of tasks being checked" (1995, p. 14). With smaller crew sizes and a reduction in shared language on today's cruise ships, communication failures and breakdowns are inevitable.

Changed Patterns in Ship Registry and Safety Standards

Passenger safety is obviously a high concern of all the cruise lines, and most companies can boast of good safety records. However, safety is a cost of doing business that yields no measurable return. Consequently, the associations of shipping corporations closely monitor safety mandates to avoid unexpected imposed costs. Organizational representatives fight to maintain the status quo and are bitterly opposed to any improvements in safety standards that would increase costs even slightly (for example, numbering deck levels to help passengers determine whether they should go up or down; numbering passenger cabins so that passengers can easily orient themselves to port and starboard).

Arguments are heated over the cost-to-risk factors. Opposition to increased safety costs and increased governmental regulation is particularly strong from third world nations and from nonvoting trade associations, such as the International Council of Cruise Lines. Adding to these voices are the national delegations to the IMO[2] that are dominated by shipowners. As a result, parochial economic interests may claim a higher priority than safety.

Because opposing voices are so numerous and—in the case of the trade associations—so well-funded, the international standards for passenger safety that have been voted into the SOLAS Convention[3] of the United Nations provide only a minimal level on which all members can agree. Enforcement of the agreements is the responsibility of the nation in which a ship is registered. There is no international enforcement agency.

Individual nations, particularly some Northern European nations and the United States, have mandated higher safety standards than SOLAS for passenger

[2]The IMO is the maritime branch of the United Nations. Membership is open to all members of the United Nations with maritime interests. At the March 1995 meeting, attendees included delegations from twenty-seven member nations and representatives from nineteen major international trade or nongovernmental organizations. National delegations typically included spokesmen who have had extensive experience as ship captains. Nongovernmental spokesmen represented such varied interests as the Commission of the European Communities (EEC), League of Arab States, Oil Companies International Marine Forum (OCIMF), and the International Council of Cruise Lines (ICCL).

[3]The acronym SOLAS stands for Safety of Life at Sea. The SOLAS Convention is a treaty setting forth operating guidelines that have been agreed on by 139 nations. The IMO administers but does not enforce the SOLAS guidelines. Once a SOLAS guideline has been established among the member nations, all member nations follow the guidelines and do their own enforcing.

ships sailing under their country's flags. However, since tax costs can be kept to a minimum by registering ships to nations with the most favorable tax laws, most of the passenger ships in the world currently are registered outside the United States and operate under widely varying safety standards.[4]

In short, passengers today can cruise safely only to the extent that the shipping companies make passenger safety a priority. In a 1995 statement to the SEATRADE Conference in Miami, Rajiv Khandpur of the U.S. Coast Guard warned that, despite all efforts of governments and shipping associations to ensure passenger safety,

> *in the end it is each individual company that will ultimately decide the level of safety which provides the best tradeoff for the company between being competitive, profitable, and maintaining their reputation and goodwill. It is at this organizational level that poor decision and bad management can translate into unsafe practices at the operational level.*

Growth and Risk in Passenger Ship Traffic

Simultaneously, the international cruise industry is in the throes of massive change. Business has been booming. In the past two decades, customer bookings have increased ten-fold. According to U.S. Coast Guard data, the number of U.S. passengers vacationing on cruise ships grew from 2 million to 4 million between 1983 and 1993. The Cruise Lines International Association saw this number hit 8 million by the year 2000. With 5 million customers in 1997, the market still has significant room for expansion as the Baby Boom generation reaches retirement years, since only 8 percent of North Americans have taken a cruise to date.

To fuel this growth in passenger traffic, passenger ship companies have developed glamorous advertising themes, which lead passengers to overlook the normal risks of a ship at sea. In cruise line advertisements, the sky is always blue, the sea is always calm and inviting, and well-groomed hotel staff provide services to passengers in luxurious settings. As a result of these advertising ploys, passengers have come to expect comfort, luxury, and entertainment on cruises and have come to lose the sense of life-threatening risks that accompany travel at sea.

---

[4]Third world nations that rely extensively on ferries for transportation are among the worst offenders of passenger safety standards. On May 17, 1995, a Reuters report of a Philippine ferry disaster stated: "Sea tragedies are common in the Philippines, a nation of more than 7,000 islands where ferries, often badly maintained and poorly equipped, are one of the most common forms of public transport" (Romeo Ranoco, 1995). In that particular "common" tragedy, at least forty-four people died. On September 23, 1998, the Philippine Maritime Industry suspended passenger operations of the Sulpicio Lines after that shipping line lost thirty passenger ships at sea, of which twelve were RO-RO vessels (like the *Estonia*). Sulpicio was also the owner of the *Dona Paz* ferry which, in 1987, collided with an oil tanker resulting in the deaths of four thousand people.

Although cruise ships departing from U.S. ports usually require passengers to attend safety training sessions, such sessions are optional—not mandated by SOLAS—and not standard procedure throughout the international cruise industry. On many cruise ships in Europe, every possible strategy is used to diminish the perception of the normal risks that accompany travel at sea. Nightclubs, gyms, putting greens, conference centers, and entertainment fill every waking moment. In some European ports, safety instructions are broadcast over loudspeakers to passengers who are simultaneously distracted by open bars, rock bands, and topless dancers. To maintain low daily rates on these ships, the cruise industry must make its profit by getting passengers to spend money while on board or on islands owned by the shipping organization.

In light of recent cruise ship problems and the consequent passenger complaints, it appears that passengers do not have realistic notions of the risks at sea. In the event of a fire at sea, for example, many passengers unrealistically expect full service to continue, as well as chilled beverages, electricity, and toilets that flush. For example, after her luxury cruise ship was stuck for a day on a shoal off Nantucket Island, a passenger groused, "I lost a day's pay and I have to pay a sitter an extra day—and the sitter had plans."

In reality, even the best cruise ships experience occasional problems.. Between 1994 and 1998, cruise ships sailing out of U.S. ports reported numerous problems that jeopardized the safety of passengers. Although none resulted in major disasters, some of the incidents have included:

- In July 1998, a fire aboard the Carnival Corporation's *Ecstasy* caused 60 passengers to be taken to Miami hospitals to be treated for smoke inhalation.
- At least two incidents were reported by the Associated Press in 1996. In July, five people died and another sixteen injured when a fire broke out aboard a Commodore Cruise Lines ship in Alaska. In addition, a fire broke out in the engine room of the Princess Lines' *Golden Princess* on the second day of a ten-day trip from San Francisco to Alaska, forcing cancellation of the trip for 839 passengers.
- In June of 1995, the *Star Princess* of Princess Cruises struck a rock off Alaska, gashing its underbelly and curtailing the journey for 2226 passengers and crew.
- The same month, 1760 passengers on Carnival Cruise Lines' *Celebration* were evacuated after a fire disabled the ship and left them without air conditioning, running water, hot meals, and other comforts for two days. (The *Celebration*, which is registered in Liberia, had run into a Cuban cement carrier in 1989, killing three people on the Cuban ship.)
- Also in June 1995, Majesty Cruise Line's *Royal Majesty* ran aground off Massachusetts. The 1500 passengers waited a day before higher tides permitted towing the ship.
- In yet another June 1995 incident, the *American Queen* paddleboat—full of travel writers seeking to chronicle the joys of riverboat cruising—got stuck in mud on its maiden voyage on the Ohio river.
- In December 1994, the world's most famous ocean liner, the *Queen Elizabeth 2*, suffered a much publicized Atlantic crossing at Christmastime, with incom-

plete renovations, brown running water, exploding toilets, and garbage spilling into the hallways.

- The *QE2* also hit uncharted rocks two years earlier off Martha's Vineyard, forcing evacuation of the 1824 passengers and repairs costing $13.2 million.
- Other 1994 incidents included an outbreak of Legionnaire's disease on Celebrity Cruises' *Horizon* and an outbreak of intestinal illness among 400 passengers aboard a Royal Caribbean Cruise Line ship sailing from Los Angeles.

Despite the long list of problems, industry spokesmen have been sanguine about the risks passengers face. Cynthia Colenda is president of the International Council of Cruise Lines, a powerful industry group based in Washington. Commenting to reporters on the array of cruise line accidents during 1995, she minimized the problems: "It's just a bad spate of incidents," she said. "Our industry still has the best safety record of any other mode of transportation."

Carnival President Bob Dickinson expressed similar confidence in 1995 when queried about the control room fire on the *Celebration*: "Things do go bump in the night when you're dealing with electrical and mechanical systems." He can afford to be cheerful: With a 36 percent market share, Carnival Lines reported 1997 revenues of $2.45 billion.

Recipe for Disaster

The combined influences of these economic factors have created a potentially disastrous situation. At the point of a fire or a major mechanical catastrophe, things do not just go "bump in the night," as Carnival Line's Bob Dickinson trivializes. Rather, because there is no common crew language on most passenger vessels today and because of an overwhelming dependence on technology to guide ships through treacherous weather, the component elements are in place for the world to see far more tragic accidents such as the sinking of the *Estonia*. And, as the capacity of ships expands to carry even greater numbers of passengers, the potential escalates for greater and greater loss of life at sea.

The Sinking of the Estonia

On September 28, 1994, more than 900 people died when the luxurious passenger ferry *Estonia* sank on a voyage from Tallinn, the capital of Estonia, to Stockholm (Figure 10.1). Only 137 people survived; 100 bodies were recovered, and about 810 persons were presumed to have gone down with the ship. The map on page 134 shows the Baltic area and the two port cities, Tallinn and Stockholm.

The passengers included 552 Swedes, 163 Estonians, 29 Lithuanians, and smaller numbers of Finns, Germans, Norwegians, Britons, Dutch, Danes, Spaniards, Latvians, and Ukrainians. In the days following the tragedy, newswire services were filled with the survivors' accusations: no alarm had sounded; crew members had saved their own lives, but had not warned passengers. According to the sole

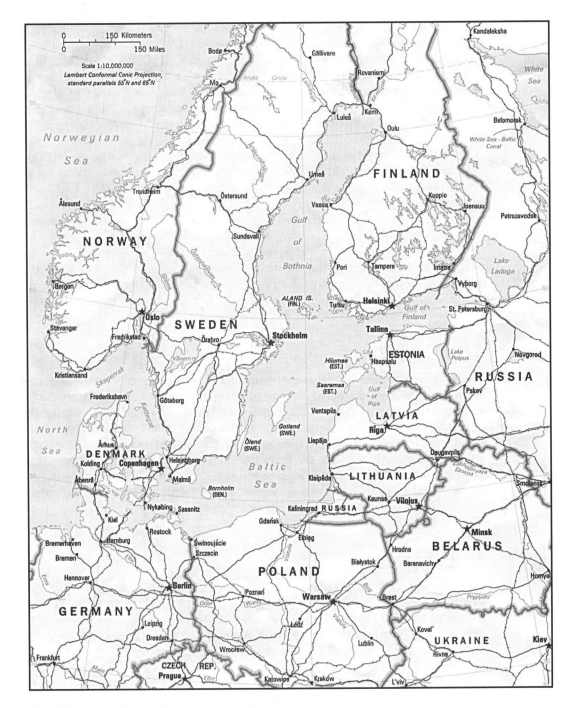

FIGURE 10.1   The Baltic Sea Area

British survivor, Paul Barney, "I heard no alarm whatsoever. All I heard and managed to get translated for me was that it was an emergency, by which time the boat was already on its side."

Within days of the sinking, underwater videos were taken to document the most likely causes of the accident. Five days after the tragedy, investigators reported that locks on the huge front cargo door of the ferry had failed during a storm, letting in a flood of water that sank the ship. According to the official statement released by the investigation team from Finland, Estonia, and Sweden:

> *The bow visor has fully separated from the rest of the vessel. The water-tight bow ramp that was located behind the visor is still in place, although there is a gap of about one metre along its top edge which allowed water to flow onto the car deck. . . . The bow visor became detached from the vessel as a result of the failure of the bow visor locking devices. Part of its rubber remains in place, but part is missing.*

The immediate cause of the disaster, then, was determined to be a mechanical failure.

Communication Analysis of the Case

The loss stunned Northern Europe. By most accounts, the fourteen-year-old German-built *Estonia* had been well designed and carefully maintained. Its engines, lifeboats, and lifejackets were all in order. The ferry had been inspected by two Swedish nautical engineers during a surprise presailing check that was part of a training program for Estonian maritime inspectors. Overall, one of the inspectors wrote on the report, the *Estonia* was in "almost perfect condition."

As more news appeared on the wire services, however, it became increasingly clear that human error and communication failures had significantly contributed to the extent of the loss. Numerous public statements suggested that perceptual differences clearly had played a role in the tragedy. Semantics, language differences, and the perception of meaning may have made a life-or-death difference in this case. Was the ship's condition "almost perfect," or was it "slightly out-of-code"? The way in which risk levels were verbally expressed could easily have conveyed false assurance.

The most obvious communication failure was the inability of the crew to communicate with most of the passengers. According to National Public Radio (Washington, D.C.), an all-Estonian crew had recently replaced better-trained Swedish crewmen. Aside from their maritime skills, most of the Estonian crew had little knowledge of either Swedish or English—the common emergency languages that most European passengers would recognize. Even the voice giving the Mayday call spoke first in Estonian, then in Finnish, reporting that the ferry was listing sharply and had lost power in its engines.

As news continued to flow out of Europe, information emerged about other communication problems that had contributed to the sinking of the *Estonia*—problems in communicating across multiple organizations, differing perceptions of risk, weaknesses in crew training, and shortcomings in electronic and mechanical communication systems.

Problems in Communicating Across Multiple Organizations

Several organizations were involved in verifying the safety of the *Estonia*. In addition to the company that owned the *Estonia*, three different organizations verified its safety: (1) a classification society, (2) the safety administrators of each maritime nation, and (3) the International Maritime Organization (IMO). A classification society is a mutually owned company to which shipowners subcontract responsibility for enforcing technical standards for their vessels. If classification society inspectors deem a ship fit to sail and correctly maintained, they issue certificates showing it meets the national and international rules that apply.

When so many organizations are involved, conflicting jurisdictional interests and judgments are inevitable. In such situations, a common communication tactic to reduce conflict at the face-to-face level of interaction is to report only the most serious violations. In the case of the *Estonia* and similarly designed European sister ships, the safety flaws discovered during inspections had not been considered serious enough to report.

Differing Perceptions of Risk

To illustrate both the problems in organizational communication and the conflicting perceptions of risk, a record follows of statements that were made at the time of the disaster:

A senior mate who formerly served on the *Estonia* told reporters that an automatic system with elaborate safety checks would have made it impossible for a crewman to shut the door improperly.

His comment, however, was contradicted by Seamen's union leader Anders Lindstrom. Lindstrom was quoted by the Swedish TT news agency as saying that, a day before the accident occurred, two Swedish safety inspectors had spent five hours examining the boat with a group of Estonian trainee safety inspectors. According to the union leader, the inspectors had indicated that the key seal that makes the loading ramp entrance watertight at sea was "not in satisfactory condition."

One of the inspectors, however, recalled the situation quite differently. Ake Sjoblom, a chief inspector with Sweden's Maritime Safety Authority and an expert on Baltic ferry safety, told Swedish television, "We saw nothing that gave us a hint that something would go wrong." In another comment to the Finnish FNB news agency in Estonia, Sjoblom said, "We saw aging and worn out lashings and seals which had been damaged on board the *Estonia*. But none of the faults was so big it could have caused the disaster. . . . A rubber packing in a seal of the bow visor in the inner ramp entrance was broken, but only partly. It was a bagatelle [a trifle] and we directed only a minor remark to the accompanying [ship's] officer. . . . That remark was not of the significance that would have been given to a [fault constituting a] safety threat." In sum, the two inspectors "got the impression that this was in the main a well-maintained ship."

Spokesmen for the Swedish partner-owner of the *Estonia*, Nordstrom and Thulin AB, also revealed sharply differing perceptions of the dangers. On hearing of the sinking, Estline executives, owners of the *Estonia*, were stunned and disbelieving. "Theoretically, it could not go down at all," said Johannes Johanson, managing director of the Estline. "All the passenger ferries are built in such a way that it is practically impossible."

Echoing these comments, Technical Director Sten-Crister Forsberg insisted that the ferry was in excellent condition overall. "The ship was very well-equipped, fulfilling all national and international rules with a very competent crew." Forsberg absolved his company of blame, saying there might have been a "failure or design problem in the bow doors," but he ruled out a failure of the rubber seals surrounding the doors. He maintained that the seals were within safe limits. "I can agree that the equipment was not doing its job since so many people died, but it is up to the rule makers and designers to look into this. I am quite sure that the aftermath of the tremendous tragedy will result in stricter regulations for life saving equipment."[5]

Swedish co-owner and managing director Ronald Bergman said the ship was last inspected less than one month earlier, on September 9, for its most important stability and seaworthiness certificate, known as a Loadline Certificate. "Everything was in perfect condition," Bergman said. He expressed anger that his company had bought the ship and sailed it, unaware that it had a structural fault that probably caused its loss. He was also angry that near misses involving involuntary opening of bow doors on sister ships owned by his rivals were not brought to his company's or the public's attention. (His allegation was subsequently confirmed by Swedish and Finnish companies who have admitted to safety authorities they did not report some of the near misses fully.) Bergman expressed his dismay at these lapses in accident reporting and regulation: "When we buy a ship and have all the [safety] documents, we think it's safe. . . . I think the responsibility lies with the owners who have not reported [near misses] and also with authorities who have not taken proper action, and with the classification societies who have a big responsibility."

In sum, every person who might have had firsthand knowledge of existing hazards not only denied responsibility but felt that others were at fault. Following the pattern that has been revealed through other crisis communication research, the safety faults discovered by the Swedish safety engineer were considered too minor to warrant communication onward.

---

[5]Reports since the sinking of the *Estonia* have made it clear that the International Maritime Organization (IMO), the UN agency responsible for maritime safety and pollution, has required lower safety standards than individual European nations have set for their own vessels. Britain and most other northwest European countries have adopted standards which are considered about 5 percent tougher than the IMO requirements.

Weaknesses in Crew Training

Sometime after midnight, in the engine room, "Estonian ship's machinist Henrik Sillaste noticed via closed-circuit television that water was washing in through the bow door. He turned on the bilge pumps." When the water became knee deep, Sillaste rushed from the engine room to a life raft. The Mayday signal was not given until 1:24 A.M., fifty-four minutes after the car deck became knee deep in water.

There is no news report of the methods Sillaste may have used to attempt to signal the captain, passengers, or crew. According to passengers, no general alarm was given before the sinking. No sirens or bells were sounded. It is possible that Sillaste had not been trained in life-saving operations, under a presumption that an engine room worker would not need to alert passengers to danger. On most ships, only the captain can authorize such a signal, and, at that hour, the captain was most likely asleep. It is also possible that crew members were insufficiently trained in emergency evacuation procedures, especially with multinational passengers and crew.

Failures in Emergency Communication Systems

At the most basic safety level, the evidence suggests that the *Estonia* was well equipped with sufficient life jackets and rafts. Major flaws, however, were found in a wide range of communication systems that should have been regularly reviewed for effective safety.

Effective emergency systems presume that all mechanical communication systems are in good operating order and that crew members are trained both in operating emergency equipment and in methods for saving passenger lives. However, based on available news reports, little thought, preparation, or inspection had been given on the *Estonia* to emergency communication needs.

Mechanical Communication Flaws

Several of the emergency broadcast systems were not working on the *Estonia*, and life rafts were not well equipped with emergency signaling systems. The only warning of the disaster to authorities on shore was a distress signal heard at 1:24 A.M. on an ultra-high-frequency radio channel used only for emergencies. The Swedish news agency revealed that this distress signal didn't reach rescue stations in Sweden because the ship radio's broadcasting range was too short.

The voice from the *Estonia* that called the Mayday signal was unable to give the ship's location to another ferry, about fifteen nautical miles away, because of the blackout. When the engine stopped, the main generator stopped, which would have cut power to the navigation equipment, including the Loran or GPS equipment. The Mayday voice guessed at a location that later turned out to be off by about ten miles.

Suggesting problems in crew training, Russia's marine rescue service reported that the *Estonia* had failed to send a distress signal into COSPAS-SARSAT, an international rescue system. This system has at least seven Russian and U.S. satellites in orbit to pick up signals from ships and aircraft in distress around the world. The Itar-Tass news agency quoted a duty officer at the Moscow State Marine Rescue Coordinating Centre as saying that "a special radio device [aboard the *Estonia*] designed to send distress signals and exact coordinates of the ship into the satellite-based system had failed." A report from the Swedish TT news agency also stated that a "radio designed to send out SOS calls wasn't working."

Subsequently, the IMO investigation revealed that the device was still in its original packing container and had never been activated. U.S. Coast Guard officials report that this Emergency Position Indicating Radiobeacon was designed to deploy automatically from a sinking ship and automatically start broadcasting. However, if the beacon had never been unpacked or properly activated, that failure could conceivably have been related to the crew's language limitations. Operating instructions would have had to have been written in Russian or Estonian—an unlikely possibility.

Finally, despite a feverish search that included rescue divers, twenty helicopters from six countries, at least twenty surface craft, and an airplane, only 139 people were saved. While some of the life rafts had flares, most survivors had only tiny rescue lanterns (position-indicating lights) attached to life jackets and rafts. There was no other means of signaling the location of the ship or life rafts to searching rescuers (Figure 10.2).

FIGURE 10.2   Close-Up of Baltic Sea Area

Background for Additional Analysis

The passage of time has allowed greater investigation of the facts surrounding the *Estonia* disaster. It is now possible to consider a much wider range of information to see what other factors may have had an influence on the tragedy. These include relevant economic factors that may have led to a diminished perception of risk, or a diminished way of describing risk; and the International Maritime Organization's investigation, the role of human error, and unresolved communication issues.

The Effect of Economic Factors on Risk Perception

Economic factors can affect the way in which both safety and risk-level are perceived. In the case of the *Estonia,* four key economic factors may have contributed to the willingness of managers and inspectors to minimize the actual risk level:

1. The Estline appears to have had a monopoly on newly negotiated ferry routes between the capitals of Sweden and Estonia.
2. Estonia was under pressure to increase tourism.
3. Prior to the disaster, the Swedish co-owners of Estline were anticipating a year with no profits.
4. To stay competitive in the European ferry market, roll-on roll-off (RO-RO) ferries like the *Estonia* have been widely used, despite known flaws in their design.

In a joint economic venture starting in 1990, Nordstrom and Thulin, a Swedish ship-owning company for 125 years, joined with the government-owned Estonian Shipping Company as equal partners in the Estline ferry line operation between Stockholm and Tallinn. Estline was awarded a ten-year concession for this route. The service was the first regular shipping link between these two European capitals in the previous fifty years. The *Estonia,* one of Estline's ships, was classed with Europe's large, luxurious cruise liner ferries.

Expectations ran high for this new shipping route, especially in Estonia. In June 1993, sixteen months before the *Estonia* tragedy, Estonia, Latvia, and Lithuania had begun an intensive campaign to increase tourism, trade, and shipping from Tallinn, the capital of Estonia, all the way to Warsaw.

For Estline's Swedish partner, the economic picture was far less optimistic. Prior to the accident, Nordstrom and Thulin, had been forecasting a zero profit for 1994 because of the depressed state of the tanker market in which the company was a major participant. Although it is not known if the Estline investment was contributing to the company's economic difficulties, available information suggests that, through the first six months of 1994, the line was operating at far less than 50 percent of passenger capacity.

Within two weeks of the disaster, Nordstrom and Thulin cut its losses and decided to withdraw altogether from passenger shipping. All shipping service between Stockholm and Tallinn was suspended, since the Estline's second ferry ran aground outside Stockholm and had to undergo repairs. Following the decision to discontinue with Estline, Nordstrom and Thulin said it expected to lose between 70 million and 100 million Swedish kronor ($7 million to $14 million) in 1994.

An additional economic factor revolves around the inherently hazardous design of the *Estonia*. The ferry was operating in a European market that had come to expect fast port turnaround times. To increase the rate of passenger travel, ports had begun to brag about how time-efficient ferry travel could be. To cut port turnaround time to a minimum, RO-RO ferries like the *Estonia* are designed more for speedy loading and unloading than for water safety, with vehicle entry doors at both the bow and stern. Cars drive on at one end of the ship and off the other end. There are no watertight bulkheads, or baffles, to interfere with the easy flow of vehicle traffic on ship decks.

However, naval architects know that, as a result of this open space, a moving mass of water can become an overwhelming destabilizing force in these ships' open holds. Architects make the comparison between carrying a flat, shallow pan of water and a divided ice-cube tray: the shallow pan is difficult to carry without spillage.

Despite the known hazards, 4500 ferries with this design continue to operate worldwide, and operators have been resisting the use of baffles because they would interfere with the efficient movement of vehicles through the interior. Any change in these ships' design would be extremely costly.

In sum, the design hazards on the *Estonia* were known. However, the Estonian partners of the Estline would have been unlikely to pay much attention to the hazards since they had a rare opportunity to capitalize on a new shipping route. The Swedish partners would also have turned a deaf ear to minor safety violations since their investment in this passenger shipping business was their only hope for 1994 profits.

The IMO Investigation, Human Error, and Unresolved Communication Issues

Correcting human error is far more difficult than correcting mechanical problems. To begin with, perceptions of human error appear to be dependent on the specific culture investigating the ship's sinking. For example, Estonian police apparently view human error as voluntary behavior. After the sinking of the *Estonia,* they went on record as saying that "if human error were to blame, those responsible could be jailed for up to 10 years."

Others view human error as a consequence of insufficient training. In a painfully ironic message written before the sinking of the *Estonia* and delivered on September 29, 1994, the day after the disaster, William O'Neil, the Secretary-General of the IMO, said it was often claimed that up to 80 percent of accidents at sea were caused by human error. "If we sincerely want to stop accidents from occurring, then I think it is obvious that we should concentrate our efforts on eliminating human error" by raising standards of crews throughout the world. Mistakes are usually made, he said, not because of faulty, deficient, or inadequate regulations but because existing regulations and standards are ignored. O'Neil said implementation of regulations had in the past proved to be the weakest link in the safety chain.

Later, O'Neil issued a statement calling for an IMO panel of experts to review all aspects of ferry safety. The items to be addressed included

1. Evaluating life-saving and evacuation arrangements
2. Assessing on-board communication issues, especially where multinational crews and passengers are on board
3. Revising the procedures for reporting safety incidents involving ferries and the actions authorities should take on receiving these reports.

After an extensive investigation by an IMO international team that included the U.S. Coast Guard, recommendations were made in March 1995 to address and attempt to correct some of the dangers in RO-RO ferries. At a March 1995 meeting of the Safety Awareness and Emergency Training (SAET) Subcommittee of the Lifesaving, Search, and Rescue (LSR) division of the IMO, cruise industry representatives vehemently opposed the RO-RO panel's recommendations as unnecessary and too expensive to implement. Despite their protests, the recommendations were shepherded through and were eventually approved by the IMO.

To illustrate the difficulty in implementing communication change on an international level, Table 10.1 describes four representative proposals brought up in the March 1995 SAET Working Group. To any U.S. communication scholar, the issues are obvious and need correction. None of the issues, however, was resolved; all were tabled indefinitely.

International Interpretations of Communication

This case has viewed the term *communication* in its broadest sense, as it is used within the U.S. academic field of communication. It is important to recognize, however, that outside the United States, the term takes on far more limited meanings and may be used only to refer to a specific language (e.g., French) or to data or radio communication *messages*. In contrast, this case has viewed *communication* as an interactive thought-transmission process that takes into consideration all components of the communication process: sender, receiver, message, channel, noise, feedback, situational context, encoding, decoding, and such other variables as status, power, gender, interpersonal relationship, cultural differences, and nonverbal communication. The term encompasses both human and nonhuman communication.

A vast number of communication issues surrounding multilingual crews remain to be addressed. For example, in the SOLAS regulations, the word *communication* is used primarily to refer to the use of communication *equipment* used on board ships.[6] Basic safety training required for all seafarers only requires that the trainee "be able to communicate with other persons on board on elementary safety matters" (STCW/CONF/5/Rev.1, ANNEX, p. 104, Section A-VI/I). No measurement is identified for that standard other than for communication to be "clear and effective at all times."

---

[6]See SOLAS Reg. III/6.4.1 or MSC Circ.617.

TABLE 10.1   SAET Working Group Proposals

Issue	Resolution of the Issue
A suggestion was made by the United States to clarify the standards that communication must be "clear and effective at all times" (e.g., understandable with no more than two repetitions).	The ship captains present at the Working Group insisted that such a standard would be too lax. They insisted that the standard for communication must be that no repetition would be necessary "because it *must be* (i.e., would be) clear and effective at all times." There was no recognition by the ship captains that orders might be neither clearly stated nor accurately comprehended. They did acknowledge that orders might not be *heard* due to noise from high seas during a storm.
A suggestion was made by the United States and endorsed by the representative from Poland that the SOLAS-mandated term, *muster,* is neither universally understood nor, in many languages, translatable. The French representative stated that *muster* cannot be translated into French. The German representative reported that Germany resolved its translation problem by using a German word that means "assembly." The U.S. representative requested that the word be changed to "assemble/assembly station." In response, the British representatives stated that millions "have been trained to use" the term *muster* and that "all speakers of the English language understand what *muster* means."	After extensive discussion, the group remained divided on the issue.
The United States proposed that debarking ships provide printed safety information in the language of the two primary ports (i.e., initiating and terminating) as well as in English.	After extensive discussion, no agreement was reached.
The United States proposed that a standardized emergency vocabulary (i.e., 50 words) be established for required learning by all seafarers. The United States also proposed that a standardized set of nonverbal signals be developed and taught for use in emergency conditions for directing passengers to safe areas.	Discussion ended when the representative of the international cruise lines labeled both ideas as "impossible."

Some progress has been made in terms of teaching ships' officers English as the international language of navigation. For example, the World Maritime University trains officers in English vocabulary, usage, and pronunciation. However, the program does not appear to address other essential communication aspects of an emergency situation, such as

- Early identification of a need for communication
- Audience/situation analysis (especially mob control)
- Selection of and limitations of message content
- The importance of continuing communication with passengers throughout a crisis situation.[7]

To date, no requirements exist to inspect mechanical communication systems that are essential in emergencies: radio-signalling systems, satellite or GPS systems, sirens, public address or loudspeaker systems. And, no funds have been made available to the World Maritime University for developing an English language training program for seafarers, or for determining a standard vocabulary or communications procedures for emergency conditions.

In addition, research is almost non-existent in other communication areas that impact passenger safety, such as

1. the most effective ways to communicate safety instructions to passengers under non-emergency conditions;
2. how much and what kind of information a ship's captain should provide to passengers as an emergency unfolds;
3. what combination and sequence of communication channels are the best to use;
4. what minimal technical standards should be mandated for the audibility and intelligibility of emergency information;
5. how many languages and which ones should be used to communicate emergency instructions to passengers or to write technical operating manuals for multi-lingual crews;
6. what nonverbal signals should be taught to all crew for directing passengers in emergency conditions.

Conclusion

Continued research is essential to determine more precisely the role that communication failures regularly play in creating disasters, escalating crises, interfering with crisis control efforts, and increasing fatalities. Through the identification of common patterns of communication failures, guidelines can be developed for safety managers to reduce risks of major disasters. By acquiring a better understanding of the

---

[7]In a 1976 prize-winning Danish dissertation on recent ship disasters, the researchers reported that passengers need far more information than is typically available to them and recommended that "the information task [be] incorporated as a specific position in the muster list [i.e., a job be created as Information Officer]." There is no evidence that this recommendation has been implemented on any cruise ships to date.

role communication failures play in crisis management, loss of life and property can be prevented, crisis control efforts can be facilitated, rather than impaired, and fatalities can be reduced.

Questions for Discussion

1. In the case of the *Estonia,* how could communication have saved more passenger lives? What kinds of communication?

2. How do you think that switching from an all-Swedish crew to an all-Estonian crew made a difference?

3. In what particular stage of economic and political development was Estonia at that time?

4. What communication strategies can senior managers use to learn of problems that exist at lower levels of their organizations, especially problems that put the organization at risk?

5. How could lateral scrolling news screens with multilanguage translations be used in public transportation (or other settings) to inform the public of danger? What other new communication devices and technology can be used to span language differences during crises?

6. Nordstrom and Thulin was an old, established ship-owning company. Its primary business was tanker shipping when it decided, in 1990, to move into the passenger cruise business. How do those two types of businesses differ? How might another company that is considering a move from its traditional type of business to a new type better prepare for those differences?

7. Should manufacturers of safety equipment used in public transportation be required to publish operating instructions in languages other than English, Spanish, French, German, and Japanese?

8. What laws should be developed to protect both the public and transportation companies from risks or injury due to inadequate translation?

9. What methods can be used in a crisis to compensate for language differences? Consider an organization with which you're familiar, such as a hospital, an office building, or a school. In case of a fire, tornado, explosion, or gun threat, how might you evacuate people who speak languages other than your country's language? What communication devices are already in place for such people to reach safety by themselves? Should additional safety devices or methods be added?

Writing Assignments

1. Interview an executive to learn more about how cost-versus-risk decisions get made. Ask such questions as: When do safety precautions reach a point of costing too much to justify the expense? Who makes the cost-versus-risk decisions in this organization? What methods are in place for communicating with employees and their families in the event of a crisis? Ask for a copy of the company's crisis plan so that you can study it in class. Discuss your findings in small groups in class.

2. Identify an organization that has reduced safety standards to maintain profitability. Then identify one that maintains high safety standards to maintain its reputation or to protect its workers. How do those two organizations differ in terms of executive leadership, government regulation, and profit margins?

3. Select an organization with a high volume of multilingual public contact. Design signage for them that would reduce risk to the public in case of a crisis.

4. Visit the manager of your local shopping mall. What communication plans are in place for evacuating the mall in case of a fire, earthquake, or explosion?

5. Internationally, all transportation companies depend on passenger safety to stay in business. In a team, consider one transportation industry—railroads, airplanes, or ships. Select companies in that industry that are the safest and the least safe, and examine the marketing literature—frequent flier newsletters, brochures, advertisements, Web site information—from those companies to see how safety messages are addressed, either directly or indirectly.

6. In many industrial accidents, the way managers are compensated can be a contributing factor to safety or its lack. That is, if managers are directly rewarded for safety control in their operations, safety becomes a high priority. If, on the other hand, managers are primarily rewarded for cost-cutting and high levels of production, and if safety is not directly linked to a manager's performance and compensation, safety concerns can easily be dismissed or set aside for cost-saving reasons. The outcome can be that a manager may receive more personal compensation by postponing safety-related repairs. Select an organization and ask its managers if their salary increases are directly linked to safety, risk, or loss. Prepare a presentation for management on their exposure to risk.

Additional Sources: Issues Relevant to the Case

Bajak, F. (1994, October 1). The last night of the Estonia—and of 900 souls. Associated Press, to Mercury News Wire Services.

Baltic disaster survivor criticises ferry design. (1994, October 1). Reuters.

Cut human error to stop ship accidents, says IMO. (1994, September 28). Reuters.

Dahl, F. (1994, October 1). Checks on Finnish ferries show wear in gate locks. Reuters.

Fearn-Banks, Kathleen. *Crisis Communication: A Casebook Approach* (Mahwak, N.J.: Lawrence Erlbaum Associates), 1996.

Ferry sinking probe could lead to jail terms. (1994, September 28). Reuters.

Greeenwald, J. (1998, May 11). Cruise lines go overboard. *Time*, p. 42.

Grounded cruise ship returns to port. (1995, June 12). Associated Press.

Hockstader, L. (1994, September 9). Disaster hit like lightning, dooming hundreds on ferry. *Washington Post.*, to Mercury News Wire Services.

Huddart, A. (1994, October 1). Estonia's Swedish owner tormented by "design flaw." Reuters.

Huddart, A. (1994, October 1). Search team hopes to film ferry wreck. Reuters.

Huuhtanen, M. (1994, October 3). Locks failed on ferry Estonia doors. Associated Press.

Huuhtanen, M. (1994, October 4). Authorities scrutinize, seal ferry doors. Associated Press.

IMO says ferry passengers need safety assurances. (1994, October 7). Reuters.

Jackson, J. O. (1994, October 5). The cruel sea. *Time*, to AOL.

Khandpur, R. (1995, April). *Passenger vessel safety—a human factored systems approach.* Unpublished paper presented at the SEATRADE Conference, Miami, FL.

Le Gouard, Y. (1995). Porte-conteneurs l'armada des '5000 boites' entre en scene. *Journal de la Marine Marchande,* p. 980. In K. Porter, *Onboard communications of multilingual crews: Feasibility study* (1995). Unpublished paper, World Maritime University.

List of Maritime Training Institutes. (1994). IMO.

Lynn, E. M. (1986, April 13). Decision makers should listen to what the troops are saying. *Los Angeles Times,* pp. 1 ff.

Madsen, F., & Harbst, J. (1976). The behavior of passengers in a critical situation on boartd a passenger vessel or ferry. Danish Investment Foundation. (prize dissertation, awarded 1991)

Partial text of statement from Estonia ferry inquiry. (1994, October 3). Reuters.

Porter, J. (1994, October 10). Owner of ill-fated ferry to quit passenger shipping. *London Journal of Commerce* to AOL.

Porter, J. (1994, October 11). Janet Porter column. *London Journal of Commerce* to AOL.

Porter, K. (1995). Onboard communications of multilingual crews: Feasibility study. Unpublished paper, World Maritime University.

Romeo Ranoco. (1995, May 17). Reuters Variety News Service. Washington dateline. AOL via Mercury News Service (June–July 1995).

Reed, T. (1995, June 22). *The Miami Herald.,* Business News.

Russian rescuers say ferry sent no distress signal. (1994, September 28). Reuters. (Moscow) to News Wire Services.

SOLAS Convention. (1995, July 17). Reg. III/6.4.1 or MSC Circ.699. International Maritime Organization.

STCW Conference 5. Annex (Rev.1, p. 104, Section A-VI/I). International Maritime Organization.

Stevenson, R. D. (1994, September 29). Water rushing into hold may have led to sinking, ferry owners say. New York Times News Service.

Swedes found "minor faults" on Estonia on Tuesday. (1994, September 28). Reuters.

Tanner, A. (1995, June–July). Reuters/Variety News Service.

Winsor, D. A. (1988). Communication failures contributing to the Challenger accident: An example for technical communicators. *IEEE Transactions on Professional Communication, 31*(3), p. 101.

Wigglesworth, Z. (1993, December 20). Finland near to getting commercial route through republics. Mercury News Service.

U.S. Coast Guard Sources

Markle, R. L., Chief, Lifesaving and Fire Safety Standards Branch.

Khandpur, R., G-MOC-2.

Personal Contacts, International Maritime Organization, London (1995)

Captain Peter Olsson, Executive Officer, Maritime Division, German Federal Ministry of Transport, Bonn.

Comments by Captain Ole M. Brakstad (Norway) and Captain Guy Mickelsson (Finland) to the Safety Awareness and Emergency Training Sub-Committee of the LSR, March.

Chapter 11

Risk-Based Design in a Pipeline Engineering Project for Colombia

First Do No Harm

LINDA DRISKILL
Rice University

FRANK DRISKILL
Brown and Root Energy Services

Abstract: This case involves a student intern in a U.S. engineering design team preparing a portion of a wells and pipeline project to be built in Colombia. The firm's client companies are headquartered outside the United States. Leigh's success depends on catching on to the cultural beliefs of coworkers and clients because these beliefs affect engineering decisions. This case consists of three parts. In Part 1 students role-play a meeting or discuss the effects of cultural attitudes on engineering choices; in Part 2 students apply this knowledge in recommending a design change; and in Part 3 students consider ways of including risks to the environment and native people in their recommendations for the layout of a facility. All the information necessary for composing the recommendation for a design change is contained in the narrative and is accessible to people with no engineering background.

Note: The reader of this case must be a cultural detective, searching for the beliefs of people who either are from a particular country or who have experience dealing with people from various countries. Even though the central person in this case, Leigh Hadawy, is working in a U.S. office, many of Leigh's coworkers did not grow up in the United States and the client companies are headquartered outside the United States. Leigh's success as a summer employee depends on catching on to the general beliefs of coworkers and clients because these beliefs affect decisions about technological approaches. Many students think that all engineering and scientific decisions are value free—absolutely right or wrong in terms of good science—but this is not the case. It's somehow easier to understand that bowing or shaking hands is culturally prescribed; it's not as obvious that using a recommended practice approach or a safety case approach might also be the result of where an engineer is from and his or her culture values.

Background for the Case

This case illustrates that international communication depends on the national and cultural backgrounds of participants. The case also illustrates that many technical decisions that are routine or noncontroversial in a single country must be negotiated in international projects. This negotiation in international projects increases the amount and importance of communication.

This case consists of three parts: (1) Learning How Stakeholders' Cultures Affect Hazard Mitigation Design Approaches, (2) Analyzing Risks, Costs, and Ethical Issues to Recommend a Design Change, and (3) Balancing Security and Environmental Effects at the Flowlines' Central Processing Facility. In Part 1 students role-play a meeting or discuss the effects of cultural attitudes; in Part 2 students apply this knowledge in recommending a design change; and in Part 3 students consider ways of including risks to the environment and native people in their recommendations for the layout of a facility.

Multinational Collaborations

For large projects, such as developing an oil field in a remote location, many countries look to multinational petrochemical companies for necessary capital and expertise. Through joint ventures with a multinational company, usually headquartered in one of the more industrialized nations, resource-rich countries can reap the benefits of their natural mineral base.

The engineering work on such large projects includes

- Drafting the project requirements
- Creating the general, front-end design
- Turning the front-end design into detailed designs to guide construction and operation.

The engineering work may be divided among several companies (see Figure 11.1). If the principal owner firm does not choose to oversee the project, another company may be selected to oversee the whole project, even though it does not conduct the engineering or construction work in any of these phases (Company A in Figure 11.1). Either the principal owner or a consulting company (Company B) will prepare the list of requirements for the project, which may be two hundred pages long. Once the requirements have been determined, companies may compete to perform various parts of the project, and contracts will be awarded. One engineering company (Company C) may receive the contract for the first stage of the design process, called the front-end design, which involves the general plant design. Another engineering company (Company D) may do the detail design. In the detail design, the specifications of the front-end design are transformed into drawings and detailed specifications from which equipment can be ordered and construction firms can work. Although some of the giant engineering firms are capable of taking even the biggest projects from concept through construction to start-up operation, it is a fairly common practice to use more than one firm in a check and balance strategy. When several companies are involved, differences in methods and standards must inevitably be negotiated.

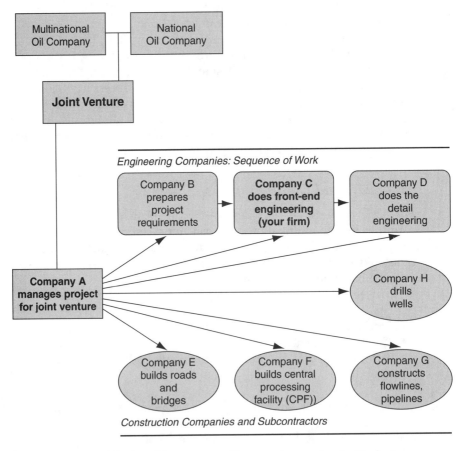

FIGURE 11.1   **Relationships among Companies on Large Projects**

Project Communication during Front-End Design

During the front-end design, frequent meetings must occur between engineers of the principal firm, the managing firm, and the front-end design firm to ensure that the design choices meet legal codes and regulations, minimize political and environmental hazards, agree with the principal owners' standards and recommended practices, and lead to cost-effective operation over the years. Every change to the original requirements must be written down and incorporated into all the other specifications, drawings, and documents affected by the change. Comprehensive management of change (MOC) systems may be adopted to track these changes. The proposals, drawings, memos, reports, procedures, and manuals in a major project run to thousands of pages and hundreds of thousands of e-mail messages and other communication notes and transmissions.

This case will introduce only a few of the documents of a major project, but it is important to understand how the situation in this case fits into the larger project as a whole. Because joint ventures and major projects typically cause people from several companies to interact, and since these are often international projects, each part of the project may contain intercultural and international communication challenges. Documents may be produced in one or in several languages.

This case begins after the project requirements have been written and during GreenTree Engineering's work on the front-end design of a portion of a transportation project (a wells and pipeline project). The overall project involves pumping fluids from wells in low-lying eastern Colombia, South America, to a nearby central processing facility or separation station where water and natural gas are removed. Then the crude oil is lifted across the mountains by pipeline to a port in northern Colombia on the Caribbean coast where crude oil may be shipped around the world. The water is treated at the separation station and returned to the environment; the natural gas is compressed and reinjected into the oil field to maintain pressure and ensure that more of the oil is recovered.

Identification of People in the Case

GreenTree Engineering Personnel

- Leigh Hadawy, a summer intern majoring in mechanical engineering and economics at the university (central character in this case)
- Cran (Crandall) Fairchild, Department Head, Engineering Design—head of the front-end design project and Leigh's boss at GreenTree Engineering
- Rocky Crespo, a young engineer who works in Fairchild's department
- Connie Staples, a GreenTree design engineer from the United States
- José Sanchez, a GreenTree design engineer from Mexico with experience working with Colombia
- Rich Nelson, a GreenTree design engineer who likes API-recommended practices

- Ross Dunbar, a Scotsman who worked in the GreenTree front-end design group
- Hazel Chang, the other intern in the department
- Hazel's supervisor, Devicka Persault

Other Personnel

- Monique Reilly, the Celtic Oil–Colombia Petrol joint-venture project manager
- Dalkin Hopwood, Project Manager for Berber Engineering, the company that is managing the project for the Celtic Oil–Colombia Petrol joint venture.

Part 1: Learning How Stakeholders' Cultures Affect Hazard Mitigation Design Approaches

After completing the sophomore year in a mechanical engineering program, Leigh worked at GreenTree Engineering, one of the major multinational engineering and construction firms, doing minor drafting and routine calculations. This summer Leigh is back at GreenTree after an exciting junior year taking more advanced engineering and some economics courses. Leigh is hoping to gain significant job experience. The internship is in a project design group internship working on the Joint Venture Fluids Gathering Project for the Colombia Transportation Project.

"Glad to have you," lead engineer Cran Fairchild welcomes Leigh. "Your double major in mechanical engineering and economics will make it easy for you to take hold here. In the next few months, we'll be developing the front-end design for Celtic Oil–Colombia Petrol, a joint venture that plans to link a string of oil wells in the eastern jungles of Colombia to a destination in the northwest with a pipeline. It's a bold project. I'm glad we're just doing the front-end engineering for the fluids gathering portion on this baby." With that, Fairchild answers a phone, leaving Leigh to wonder why the company hadn't been bidding on the rest of the project. Surely a firm as big as GreenTree is big enough.

Later Leigh learns more from Rocky Crespo, a young engineer who also works in Fairchild's department. "Take a look at this map," Rocky says, pointing to the computer screen. Here's Bogota, the capital of Colombia, and here's the project, way out here across the mountains in the jungle near the Venezuelan border (see Figure 11.2). Some of the roads in between are controlled by guerrillas. Last year two oil company engineers and their driver were kidnapped right along here," he said, pointing to a secondary road.

"Were they from GreenTree?" Leigh asks.

"Not ours, Berber Engineering people. That's the same company [Company A in Figure 11.1] that's managing this project for the joint venture. To get out here, the project engineers will have to go by helicopter. Same for the technicians who will maintain the flowline pipes and routinely check on the wells after the construction is done."

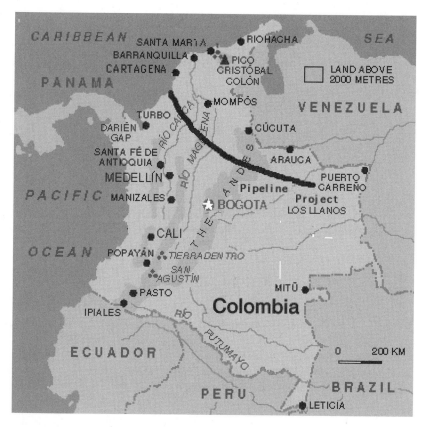

FIGURE 11.2 Map of the Project's Location

Another engineer, Connie Staples, chimes in: "They ought to get hazardous duty pay, don't you know? If the helicopter doesn't crash and if the guerrillas don't get them, they could always be blown up."

"Blown up?" Leigh echoes, startled.

"Yea, that area through the mountains is an active seismic region. Mild earthquakes are common, but even a mild earthquake could rupture a flowline pipe or cause a well blowout. Some job, eh?"

Leigh begins to see what Fairchild meant about not really wanting anything to do with the later parts of the project. However, the new information does color with excitement the somewhat routine process of setting design parameters, making sure the designs meet the various requirements and safety codes, and determining the overall layout. Leigh looks at the diagram Rocky handed out that shows a schematic drawing of the eighteen wells, each with its own flowline running to the central processing facility (CPF) (see Figure 11.3).

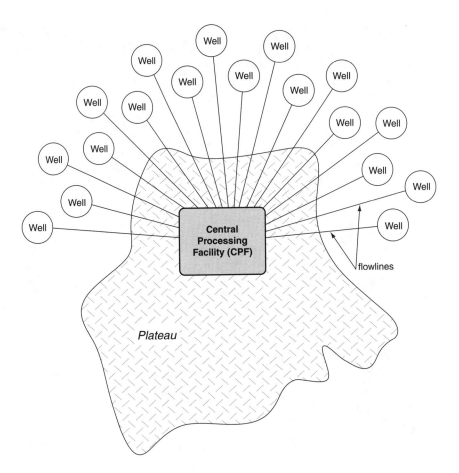

FIGURE 11.3 Schematic Configuration of Wells, Flowlines, and Central Processing Facility (Separation Station) on a Plateau

From what Leigh has read in the project materials from Fairchild, Leigh can already see that the hazards Rocky and Connie had mentioned only increased the already serious technical challenge. The flowline pipe would carry petroleum at 95 kilograms per square centimeter pressure (the limit of the American National Standards Institute or ANSI class 600 specification for the flowline). Oil spills, should the flowline pipe be ruptured, would be especially costly and hard to cope with because of the remote location. The terrain, although covered with jungle, is hilly—nearly mountainous in parts. Leigh looks over the computer files that already have been created for the project, knowing that Ross Dunbar, a Scotsman who worked in the group, will be back in an hour to tell what the internship job, in particular, will involve for this project.

Leigh Digs Out Project Background by Reading Project Documents and Asking Questions

Leigh feels a bit daunted. The project requirements document runs over sixty pages and includes background on the project, a policy statement, and page after page specifying the information that will be generated during the engineering phases. It describes the specifications format, the software standards for electronic transfer of information, and the types of documents that will be created. These documents will describe the control system, equipment, instruments, fire and gas protection, telecommunication systems, and electrical, mechanical, and piping systems. Civil and structural documents, corrosion inspection, certification processes—all have to be documented and reported on. Leigh decides to try at least to cover the background on the project before Dunbar returns.

The style of the introduction surprises Leigh. It seems legalistic:

> *Engineering information required for the safe and efficient operation, repair, and modification of the facilities comprising the Well Fluid Gathering Project for the duration of its operating cycle are detailed in this document. Key terms used within this document are defined in the glossary (see Appendix B). All engineering information will be collected in accordance with the requirements set forth in this document. Any deviation must be recorded and approved by the Project Manager or the Project Management Company's designee. The information shall be developed according to the Engineering Information Table shown in Figure 2. This table details the information to be handed over to the Operator and includes the following equipment data: . . .*

Leigh sighs, thinking how *engineering* textbooks had been dry; the project background section is even worse. However, the legalistic tone makes it clear that engineering work has to be done to contract specifications:

> *All documentation will be uniquely numbered (coded) to one numbering system to enable retrieval/sorting by system code, document type, discipline, order number, manufacturers' equipment number, sequence number, and revision (as built status). All documentation shall be catalogued in a Master Document Register that will be provided in an electronic relational database . . . .*

It makes sense, of course, that everything on a project this large has to be tracked, but that aspect of an engineering project had never occurred to Leigh as students worked on course projects at school.

"All right, mate," Ross Dunbar booms as he enters Leigh's cubicle after his meeting. "Time to get you started." He puts some folders down on Leigh's desk: "Here you've got the makings of a fine dispute.

"If we were designing this pipeline and these wells for offshore on the Texas coast, we'd use the American Petroleum Institute's Recommended Practice 14C. API RP 14C was developed after literally years of meetings by a committee made up of representatives from most of the major companies, both oil companies and engineering companies. The 14C standard was developed for the temperatures and conditions of the Gulf of Mexico, and you can see from the project map that part of northern Colombia lies along the Caribbean. However, the RFP [request for proposal] from Celtic Oil–Colombia Petrol doesn't call for that standard. They want to take the British approach and do a 'safety case'—that's a special safety analysis of the data on a particular project.

"The safety case is the method the British developed after a terrible disaster in the North Sea at an offshore platform called Piper Alpha. After that catastrophe, they replaced API RP 14C because it wasn't developed for North Sea conditions. For example, if a worker falls off an offshore platform in the Caribbean, he or she can survive for quite a while because the water's pretty warm. However, in the North Sea a worker has to have safety gear to conserve body heat. In the North Sea, death could be less than thirty minutes away once your body hits the water. So they now take a different approach to safety, and what they've asked for leads to a couple of interesting problems, one of which I'm going to give you to think about.

"We're going to have a meeting with the engineers from Celtic Oil–Colombia Petrol, and Berber Engineering about whether we should follow API recommended practices or do a risk analysis to justify our design choices. That meeting is scheduled for 3 P.M., and I want you to sit in as an observer because it will help you understand the risk-based design questions in front-end engineering. You might want to get some more insight from José Sanchez, whose cubicle is over near the window, and from Rich Nelson who has the cubicle next to José. You'll get opposite ends of the spectrum in their views."

Leigh decides to see what Rich and José have to say and walks through the maze of cubicles to find them. José is just getting up from his desk as Leigh approaches. "I've got to catch lunch early," he responds after Leigh greets him and gives him a brief version of Ross's instructions. "Come on down to the cafeteria, and I'll try to explain how the client will see it."

Over lunch, José tells Leigh about his work on another project in Bogota last winter, then says: "After working with the Colombians, I can predict that Celtic Oil's engineers will probably see eye-to-eye with the Colombians on this matter, even though you wouldn't expect it. The 1987 Piper Alpha disaster in the North Sea, where 167 people died, caused a ton of bad press around the world. It was portrayed in the press as a case of both engineering shortcomings as well as operational problems. So they developed the safety case approach in the hope of having every installation built to meet the conditions that a particular project might have to withstand. [See the reference list for newspaper articles on Piper Alpha.] The engineers I worked with in Bogota also would like that approach, because they are suspicious of universal standards. They're more likely to say that the truth depends on the circumstances; they'd prefer to work out a solution each time.

"And who can blame them? In Colombia things are more as they are in Mexico, where I grew up," José tells Leigh. "Development occurred gradually in Mexico, with different plants being built at different times and with different designs and standards. Older plants don't have the same size fittings or equipment, and so it makes sense to favor a case-by-case analysis and to make a specific solution to everything. It was like that in the Bogota deal I was in on, too. You know, I think it was the United States that invented the slogan, 'One size fits all.' And some people are just more willing than others to admit old sayings aren't always right."

"Yeah," Leigh replies with a laugh, "things may be changing even in the United States. The gloves I bought for my sister at Target said 'One size fits *most.*' They've dropped 'One size fits all."

José does have a point, Leigh decides. Conditions everywhere can't be like those in the Gulf of Mexico; but how different are things going to be in a country that edges the Caribbean? Why wouldn't the API RP 14C be just fine in Colombia? José's meeting is about to start; no more time for questions.

When Leigh gets back upstairs, Rich Nelson gives the opposite side of the argument. "I've seen too much disagreement over what a set of facts means to trust this safety case process. It would take a really brilliant engineering team to make me feel as good about a committee decision as I would feel about a design that met a universal standard that had been hammered out by representatives from a whole slew of companies over a period of years. I mean, the level of expertise that's rolled into an API recommended practice is awesome. And if it comes into court in the good old US of A, I'm going to feel much better telling the judge or the jury that the design team went down that checklist and answered every item on it. There's a right way to do things, and I want to do it that way." Leigh can see from Rich's straight posture and bearing that integrity is critical for him.

Rich pulls out a proposal that had been developed last year for a project not far out in the Gulf, and sure enough, Leigh can see that it documented full compliance with API RP 14C. The checklist portion of the document, which is numbered API RP 14J, is attached to the front of the proposal. "It's actually easier to reach technical decisions with a checklist, " Rich tells Leigh. "There are a lot of intangibles on which people can't agree. This kind of approach forces them to focus on the technical questions: how much, how many, what pressure—the things that *really* affect whether something works the way it needs to. That's why I like it. When you're at the meeting, you'll see that raising the safety case approach brings a lot of nontechnical elements into play that really don't bear on the design." With that, he sends Leigh off to look at the file before the meeting.

Background for Analysis

Much of what José and Rich said reminds Leigh of readings assigned in a cultural anthropology class from Franz Trompenaars' and Geert Hofstede's books, which compare countries on the basis of several cultural features. One of those features was a culture's view of truth. The United States, Leigh remembers, tends to believe in universal principles, whereas Latin American cultures seem to take a more relative or situational view of what is true. In addition, the United States and the British (along with the Germans, Swiss, Israelis, and Scandinavians) tend to look at technology as a means of controlling nature, whereas many Latin American cultures expect nature and situations to control them, with technology as a neutral element in the scheme of things. Could attitudes toward truth and technology be at work in the comments around the office? School and work seem to be coming together in an unexpected way here. What should be made of the British viewpoint? If the United Kingdom is a control-of-nature, universalist kind of culture, why are the British committed to the safety case process? What would they be likely to favor in a negotiation over the implications of risk for this project's front-end design? How much would they care about worker safety? Would a class-conscious society that cheered for royalty care if a trained technician fell victim to an earthquake or terrorist attack? Leigh's anthropology course seems to take on a new relevance as thoughts about these recent conversations flood back.

Questions for Discussion: Cultural Views of Stakeholders

Note: Use the following questions to make sure you understand some of the basic cultural views that different stakeholders in this situation have. You may want to reread the case so far or look at some of the readings listed at the end of the chapter, especially Trompenaars' and Hofstede's books, if you need further elaboration.

1. How do the principal national cultures (United States, Britain, Columbia, Mexico, Venezuela) in this case view the nature of truth? Which countries hold similar views of truth? What did people say in the case that led you to make that inference?

2. How do Latin American cultures tend to differ from the United States and the British in their beliefs about the role of technology? Is technology a positive, a negative, or a neutral element in the scheme of things?

3. How could attitudes toward truth and technology in this situation influence the stakeholders' attitudes toward safety and disaster prevention? What should be made of the British viewpoint? If the United Kingdom is a control-of-nature, universalist kind of culture, why were the British committed to the safety case process?

4. What would Celtic Oil's representatives be likely to favor in a negotiation over the implications of risk for this project's front-end design? How much would they care about worker safety? Would a class-conscious society that cheered for royalty care if a trained technician fell victim to an earthquake or terrorist attack?

Writing Assignment

Write a memo summarizing the cultural positions of Celtic Oil, GreenTree Engineering, and Colombia Petrol with regard to truth, technology, and project hazards.

Questions for Discussion: Role-Play
the Intercompany Meeting That Leigh Observes

1. One way to internalize another culture's beliefs is to "walk a mile in the person's shoes"—to try to pick up clues about the other person's beliefs and act them out in a scene or role-playing activity. Form a group of six or more people, and ask group mem-

bers to role-play a representative of one of the stakeholders: Colombia Petrol, Celtic Oil, Greentree Engineering, and Berber Engineering. One person should play Cran Fairchild as moderator. Before the group meets, each person should make a list of the concerns and values his or her company might have about ensuring safety on the fluids gathering project. Their experiences have been different. For example, Berber Engineering had two people kidnapped last year. That should influence their ideas about safety. The people from Colombia Petrol aren't likely to want to admit the guerrillas are a big threat. And so on. Rereading the information given so far should help you imagine the interests of the stakeholder representative you're assigned to role-play. As much as possible, try to understand and adopt the feelings and beliefs of that person. Imagine the gestures, expressions, and personal style of these individuals, and think about what they would say.

2. Cran Fairchild should begin the meeting by thanking everyone for attending and bring up the issue: "The present contract calls for a safety case, but in this hemisphere the more common practice is to use API RP 14C." Naturally, the client will have the last word, but in a real sense, this matter is like a hundred others in a huge project—the method is there to be negotiated among the parties. It's not a legal matter, but an engineering decision. The success of the role-play will depend largely on your ability to put yourself in the shoes of each party and represent the interests and concerns. As your instructor directs, you might take fifteen to twenty minutes to consider the pros and cons of the options.

Writing Assignment

After the group discussion, write a memo summarizing the participants' positions and explaining the consensus the group arrives at. Turn in the memos. Your instructor may want to demonstrate to you later how closely the group members' memos agreed on what was said in the meeting.

Part 2: Analyzing Risks, Costs, and Ethical Issues to Recommend a Design Change

Ross Dunbar meets Leigh the next morning. He says, "For the time being, until the joint-venture client, Celtic Oil–Colombia Petrol, makes its decision about the safety approach, we're going to proceed by collecting the data we would need for a safety case analysis. Here's the issue."

The pressures in the well can be very high, say, 3000 pounds per square inch (note: U.S. measurements; not the metric system). The wellhead has a throttle or choke valve that reduces that pressure to something more manageable. If the choke didn't work, the full 3000 pounds or whatever the petroleum was under would slam through into the flowline pipe and burst it. To make sure we don't have a blowout, we can use a High Integrity Protection System (HIPS), which means we would put additional valves on the wellhead, and if the valve reads a pressure higher than its set point, it will close down the well and shut it off. We can't rely on just one valve to do that, of course, because any one valve could fail. A HIPS at the wellhead might require triple redundancy. Out there in the jungle, you don't want anything to go wrong at the well, so you make sure there are two additional backups for everything—that's what triple redundancy means. Of course, any system is only as good as the reliability of its weakest piece, so each and every component in the HIPS must be reliable. In short, we either have to use a High Integrity Protection System or build a heavier flowline pipe; each has its costs—in money and in risks to people."

"If we use a HIPS, a trained technician, who is a person with more than a little experience," Ross's craggy eyebrows rose to stress his understatement, "and usually with some formal education, say a couple of years, a really valuable person, will have to come to each well every three months. The joint-venture philosophy is that it's worth up to maybe $10 million dollars to save that person's life—to make it safe for him or her—but they would rather it didn't cost more than $1 million. Now, there are eighteen wells attached to this pipeline. Seventy-two times a year this person will have to risk a helicopter flight, terrorist attacks, seismic instability, and equipment malfunction in order to make the equipment assessment—run tests on every part with the help of an assistant. As it stands, the seismic activity is so high that the greatest threat to a senior technician and the assistant is from some movement along an active fault.

"The inherently safer alternative is to build a heavier flowline pipe that would withstand most seismic activity as well as the full wellhead pressure. It would even resist most terrorist attacks unless they have very sophisticated explosives. We could change the specifications from 600 grade to 1500 grade ANSI.[1] A flowline pipe that thick should withstand most seismic events. There's a copy of *ANSI/ASME B31.4 Liquid Transportation Systems for Hydrocarbons, Liquid Petroleum Gas, Anhydrous Ammonia, and Alcohols* over there on the bookshelf, by the way. You probably had one in your college library, too. That way a HIPS wouldn't be absolutely necessary.

"To figure the safety risk with the British approach they've recommended, you would multiply the probabilities of the various events by the associated costs. If the probability is less than 0.001 (one in one thousand), for example, 10^{-4} or 10^{-5}, an accident should not cost the company more than they would have to pay to prevent the accident. Their managers would say that unless the chances are higher than one in one thousand, there isn't any extra money to make the design safer. That $10 million I mentioned is a figure that you could use in the risk assessment."

Leigh Is Assigned to Draft the Change of Design Memo

Note: In the section of the case below, Dunbar assigns Leigh the job of analyzing the safety case issues, writing up the analysis, and giving a brief presentation about the analysis. If

---

[1]The American National Standards Institute began in 1917. It develops consensus among professional practitioners for drafting standards for projections, various types of sections, dimensioning and tolerancing, representation of screw threads, all types of fasteners, graphic symbols for various specialties, and a great deal more. Other industrialized countries have similar institutes, such as the British Standards Institution and the Deutsches Institut für Normung (German Standards Institute).

your instructor gives you this assignment, follow Dunbar's instructions as if you are Leigh. Even if you are not given this presentation assignment, you should read this part of the case because understanding it is essential to later assignments as well.

"To give you some practice, I want you to present the safety case issues to the project proposal team—that's about five people, all Greentree people—three from the United States, one from Mexico, and one who used to work with Celtic Oil. Tell the team (1) whether the risks to personnel are large enough to justify spending money to fix them, and (2) how the risks and costs associated with a HIPS on each of the eighteen wells compare to the risks and costs of building a heavier flowline pipe.

"Your analysis and presentation will be the basis for their discussion. Somewhere in this stack you'll find the table that Charlie worked up after a conversation with the JV (joint venture) representative. If we recommend a design that's too expensive, the JV might cancel the contract. However, money isn't everything; GreenTree usually tries to advocate safety for its own sake."

Leigh hunts through the stack looking for a page with a table headed Colombia Well Fluid Gathering Project Risk to Individuals Projection or RIP Profile (Table 11.1). When it finally is found, it is obvious that Leigh will have to have some help making sense of these columns. Leigh remembers that José had had some experience with the safety case approach and heads for his cubicle.

"Say, José, can you explain this to me?" Leigh asks.

José looks at the table and points to the columns: "What you see here are the risks to individuals probabilities, or RIPs. Different kinds of jobs have different RIPs. People who work or live near the plant are more likely to be affected than people who are not nearby, which is what you would expect with explosions. And of course, the soldiers who guard the facilities are going to be more at risk from terrorist attacks than the ordinary workers—they're the militia referred to under Category of Personnel.

TABLE 11.1   Well Fluid Gathering Project Risk to Individuals Projection or RIP Profile per Year

Category of Personnel	RIP for Earthquake and Terrorism	RIP Excluding Earthquake and Terrorism	Total RIP Including Earthquake and Terrorism
Supervisors	1.0×10^{-3}	1.3×10^{-4}	1.1×10^{-3}
Process plant operators	1.1×10^{-3}	1.0×10^{-4}	1.2×10^{-3}
Flowline technicians*	1.4×10^{-3}	1.3×10^{-4}	1.5×10^{-3}
Militia	3.5×10^{-4}	1.0×10^{-5}	3.6×10^{-4}
Management and clerical	3.5×10^{-4}	1.0×10^{-5}	3.6×10^{-4}

*Flowline technicians' risks based on seventy-two trips/year

"Celtic–Colombia set out in the requirements that we should tolerate risks that are lower than 1.0×10^{-3} but that we could design in safety systems to reduce any risks greater than 1.0×10^{-3}. As you can see, the risk from accidents at the well, process failures, and flowline incidents would mostly be tolerable, but when the risks of seismic activity and guerrilla attacks are figured in, the risks get into the higher mitigation range; our safety case has to recommend to Celtic whether to build a heavier pipeline or put in a HIPS.

"You'll have to decide how well a HIPS lowers the risks to personnel as a whole, since the technicians will have to make seventy-two trips a year to check on the HIPS equipment. That added risk determines their chance for harm if we don't use a HIPS. Using a thicker pipe in the flowline would eliminate that risk to technicians, since you would leave the HIPS out. There are other figures in the file that tell how much the HIPS for each well costs and some estimates on how flowline costs go up if we use the higher ANSI standard for the pipe. Work out the numbers and see what you think." Leigh grins ruefully at José and looks again at Charlie's table.

The note at the bottom of Charlie's table reads: "Celtic wants risk managed in the most cost-effective manner." Leigh knows that 10^{-4} means one in ten thousand, while 10^{-3} means one in a thousand. Earthquake and terrorism will probably affect some of these workers by a factor of ten. Of course, not all the personnel will be affected equally. Furthermore, there are more people in some categories than others, as illustrated in Table 11.2.

When Leigh checks with Rich on what to do with these numbers, he says to count on a maximum of four persons in an event at a well, where the risk of seismic events would be greatest. However, the number of people who might be hurt at the CPF would depend on how many people were in the facility at the time and how far away the others are. With the plateau being as small as it was, at least one-fourth of them might sustain injuries in a guerrilla attack.

Leigh finds another sheet in the file that says the cost per well for the HIPS system over the standard instrumentation that ordinarily would be chosen would be $30,000. That would mean an additional cost of $540,000 to use the HIPS, plus an additional operating cost of $10,000 for HIPS reliability maintenance, or $180,000 for eighteen wells ($1,800,000 over the ten-year life of the project). The estimated

TABLE 11.2   Annual Project Staffing Requirements

Type of Personnel	Number of Personnel
Supervisors	3
Process plant operators	13
Flowline technicians	4
Militia	20
Management and clerical	4
Nonmilitia total	4

costs for heavier flowline pipe, including installation, will go up by around $1.50 per foot, or $8000 per mile. Since the average distance from a well to the Central Processing Facility is twelve miles, that's $96,000 extra expense per well; with eighteen wells in the system, heavier pipe in the flowline would cost an additional $1,728,000.

Leigh remembers that Celtic–Colombia said it would be willing to invest $1 million to protect a worker's life, but also that it might be willing to pay up to $10 million over the ten-year life of the project. Leigh has read that the construction risks are covered by other provisions and that the pipeline that took the oil away from the CPF to the coast has a much lower risk to personnel because of the lower maintenance required and because of fewer seismic risks going away from the mountains, but still, nothing was said about environmental risks there, either.

Leigh asks Dunbar for a little more guidance. Ross explains, "These costs, of course, are capital costs; they only occur once, except for the maintenance, whereas the risk of loss is an annual hazard. The project is designed as a ten-year life, but the estimates show the breakeven point at the end of three years. Since the total well fluids gathering project is estimated to cost $1.2 billion, they're expecting a net profit of at least $400 million per year in the first three years. Is a half-million-dollar additional cost a good insurance policy for a $400 million annual net profit? A million? Two million? You'll have to come up with a proposed answer for us."

Leigh Compares Risk Mitigation Strategies

Connie Staples hurries into Leigh's cubicle carrying a stack of drawings and asks, "How's it coming?"

"How do you decide whether something is worth doing?" Leigh replies, answering Connie's question with another one. "The lower cost option with HIPS appears still to have a greater risk to people; if we put heavier pipe in the flowlines at higher cost, they simply won't have to have technicians down at the wells. Rich tells me they'll just use daily flyovers to monitor guerrilla activity."

"Well, you're right that there's a human risk that would be hard to tolerate, even when the probabilities were low," Connie replies. "But have you considered some of the other risks? For instance, suppose the guerrillas are successful and blow a hole in the pipeline. We'll have the fluids in the pipeline, under pressure, maybe ten miles worth of moving oil and water spilling out into the watershed. That's a risk to the environment. Have you built that into any of your tables? Has the client built that concern into the project requirements? Maybe you ought to bring it up when you write up your safety case analysis proposals."

Background for Analysis: Ethics Concepts

Note: Use the questions that follow this general overview of the assignment to evaluate the safety issues as they can be formulated from the data you have been given about the two mitigation alternatives. Use the background for analysis to consider the ethical issues of the project as well. Be sure to formulate and consider any additional questions that have occurred to you. If your instructor directs, discuss these questions in a group or among the class as a whole. Otherwise, analyze the issues for yourself.

Leigh is reminded that the ethics professor kept emphasizing how new scientific discoveries have created new ethical issues in medicine. People who would have died twenty-five years ago can now be treated. But these possibilities raise ethical questions about who should receive care, who should pay for it, and when is it ethical to prolong life. It looks like the new global economy and the technology of the energy business are also bringing up new ethical issues. The Colombians will benefit from taxes and from profits, but there will be risks, too.

Other reasons for moral decisions, besides avoiding harm, involve intentions, severity of potential effects, ideals or standards, duties, and rights. This project clearly involves standards—too many, Leigh feels at first. Ideals don't seem to be on the table, the kind of things that address the highest conception of human behavior, such as compassionate sensitivity to others' needs. The environment hasn't been on the table so far, either. Maybe Leigh ought to figure that in. However, professional codes and national codes are certainly in evidence.

Students in the ethics class read Lisa Belkin's book, *First, Do No Harm*. Leigh doesn't see anyone intentionally advocating harm in the project, except the guerrillas, of course. However, Leigh recalls that some situations contain a dilemma, a problem for which all solutions are bad in one way or another. Leigh wonders whether there's dilemma in this project, or just a choice.

Lawrence Kohlberg's theory of moral reasoning was another favorite of Leigh's ethics professor. It suggests six primary levels of moral reasoning that people learn sequentially as they grow up, as shown in Figure 11.4. Although a mature person may at times use different levels of reasoning, he or she will typically tend to argue at one level. Would the client engineers tend to want to create new rules or hang on to old ones in making the design choices?

In the lowest two levels of Kohlberg's model, a person is mainly concerned about his or her own welfare, to obtain rewards or to avoid harm. In the next two levels, the influence of a group is dominant. The older child is taught the rules of his or her family and the codes of small organizations such as a scout troop or school team. During the high-school years, the laws of state and nation are learned, and decisions are often based on contractual or legal requirements. Because an individual in the United States is guaranteed certain rights by the Constitution and by other legislation and ordinances, and because laws may create certain obligations or duties, the third and fourth stages of moral reasoning are called rule-governed. The fifth and sixth levels are law-creating levels.

At the fifth level, new laws may be enacted to deal with new ethical problems, such as who can receive new and controversial treatments. And at the sixth level, the concerns of many countries and peoples, the environment, and the future of the planet may be the top priority. So as one moves up the ladder, the reasoning is based on self-interest, group interests, and, finally, global interests.

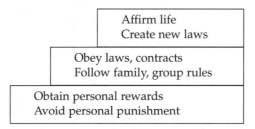

FIGURE 11.4 **Kohlberg's Ladder of**
Moral Development

Questions for Discussion

1. What level of ethical reasoning would the proposal committee take? Would it be the high view (level five or six)? At what level are the GreenTree employees likely to argue? How will the discussion change if three members of the committee are from the United States and two are not?

2. What about the clients? What are people with varying views of the nature of truth and technology likely to think about the ethical aspects of this project?

3. Which is better, a HIPS or a stronger flowline pipe? Leigh recalls that the point of a safety case is to make the design fit the situation. The environment is part of the specific situation here, Leigh thinks. Balancing rights and duties, pursuing ideals, and discovering the best use of technological discoveries and resources would be an ethical challenge in students' later careers, the ethics professor had said. Here they are—on her first day on the job.

4. The key concept is that all situations involve stakeholders—people who have an interest in how the situation turns out. Who are the stakeholders in such a huge project as this? The companies, the workers, the engineers, the government, the media, the guerrillas, the lawyers—how can one get a handle on all of these people?

5. The presence of many stakeholders complicates ethical decisions. Should a technician's safety boil down to dollars and cents? Should the stockholders' money be spent to protect the worker from a relatively low risk? Whose customs and needs should prevail? How could the risks be lowered for the technicians? For the environment?

Writing Assignments

Note on gender roles: Write this memo as if you were Leigh. The practice of drafting for a superior's signature tends to protect the subordinate writer of either gender in this case, because the draft will be perceived primarily as a possible communication from Cran Fairchild. In the presentation described in the case, some gender expectations might have been pertinent, but this case focuses primarily on the written products, not on gender in conversation

1. As Leigh, write a Request for Design Change Memo, but read the following information to help you understand the purpose and considerations before you begin.

"Got to get down to the question at hand!" Leigh mutters. "What does this situation call for? What hazards cost enough to be worth mitigating? Should we propose to go with a higher ANSI grade and make the pipeline more secure and more costly? Should we put in a HIPS on every well? And what will the engineers in Celtic Oil–Colombia Petrol be likely to accept? What are their predispositions? Their uncertainties? How will the project proposal committee decide on design choices, whatever they are, and make them attractive to the joint venture representatives?" The enormity of these questions makes Leigh very glad to see Cran Fairchild stop by the cubicle.

Fairchild confirms Leigh's calculation that building the flowline pipes to a higher ANSI standard will increase the flowline cost by $1.728 million, whereas the HIPS would add $540,000 installation cost and $1,800,000 additional operating costs. Fairchild lays out the assignment for Leigh in more detail: "We have to present Celtic–Colombia with a Request for Design Change Memo. You can write the first draft. It will be reviewed by the design review committee and it will have to be revised to put forward whichever decision the committee makes. However, you should go ahead and write up the memo with your own recommendations. If they're well justified, the committee may change it less than you'd think. The memo will eventually have my name on it as the sender, and the memo should go to Monique Reilly, the Celtic-Colombia joint-venture project manager and Dalkin Hopwood at Berber Engineering. Reilly will make the final decision. At the bottom of the memo put a note on this draft that says, 'prepared by Leigh Hadawy,' and today's date."

As is often the case in business, the person drafting a document is not the person whose signature will be placed on the document as the sender. In this case, the committee consists of people who are doing the front-end design itself. This committee manages the overall interaction between the rest of the design groups and the joint-venture client (Celtic Oil–Colombia Petrol). Among other things, this committee coordinates management of change requests and makes sure that changes requested by one design group are not in conflict with changes proposed by another group. All the changes have to produce a consistent final design that meets integrity standards. This committee needs to hear the safety issues involved in the flowlines design, and the committee will revise the memorandum Leigh prepares and send it to Fairchild, who may make some slight additional changes. What is a final draft for Leigh is a working or interim draft for the committee. The committee also could start out fresh, but since Leigh will already have presented the numbers in a useful form, it will almost certainly preserve parts of Leigh's memo in its final draft.

Leigh jots down the key issues:

- Whether the risks to personnel are high enough to justify mitigation, and how much could be spent, given the risks
- How much cost the company would incur with a HIPS or with a stronger flowline
- How to represent the risk to the environment and the risk to the joint venture.

That is, how much would the joint venture stand to lose if a safety event—in the euphemism used at GreenTree put it—occurred in the first three years? What would the JV stand to lose in revenues? How much would the JV lose over ten years, the life of the project, if Colombia decided to throw Celtic out over an environmental incident and not let them continue? Leigh remembers that Alaska had almost tried to kick Exxon out after the *Valdez* incident; only the enormous taxes Exxon paid to Alaska seemed to change the state government's mind. And Mobil went through a difficult negotiation in Peru in 1996.

The international challenge here is how to persuade people from three different cultures: the United States, Mexico, and Great Britain. It stood to reason that if the joint venture didn't put environmental damage in the project requirements, GreenTree would have to introduce it in a compelling way for environmental issues to be considered. In addition to the cost benefit information you've calculated, the team will be influenced by your ability to address their cultural views, which you identified in Part 1 of the case. The British and Mexican members of the team are likely to be predisposed to a situation-specific basis for the choice. The U.S. members are likely to be predisposed to an argument that rests on general principles of probability and good business.

2. Can you describe the benefits of your proposal or recommendation for hazard mitigation on this project in such a way that both groups will be convinced?

3. As Leigh in this assignment, you should organize the memo with an introductory summary that sets out the situation, the three issues, and a brief version of your recommendation. The body of the memorandum should discuss each of these matters in turn. No close or signature is needed at the end of a memorandum. Use the following headings for the memo: Date, From, To, Reference No. (Project Number for this project is 00-CC40747), and Subject. The subject description should be detailed enough to set it apart from other memos to the team about the front-end design.

4. As the instructor directs, hand in your version of Leigh's written analysis with recommendations.

5. In the meeting, Ross will give you four minutes to present your analysis of the data and your arguments in support of your recommendation. Once again, you will have to define your recommendation in terms that address the cultural predispositions of the audience. The committee will receive your memo before the meeting, so you will be reminding them of your main points. Do not read the document to them. Few professionals like to be read to. To encourage discussion, you may want to prepare overheads that will focus their attention on you and the overheads, not just on the memo. Your thoughtful analysis of the issues and your character will be important influences on the team. What aspects of your personality will be most useful to you in establishing rapport with this group?

Part 3: Balancing Security and Environmental Effects at the Flowlines' Central Processing Facility

Hazel Chang, the other summer intern in the department, has been working on another aspect of the design project. Instead of dealing with flowline pipe and wellhead systems, Hazel was brought into the small team that is designing the central processing facility that will contain the separation station. This station will remove the natural gas and water mixed in the petroleum that is pumped from the well before it is sent through the pipeline and over the mountains. The natural gas is put under 300 Kg/cm^2 pressure (note that these are metric system units) and reinjected into the formation to increase the pressure on the remaining petroleum and ensure a higher proportion of recovery. The water produced is treated and put back into the environment.

One day, Hazel stops by Leigh's cubicle. "Got a few minutes?" she asks. "Come by my cubicle and look at my screen." Leigh can see she's frustrated. "Sure, what's up? " Leigh replies.

Hazel's computer screen shows an irregular area with lots of small designs on it (Figure 11.5). "This is one of two layouts I've done," she explains. "There are awfully few possible sites for locating this separation station. We don't want to put it down in the jungle, and we finally found a small plateau on which we can put the plant. It's so far out here that we've got to include housing so that crews can live on the site. We also have to have barracks for troops, or security forces, as they're referred to."

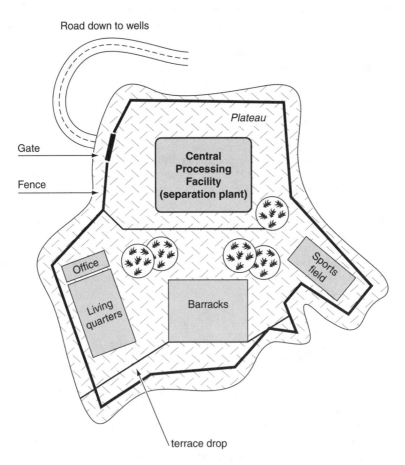

FIGURE 11.5   Plateau Plan with Trees Cut for Safety

"Army people?" Leigh asks.

"Yeah, I think a maximum of thirty soldiers has been called for, but I'm told twenty is a more likely number. My problem here is that for safety purposes I'd like to put the housing area as far from the plant as possible, right up against the fence, but since security is also an issue, we don't want terrorists or guerrillas coming over the fence into the housing area. We need a zone that can be kept under surveillance."

"Hey, I'd put the soldiers' barracks right by the gate if it were my project," Leigh responds.

"As you can see from this other drawing [Figure 11.6], Leigh, there are trees on the plateau. It slopes now, but we plan to terrace it so there will be three levels. If I cut down all the trees and put the fence out close to the edge of the plateau (Figure 11.5) it will be easier to protect the place. Anyone attacking the complex would have

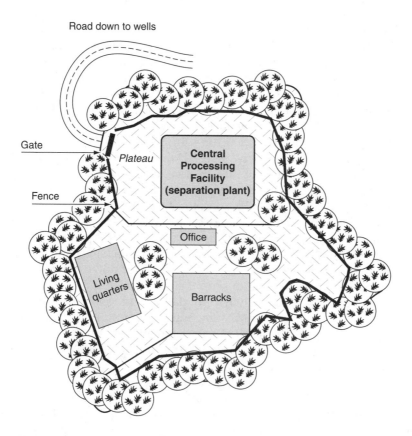

FIGURE 11.6 Plateau Plan with Trees Retained

to climb up the slope, and it's a pretty steep drop. On the other hand, if I leave the trees and put the fence inside of them it would be easier for people to climb up into the trees and get across the fence undetected. Plus, if we take down the trees the visibility goes up but the long-term effect, say over ten years or more, will be to increase the possibility of erosion, which will make the whole plateau, small as it is, less stable. Of course, the project life is only scheduled for ten years, so I don't know if anyone would care after that, although I think they'd keep pumping as long as the field was producing, don't you?

"And we've got to have some public area—you know, some kind of sports field or something, because people will go crazy being shut up in the plant or in the barracks all the time." Almost as an afterthought, Hazel said, "And we'll have to build a road up here and put a bridge across the stream. There are very few villages in this region, mostly little settlements of a hundred people or so, meager agricultural communities mostly."

Leigh studies the map and asks, "What kind of water supplies do the villages have?"

Hazel frowns and replies, "There's only one stream in the watershed. All the little villages use it. There's one about 300 meters to the southeast of the CPF property line that looks like it might have twenty or so dwellings and two little stores; I see a small school that is just off the one road that goes up to the plateau, maybe 100 meters or so, and various little residential structures scattered around within a 500 meter radius—not any above the plateau. I've seen the aerial shots, but I haven't been there, of course. But, gee, they're all so small. If we pollute the stream it's not as though there would be any municipal water treatment plants cleaning things up. There's some water treatment planned, but it is shown as an additional cost."

Without waiting for a reply, she turns toward Leigh. "What do you think of the environmental issues? The safety issues? How will we present all these complications to the client? Even if one of the joint-venture partners is the Colombian government, will it insist on protecting the environment, or will it care most about getting high revenues from the project? It sort of has two different interests here, and they may conflict. I know you took an ethics course. You mentioned that there are always three things to consider: intentions, effects, and standards or ideals. What are you guys doing about the environmental issues with the pipeline part of the project?"

Hazel continues urgently, "You know, if you cut down jungle to put through a pipeline, how are you going to keep the jungle from growing back? Use defoliants? Agent Orange? I know what my dad would say: 'Shades of Vietnam!' Is Celtic is going to put people at risk by hauling them out here and having crews working on hundreds of miles of pipeline right of way clearing brush every year? And what about where it goes through the mountains? How will you prevent erosion and destabilizing of the soil?"

Leigh looks at Hazel and laughs with amazement. "Is this a change from our numbers only engineering problems in school or what?" Leigh could tell that Hazel was alternately feeling angry and overwhelmed by the prospects that kept popping up at every turn. Guerrillas, pollution, recreation for the troops? Where to put a fence? What would the clients, Colombia Petrol and Celtic Oil care about? What position would GreenTree take? Leigh knew that GreenTree usually argued in favor of environmentally sound engineering. Here, however, the company was trying to keep the client and the company managing the project, Berber Engineering, happy.

Leigh stares at the computer screen, trying to sort out the multiple issues before trying to address Hazel's concerns. Finally, Leigh replies, "Let's get some of the other interns together tonight to talk about this. Why not a session at Birra Poretti's Irish-Italian Restaurant and Bar? This ought to keep us going through a couple of pitchers and more."

"Yea, it's too much to sort out alone. Thanks for suggesting it. Let's send an e-mail and see who can come," Hazel says, turning back to the computer screen. Leigh thinks of Birra Poretti's pizza with a smile—that alone ought to bring out a crowd.

Questions for Discussion

Note: At the after-work session, Leigh and Hazel lead the discussion.

1. What do you think of the environmental and safety issues? What's the relevance of the size of villages and the fact that there is only one stream in the watershed?

2. How should GreenTree present all these complications to the joint-venture client? Should such things be handled at a low level between project managers, or should the discussion be bumped up to a meeting of top-level executives? Latin American countries as well as Great Britain are places where status and class are given greater respect than in the United States. On the other hand, executives might ask subordinates for a recommendation, and without being familiar with GreenTree evidence, subordinates in Celtic Oil–Colombia Petrol might give bosses a negative recommendation.

3. Do you predict that the Colombian government will insist on protecting the environment, or will it care most about getting high revenues from the project? Is there a way to present these two concerns simultaneously?

4. Leigh mentioned that there are always three things to consider: intentions, effects, and standards or ideals. What are the relevant intentions, effects, and standards or ideals in locating the CPF?

5. Should environmental risks in the CPF be presented to the joint-venture client along with risks in the gathering pipeline and wells?

6. If GreenTree recommends cutting down jungle to put through a pipeline, how will the company most likely keep the jungle from growing back? Use defoliants? Maintenance crews? What should GreenTree bring up, if anything, about the environmental risks where the pipeline goes through the mountains? This isn't GreenTree's part of the project.

7. Should GreenTree write a Request for Design Change Memo to address prevention of erosion and destabilizing of the soil? Should all the environmental issues be addressed in a single memo, or should several memos be prepared?

8. How should the competing factors be weighted in Hazel's report on guerrillas, pollution, and recreation for the troops? Where should Hazel recommend putting a fence?

Which alternative layout should Hazel recommend? What would the clients, Colombia Petrol and Celtic Oil, care about?

9. What position could GreenTree take? What strategy should GreenTree take with the client? With Berber Engineering? How can the communication be managed to accomplish GreenTree's goal?

Writing Assignment

After the discussion, Hazel will use notes from the session to write an analysis of the fence-placement issue in a memo to her supervisor, Devicka Persault. If your instructor directs, write this memo and turn it in to the instructor. Use the first paragraph to summarize and the body of the memo for specific issues and details. Include a recommendation.

Additional References: Issues Relevant to the Case

Safety, Multinational Companies, and Platform Disaster

American Petroleum Institute. (1998). *Recommended practice for analysis, design, installation, and testing of basic surface safety systems for offshore production platforms* (API Recommended Practice 14C). Available Internet: http://www.api.org/programs_services/newpubs/html/14c.htm.

West, H. H., Mannan, M. S., Danna, R., & Stafford, E. M. (1998). Make plants safer with a proper management of change program. *Chemical Engineering Progress, 94*(6), 25–36.

Newspaper articles from the *Houston Chronicle* about complex interactions between multinational companies and countries, plus articles on safety rules and the Piper Alpha Disaster are available at the Houston Chronicle Interactive site: *http://www.chron.com*. The Houston Chronicle Interactive site requires users to register, but there is no charge.

Anatomy of an oil spill [videorecording] / a co-production of Oregon Public Broadcasting and Frontline. Alexandria, Va : PBS Video, c1990. VHS. "A presentation of KCTD/Seattle, WNET/New York, WPBT/Miami, WTVS/Detroit, and WGBH/Boston."

"Exxon Valdez" oil spill: report together with additional views (to accompany S. 711). United States. Congress. Senate. Committee of Energy and Natural Resources. Washington, D.C.: U.S. G.P.O., 1999

Fiery tragedy in North Sea/Rig: workers had two choices: certain death or likely death. (1988, July 9). *Houston Chronicle* [On-line]. Available: http://www.chron.com/.

Focus: International/Mobil set to drill in Peruvian jungle/Government must give final OK. (1996, July 18). *Houston Chronicle* [On-line]. Available: http://www.chron.com/.

Hazardous duty/Oil field disasters common in North Sea. (1988, July 7). *Houston Chronicle* [On-line]. Available: http://www.chron.com/.

Lawyer wants rig blast trial in Texas. (1988, July 16). *Houston Chronicle* [On-line]. Available: http://www.chron.com/.

Lost at Sea/Offshore Risks/Safety concerns rise with return of oil, gas boom. (1996, December 22). *Houston Chronicle* [On-line]. Available: http://www.chron.com/.

North Sea blast prompts calls for safety. (1988, July 9). *Houston Chronicle* [On-line]. Available: http://www.chron.com/.

Offshore rig's safety apathy gone/1988 blast catalyst for host of rules. (1992, November 29). *Houston Chronicle* [On-line]. Available: http://www.chron.com/.

Oil platform blast may cost $1 billion. (1988, July 9). *Houston Chronicle* [On-line]. Available: http://www.chron.com/.

Oil prices plunge; panic buying eases. (1988, July 9). *Houston Chronicle* [On-line]. Available: http://www.chron.com/.

Oil prices shoot up/ Platform blast hikes North Sea crude blast. (1988, July 8). *Houston Chronicle* [On-line]. Available: http://www.chron.com/.

Oil rig officials deny gas leak warnings were ignored. (1988, July 12). *Houston Chronicle* [On-line]. Available: http://www.chron.com/.

Oil rig rescue team abandons hope for 149. (1988, July 8). *Houston Chronicle* [On-line]. Available: http://www.chron.com/.

Red Adair assesses damage to platform. (1988, July 10). *Houston Chronicle* [On-line]. Available: http://www.chron.com/.

Shattered lives/Families try to cope with tragedy. (1988, July 10). *Houston Chronicle* [On-line]. Available: http://www.chron.com/.

Up to 164 feared killed in North Sea oil rig blast. (1988, July 8). *Houston Chronicle* [On-line]. Available: http://www.chron.com/.

Culture

Barnlund, D.C. (1989). *Communicative strategies of Japanese and Americans: Images and realities.* Belmont, CA: Wadsworth.

Driskill, L., & Tebeaux, E. (1999). Culture and the shape of rhetoric: Protocols of international document design. In C. Lovitt & D. Goswami (Eds.). *Redefining professional communication as an international discipline.* New York: Baywood Press.

Hoecklin, L. (1995). *Managing cultural differences: Strategies for competitive advantage.* Wokingham, England: Addison-Wesley.

Hofstede, G. (1983). National cultures in four dimensions. *International studies of management and organizations, 13,* 46–74.

Hofstede, G. (1984). *Culture's consequences.* Thousand Oaks, CA: Sage.

Hofstede, G. (1991). *Cultures and organizations: Software of the mind.* London: McGraw-Hill.

Mead, R. (1990). *Cross-cultural management communication.* New York: Wiley.

O'Hara-Devereaux, M., & Johansen, R. (1994). *Globalwork: Bridging distance, culture, and time.* San Francisco: Jossey-Bass.

Trompenaars, F. (1993). *Riding the waves of culture.* London: Economist Books.

Ethics

Belkin, L. (1993). *First, do no harm.* New York: Ballantine.

Colby, A. & Kohlberg, L. in collaboration with Abrahami, A., et al. (1987). *The measurement of moral judgment.* New York: Cambridge University Press.

Davis, M. (1998). *Thinking like an engineer: Studies in the ethics of a profession.* New York: Oxford University Press.

Pinkus, R., et al. (1996). *Engineering ethics: Balancing cost, schedule, and risk—lessons learned from the Space Shuttle.* New York: Cambridge University Press.

Schlossberger, E. (1993). *The ethical engineer.* Philadelphia: Temple University Press.

Unger, S. H. (1994). *Controlling technology: Ethics and the responsible engineer.* (2nd ed.). New York: Wiley.

Vesilind, P., & Gunn, A. S. (1998). *Engineering, ethics, and the environment.* New York: Cambridge University Press.

Whitbeck, C. (1998). *Ethics in engineering practice and research.* New York: Cambridge University Press.

Communicating the Risks of Natural Hazards:

The World-at-Large is at Stake

NANCY L. HOFT
Michigan Technological University

Abstract: This case is a true and ongoing story containing personal, scientific, and reference data that was gathered by the author and two faculty members from Michigan Technological University, who traveled to Guatemala to study volcanic hazard communication efforts, specifically those regarding the Santa María volcano. This case study tells the story of the field trip to this land of contrasts and its broader context in a United Nations' program called the Decade Volcano and in the global issues that volcanic hazard communication raises. The central question in this case study is what can international technical communicators contribute to this complex, disturbing, and simultaneously local and global tale.

Note: With the generous assistance of two faculty members at Michigan Technological University (Dr. William Rose, Jr. and Dr. Ciro Sandoval) in Houghton, Michigan, the author traveled to Guatemala from November 22 to November 28, 1998, on a grant to Michigan Technological University from the U.S. National Science Foundation, Office of International Programs.

October 24, 1902 marked the beginning of "one of the ten largest historic eruptions in the world" (Rose, 1972). This eruption produced 10^3 km of volcanic debris—enough to cover an area approximately ten times the size of Guatemala with 1 cm of ash, or enough to cover all of Guatemala with 10 cm of ash. It originated from Santa María, which as a result became "the most notorious volcano in Central

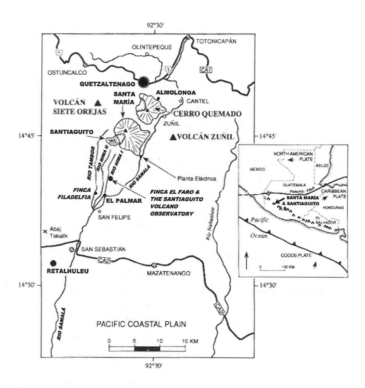

FIGURE 12.1   Map of Guatemala that features many of the places described in this case study

America" (Bennett et al., 1992). The volcano Santa María (latitude: 14.758 N, longitude: 091.548 W) is located in southwestern Guatemala, near the country's second-largest city, Quezaltenango, about 105 kilometers or 65 miles northwest of Guatemala City (see Figure 13.1). A series of earthquakes shook southwestern Guatemala, Belize, Nicaragua, El Salvador, and Mexico in the ten months preceding the October 24 eruption, foretelling the disastrous event to come. One of the earthquakes caused a Pacific tidal wave, which killed more than 150 people in El Salvador. Although documentation about the 1902 eruption is not complete, since most witnesses died in it, it suggests that more than 5000 people died from one or more related natural disasters, and several villages in Central America were destroyed or heavily damaged. The volcanic debris is known to have caused worldwide atmospheric effects. Significant amounts of ash fell as far away as Acapulco, Mexico (approximately 900 kilometers or 559 miles away). Even San Francisco, California (approximately 4000 kilometers or 2,485 miles away), reported a fine white ash falling in a light rain on January 25, 1903, which is believed to have originated from Santa María. The damage to coffee *fincas* (the Spanish word for *plantations*) in Guatemala is estimated to have been in the millions of U.S. dollars.

Background for the Case

A Trip to Santa María: Gathering Data on the Progress of Volcanic Hazard Communication in Guatemala

I arrived in Guatemala on Sunday, November 22, 1998, with travel companions, Dr. William Rose, Jr., and Dr. Ciro Sandoval. Rose is a volcanologist and professor at Michigan Technological University (MTU) who is known throughout the world for his thirty years of research about Santa María. Sandoval is an associate professor at MTU; he teaches courses in Spanish, intercultural communication, and comparative studies. I have worked as a technical communicator for over fifteen years with a specialty in international technical communication, and I am now a doctoral student in the Rhetoric and Technical Communication program at MTU. In short, we comprised an interdisciplinary team with a shared interest in volcanic hazard communication.

We had just spent six days traveling throughout southeastern El Salvador, where we met with various people from the government, universities, and the private sector, as well as with villagers in remote areas that flanked active volcanoes, to discuss national volcanic hazard communication efforts. The timing of our visit was disturbingly serendipitous. From October 22 to November 6, 1998, Hurricane Mitch—a Category 5 hurricane and the third deadliest on record—ravaged Central America with winds at 155–180 mph, causing terrible flooding, mud flows, and landslides. (Figures 12.2, 12.3, and 12.4 offer glimpses of the flooding damage in Guatemala). The estimated amount in U.S. dollars to rebuild Central America after Hurricane Mitch was $4 billion, and the estimated death toll was over 10,000 people. Needless to say, our reception in both countries was warm, since national interests in natural hazard communication, an umbrella category within which volcanic hazard communication falls, was quite pronounced.

We were met at the airport by Mr. Otoniel Matías, the section chief of volcanology at the Instituti Nacional de Sismología, Vulcanología, Meteorología e Hidrología (INSIVUMEH), a Guatemalan government agency that is similar to the U.S. Geological Survey. Rose and Sandoval organized this workshop. Matías is the only professional volcanologist in Guatemala, which is home to seven very active volcanoes. He was our guide for the next six days.

Our mission in Guatemala was to follow up on the four recommendations made in 1993 by seventy-three professionals representing thirteen countries at the Santa María Volcanic Hazard Workshop. The four recommendations were:

1. Advanced training should be offered to Guatemalan personnel to lead and maintain continuous monitoring and hazard awareness from the local perspective.
2. Trained Guatemalan personnel must receive effective support from Guatemala. Support includes, but should not be limited to, jeeps, gasoline, and a per

FIGURE 12.2   Picture shows where the river came up and took everything within a mile of its usual course.

Photo courtesy of USAID.

FIGURE 12.3   Riverbed in Guatemala.
Note the land that has been scraped away by the tremendous amount of water that rushed through this channel.

Photo courtesy of USAID.

FIGURE 12.4   Repaired bridge and swollen river underneath

Photo courtesy of USAID.

diem and salary for trained surveillance personnel. If this support is not consistent, international collaboration will be extremely limited.

3. Guatemalan agencies (INSIVUMEH, local universities, and so on) should collaborate. This collaboration should be strengthened and encouraged.

4. The CEPREDENAC organization, a Guatemalan governmental agency, should fund a volcano surveillance program for the region that should be used to help support volcano surveillance at Santa María. The program should include instrumentation and training.

What we found was encouraging. Three active volcanoes in Guatemala—Santa María, Fuego, and Pacaya—each receive regular observations to develop complete data sets of complex volcanic information. INSIVUMEH installed volcanic monitoring equipment around each of these volcanoes. Some data are sent in real time to the INSIVUMEH headquarters in Guatemala City, and other data are collected by observers who have been trained by INSIVUMEH personnel for this purpose. In addition, INSIVUMEH receives daily radio contact from these volcano observers.

A Trek through Finca El Faro

We met one of these specially trained observers at the Santa María Volcano Observatory on a walk we took through a large finca called El Faro, which offered us a close view of the many daily eruptions from Santiaguito. Santiaguito is a small volcano that has grown out of the southwest flank of Santa María. It has been active since 1922.

In addition to meeting with the observer, we were here to learn more about the recent changes to Santiaguito's behavior. These changes suggest to volcanologists like Rose that the Santiaguito area is quickly ceasing to be a safe place to live. The volcano is shedding materials in a nearby valley above *finca* El Faro, a behavior that, in addition to other volcanic and environmental observations, suggests the probability of future mud flows. *Finca* El Faro, like several properties close to Santiaguito, is in the path of imminent destruction.

The observer lives in the area and had worked in the military before being invited to join INSIVUMEH. He keeps a notebook of all of his careful observations of volcanic activity, noting sounds, smells, changes to the shape of the volcano, and so on. His other role is volcanic hazard communication. Since he lives in this area, he knows many of the people: the owner of the *finca* and his family and relatives as well as many of the people who work at the *finca* picking the coffee beans that are so important to Guatemala's economy. But more importantly, the people know him. The personal networks people build in Guatemala, as in many Latin American countries, are as complex as they are essential to survival and credibility. The observer told us about the volcanic behavior of Santiaguito speaking not only from his trained memory, but also sharing anecdotes from the people of this *finca* who knew, understood, and respected his role there.

The people of El Faro also know the land as they know their own families; changes are noticed and are shared and compared in the course of casual conversations. The observer, after all, is there essentially to help protect their families, their possessions, their livestock, and their land. He has won their trust and, in turn, helps educate people on what to look for that might indicate danger. He is, in many ways, a technical communicator.

One of the formidable challenges that this observer and others like him continue to face in communicating volcanic hazards is that the current population thinks of the Santiaguito area as a safe and relatively profitable place to live. Despite its seventy-seven years of constant volcanic activity, Santiaguito has been a safe place to live. The volcanic materials from the 1902 eruption have long been converted to rich volcanic soil that makes employment and economic opportunities like *finca* El Faro possible. Some people have lived here for many years, and others migrate into the area when there is work, such as picking coffee beans. To the local population, both fixed and migratory, the Santiaguito area means work. People do not really understand the potential volcanic hazards. They have not lived long enough to see all the normal behavior of a volcano—"sleep lots, then wake up," as Rose puts it—that occurs in geologic time, which might span decades or even centuries.

The observer also learns from INSIVUMEH personnel the possible evacuation strategies in the event of an eruption or other natural disaster, like the flooding and mud flows that resulted from Hurricane Mitch. And, as we were about to learn firsthand, recent behavioral changes to Santiaguito strongly suggest that the area is rapidly becoming unsafe. The observer's knowledge of the land, the people, and

Guatemala's natural-hazard mitigation strategies increase his value to the country and to the people of El Faro and the surrounding area.

To get to a lookout area, we had to cross the Rio Nima I on a wide swing bridge that had scars from severe flooding and erosion. I was told that we would normally drive over this bridge and up and through the *finca* to our final destination, a lookout about five miles away at an altitude of 2000 meters or 6561 feet. However, the flooding from Hurricane Mitch had wiped out the previous swing bridge, and the newly erected bridge was not deemed safe enough to support the weight of our truck. The five-mile drive became a five-mile trek. As I walked across the bridge, I could see, thirty feet down, the massive boulders that Santiaguito had spit out and that were carried to this point by a combination of gravity and water from the heavy rains running down the sides of this and several other steep mountains. And to remind me of Hurricane Mitch, I watched a tall tree sweep around a bend upstream, manage to avoid being lodged between thousands of rocks, and slip underneath my feet and bounce downstream only seconds later.

On the other side of the bridge, men and their sons loaded large pieces of wood into bound piles, which they carried across the bridge load by load by load on their backs to dump into the bed of a pickup truck. The wood, most likely, was firewood to provide light, heat, building material, and cooking fuel to the many homes here, few if any of which had electricity. Firewood is precious, and it is one of the few benefits (if it is correct to call them benefits) of a hurricane that there is a lot of potential firewood floating in the river and hidden in the jungle.

The day was hot and humid, and the air was thinning as we climbed up the trail. Women dressed in traditional Mayan garb, their children, and old men and women picked bright red berries from the coffee plants. We occasionally saw groups of men rebuilding part of the trail, most of which is packed volcanic rock from the 1902 eruption, and part of which is cobblestone to prevent further erosion from heavy rains. The trail also serves as a road up the mountain, and is probably used to truck fifty pound bags filled with ripe coffee beans. At one point, the trail narrowed. Around me steep hills were covered with coffee plants and thick forestation. A waterfall was visible in the distance. Behind me, I could see forever, it seemed. Fields of sugar cane, coffee plantations, and other signs of a healthy agricultural region quilted the landscape. If it had been less hazy, I might have been able to see the ocean.

Because it was hot and humid and the air was thin, I had to walk slowly. I was not used to this environment. Matías left the others and joined me as I lumbered along. We spoke in French, since I could not speak Spanish and he was more comfortable with French than with English. Suddenly, he told me to stop and to listen. I heard a deep, resonant rumble. *"Qu'est-ce que c'est?"* I asked. It was the voice of Santiaguito, Matías explained. Looking around again and a little more than spooked, I realized that there was no place to run, no escape, and I was too tired anyway. Matías laughed at me, explaining that Santiaguito talked a lot and that there was no danger now.

A bit farther up the trail, Matías stopped to point out four stone crosses. They were there in memory of four people who had died from a 1991 eruption of Santiaguito. The eruption caused a pyroclastic flow, the most deadly of all volcanic hazards:

> *High-speed avalanches of hot ash, rock fragments, and gas can move down the sides of a volcano during explosive eruptions or when the steep side of a growing lava dome collapses and breaks apart. These pyroclastic flows can be as hot as 1,500°F and move at speeds of 100 to 150 miles per hour. Such flows tend to follow valleys and are capable of knocking down and burning everything in their paths. Lower-density pyroclastic flows, called pyroclastic surges, can easily overflow ridges hundreds of feet high.*
>
> *The climactic eruption of Mount St. Helens on May 18, 1980, generated a series of explosions that formed a huge pyroclastic surge. This so-called "lateral blast" destroyed an area of 230 square miles. Trees 6 feet in diameter were mowed down like blades of grass as far as 15 miles from the volcano. (Meyers et al., 1997)*

The others in our group—Sandoval, a geology graduate student from MTU, and the observer—were now far ahead of us. Rose was in sight, but much farther along. It started to rain softly for the first fifty yards or so, and then turned quickly into a heavy downpour. This part of Guatemala gets 7 meters or 275 inches of rain a year. We were so high up the mountain that you could almost touch the bottoms of the rain clouds, which would have been more enjoyable had it not been for the thunder and lightning. Rose and I decided to turn back, and Matías went ahead to tell the others of our plans. As we began our descent, we had to tread carefully on the fallen leaves and branches, which often covered trenches caused from rains like this one. The cobblestone-like covering was slippery with decaying vegetation.

We were soaked by the time we reached the halfway point. The sloshing sound our hiking boots made each time we took a step was almost louder than the rain hitting the big, waxy leaves of the trees above our heads. What began as light runoff was now gushing down the trail, crisscrossing and following the slope of the land. Some runoff was three and four inches deep. By the time we reached the swing bridge an hour or so later, we noticed that Rio Nima I had swelled considerably, carrying more volcanic debris and vegetation downstream. The same men and boys we had seen carrying firewood over the bridge were now comfortably lounging under a tarp, waiting for the rain to subside so that they could finish moving their firewood. They invited us out of the rain to await our colleagues, who arrived about forty-five minutes later looking silly under the huge and edible tropical leaves they had cut to use as umbrellas.

A Visit to El Palmar

We decided to visit the town of El Palmar next, since it was close by and would offer us a view of Rio Nima I farther downstream. Two older men climbed into the back of the INSIVUMEH pickup truck to get a ride home, a common practice throughout all of Central America, since many people who live in rural areas cannot afford to buy a truck or a car. The road was very rough and flooded in several spots. The truck was in four-wheel drive the entire way.

As we approached the outskirts of the town, we drove past a sign with the government seal on it, which read that the government had condemned the area and that people should not be living there. Yet, there were some buildings with laundry hanging from rope stretched between trees, an occasional dog, and some doorways where a few people gathered, talking and staring cautiously at the government seal on Matías's truck.

We drove a bit farther into the town and parked the truck. Wet, cold, and miserable, I wasn't sure whether I was up for another walk. But I got out of the truck curious to know why the government sign had been posted. We walked toward the Rio Nima I and entered a disturbing space. Walls of buildings stuck out of the ground with no roofs or windows or any sign of habitation. Their floors were filled with a fine pumice up to the window ledges, which must have been two or three feet above the floors. A deep chasm was all that I could see of the Rio Nima I. As I approached the edge of the chasm, amidst warnings in Spanish from the two older men, I cautiously peered over and could see nothing. I could only hear the sound of a very strong river current about fifty feet below. I looked to my right and saw half of a church with a cross still atop it on one side

FIGURE 12.5   The streets of El Palmar. November 1998.

Photo courtesy of William Rose.

of the chasm, and the other half on my side. It was very still and the rain had finally stopped (see Figure 12.5).

I met up with Rose, and asked what had happened here. About twenty years ago, the Rio Nima I began to flood the town (see Figure 12.6). Volcanic debris that collects on the rim and sides of Santiaguito is carried down by all the rain this area receives each year. Over time, the volcanic debris fills the riverbed, forcing the water to overflow the banks and follow the path that gravity imposes. In addition, Rio Nima I is at a much higher elevation than a neighboring river, Rio Samal. When the Rio Nima I floods, its waters go downhill and meet those of Rio Samal (see Figure 12.7). The result of more than twenty years of heavy rains, continued volcanic activity, loose pumice, and no monetary or equipment resources to empty the riverbeds of the debris caused the sight before me (see Figure 12.8). El Palmar is now just a memory for those, like Rose, who had been there when it was filled with life.

El Palmar offers some lessons about natural hazard communication. Despite experiencing twenty years of continued environmental problems, the people of El Palmar tended to stay. Unlike *finca* El Faro, a place of seasonal economic activity

FIGURE 12.6 The town of El Palmar in 1983. The surface of the Rio Nima I was in the distance. In 1998, the surface of the Rio Nima I was fifty feet below this elevation.

Photo courtesy of William Rose.

FIGURE 12.7   Ariel view of El Palmar seen from the southeast. November 1998.

Photo courtesy of William Rose.

that tended to attract migrant workers, the town of El Palmar had a mostly sedentary population and all the goods and services to support and maintain it. Rose explains the irony: "People hate to leave a place they have lived for generations, and they will stay even if there is a lot of risk and inconvenience. During the twenty years things got worse generally, but it was just the past rainy season (May-September 1998) which really was the final *coup de grace.*" Before May 1998, there were always parts of the town that still seemed normal, and some stores were open.

Rose also explained another complication in the El Palmar situation. El Palmar is on the edge of a vast area along the Rio Nima II, which has remained undeveloped because of high volcanic risk. However, such places are a magnet to people who own no or very little land. They can herd goats, collect wood, and participate in the many seasonal and chance labor opportunities that the area affords.

We returned to the truck. Complaining about our discomfort seemed too trite after visiting El Palmar. We drove for a few more miles and parted from our two traveling companions.

To return to our hotel in Quezaltenango, we had to drive through some large Mayan towns, such as the town of Almolonga, where people have electricity and may have running water. These luxuries are not available to many people in the country. People also own vehicles. The thick traffic through the narrow stone streets often came to a standstill for five, ten, and twenty minutes while trucks and cars stopped to give passersby a lift or to just squeeze through a tiny street. The smell

FIGURE 12.8 **Santa María with the debris-choked Río Samalá in the foreground. View from San Sebastian. November 1998.**

Photo courtesy of William Rose.

of carbon monoxide was almost overwhelming. There are no emissions standards in Guatemala, and diesel fuel runs many a bus and truck. Women wore intensely colorful and beautifully embroidered skirts and tops and often had woven baskets that were filled with corn, beans, and other food balanced on their heads. The only distinguishing feature of the men was that most wore cowboy hats and looked pretty plain next to their wives and daughters. Storefronts provided glimpses of women making and heating tortillas. Men leaned against the outside walls of buildings, talking and watching all the activity, searching for something familiar.

Quezaltenango is a large city of 246,000 people, but its stunning colonial architecture is laid out like a maze. We drove down narrow streets that intersected with others, surrounded by buildings that were set close to the road. Pedestrians and bicyclists sometimes took refuge in doorways to avoid getting hit by a vehicle driving on the sidewalk as it made way for a vehicle coming from the opposite direction.

Meeting the Governor

We headed into the city of Retalhuleu the next morning, where we met with the governor of this department, which is similar to a state in the United States. The governor wore a buttoned, collared shirt that was open from the neck to the middle of his chest; his sleeves were rolled up. His shoes were worn, but his fingernails were immaculate, a sign of status among men in this part of the world. Clean and manicured hands separate those who work the land from those who do not. The governor's office was plain, dark, and dirty, and had floor-to-ceiling windows that were at street level. While we were sitting in the office, a funeral procession passed less than ten feet away from the open windows; the music blaring from one of the cars made conversation difficult. On the walls hung photographs of various Guatemalan leaders, including the president of Guatemala. The governor wore a beeper and carried a cellular phone, which are symbols of his status in urban Guatemala. There was no computer.

After Rose and Matías explained our purpose and interests, the governor talked to us about Hurricane Mitch and various government actions toward natural hazard mitigation. The government had relocated the people of El Palmar. To encourage people to leave, the government cut off all services to the area, including electricity. However, the people were starting to move back to El Palmar despite the glaring evidence of continued and growing danger and the stark living conditions. They figured that, in the event of another natural disaster, the government would relocate them again, allowing them to accumulate more land—for free—from the government. And yet, as Rose had explained, people have other excellent reasons for wanting to be in the hazard zones. From the rich volcanic soil, the consequent economic opportunities, and the complex, tight network of relationships, El Palmar was home, both economically and emotionally.

As I considered what I had seen so far in my visit to Guatemala, from the huge and profitable *fincas* to the gated, fenced, and machine-gun patrolled mansions in Guatemala City, I realized that land was at the heart of the conception of wealth and power in Guatemala. An article in *Harvard Magazine* offers this glimpse into the glaring economic divide in Guatemala:

> Today, 2 percent of the population still owns 67 percent of the land, a figure that grows more skewed over time. . . . The poverty line is so sweepingly drawn, according to a 1990 UNICEF report, that it encompasses 86 percent of the population, while coffee, bananas, and opportunities to exploit cheap labor boost the other 14 percent well into prosperity. (p. 50)

Santa María, Santiaguito, and other active volcanoes in Guatemala make this economic system possible. Like all active volcanoes, Santa María and Santiaguito are good for the earth and even good for people, despite their deadly results and influence on other natural hazards, like the flooding of El Palmar. Volcanic eruptions bring minerals and nutrients up from the inside of the earth in the form of ash and lava and related volcanic products. These volcanic products eventually break down and form a rich soil that is excellent for crops. In Guatemala, agriculture is the occupation of 58 percent of the labor force. Santa María and Santiaguito are no exception. The south side of Santa María, for example, is home to many plantations that produce coffee, cardamom, rubber, and sugar cane, for example. These plantations provide jobs for many thousands of indigenous people and produce export crops that bring income to the country. Where there is work, there is a dense population. There are more than 300,000 people in the vicinity of Santa María. There are also several significant resource investments, which include a major geothermal power facility and a hydropower facility.

Rose offered a preliminary geological explanation of what we saw at *finca* El Faro and at El Palmar, adding that we would like to see more to better understand the behavior of the Santiaguito and its effects on the flooding in the area. Matías explained how the chief of INSIVUMEH was to arrange for us to tour the area via helicopter. He asked the governor to see if he could assist with these arrangements. Given the governor's political status and connection with the military and the government, Matías, who also worked for the government, took advantage of the complex people network. The governor immediately called the local army training base, where young men and women learn to fly airplanes and helicopters. When he powered off his cellular phone, he explained that the weather continued to be good and that we could tour the area by helicopter that afternoon or the following morning. Matías was to call the army training base an hour or so later to confirm our plans. After a cordial and formal goodbye, we left the governor's office excited about the tour, but apprehensive about the weather and any last minute change-of-heart that the army commanders might have about being our hosts.

After eating a traditional Guatemalan breakfast of scrambled eggs, beans, fried plantains, and tortillas in a local restaurant, Matías went to make the phone call, and we strolled around the town taking pictures and watching the many vendors in the central park. Open air markets abound in Central America, especially in the large cities. Matías returned, explaining that we would need to be at the military training base at 8:00 the next morning, when, depending on weather, we would be airborne. We decided to spend the day doing more touring of the flooded areas.

Bridge-Building at **Finca** *Filadelfia*

We headed to *Finca* Filadelfia, another large coffee plantation. *Finca* Filadelfia, like El Palmar, had experienced significant flooding recently, and like El Palmar, this had been going on for many years as a result of Santiaguito's activities. We drove to the gated entrance of the *finca* and were met by an armed guard whose gaze moved from the government seal on Matías's truck to our faces several times while Matías requested permission to enter. Having said very little during Matías's introduction, the guard motioned with his head that we could proceed. We moved on and parked the truck near a large barn-like building. In the distance was the Rio Tambor, where a small front-end loader was straining to move a massive boulder. About a dozen men surrounded the scene. Some were in the river, moving large rocks by hand. Others stood on the banks, watching the man running the front-end loader. The Rio Tambor, we learned, had flooded and destroyed a small bridge the night before, during the same rainstorm we experienced at *finca* El Faro. These men were moving rocks in the riverbed to divert the current and hopefully reduce the amount of erosion and flooding.

About a hundred yards upstream, another group of men were building another bridge (see Figure 12.9). Matías explained that we wanted to tour the *finca* to study the causes and effects of flooding. The men still had another three or four feet of panels to attach so that we could cross. They quickly tacked down some rough boards and we thanked them as we walked to the other side.

We walked for about a mile along the edge of the Rio Tambor and through a thick forest of coffee plants with ripe red berries. We reached a large opening and saw a broad vista of the aftermath of many years of flooding. The Rio Tambor was tame now, but we could see that it had spread across a lot of terrain, decimating many acres that could not be reclaimed without significant investment and effort. We could see Santa María upstream in the distance.

We rounded a bend in the river. Before us men, old and young, most working alone, swung sledgehammers against the rocky debris that Rio Tambor left behind. They were crushing the stone to make gravel, which they could sell or barter for whatever their families needed. This was but one of the many chance economic opportunities that the Santa María area offered. Their gravel piles were three or four feet high on average, indicating a productive and exhausting day of manual labor. We guessed that these men returned to this site day after day to work the rock.

FIGURE 12.9   Rapidly constructed temporary foot bridge over the Rio Tambor, *Finca* Filadelfia. November 1998.

Photo courtesy of William Rose.

Back across the Rio Tambor, we headed farther upstream, to a small village of maybe twenty families, most of whom seemed related. We approached a one-room dwelling made of adobe that had window openings, but no windows. The dwelling's backyard had a small covered patio. Between the support posts for the roof of the patio swung a hammock on which a man rested reading an old, battered book. Rose, Matías, and Sandoval spoke with the man and his wife, inquiring about the behavior of the river during and after Hurricane Mitch. Around us and barely touching the boundary of the patio was the Rio Tambor. The flood waters had not withdrawn here yet, although the water was shallow and trees and small islands poked up through it. A dog timidly trotted across the strong current to a nearby island. Two boys played in the mud nearby, naked and loving every minute of getting dirty. Clearly, no one here was planning to relocate. This was home.

The Helicopter Ride

We were in the truck by 6:00 A.M. the next morning to head to the military training base outside of Retalhuleu. We stopped at an abandoned church along the highway to gaze at Santiaguito. Steam rose in big puffs from its mouth, usually followed by steaming rockfalls along its sides. There were no other clouds in the sky, and the wind was calm. Weather would not be a deterrent to our tour.

The entrance to the army training camp was gated, and there were three or four uniformed and armed recruits in a small security shed. Two recruits approached the truck. It took Matías quite a while to explain the purpose of our visit. This guard asked many questions and took notes, while the other guard walked around the truck. The guard with the clipboard eventually returned to the security shed and radioed our arrival information to the main building. A few moments later, he returned to the truck and gave us specific instructions on where to drive and park the truck. The other guard jumped into the bed of the truck as the gate opened.

The guard escorted us to the main building, where we were met by other personnel who explained the procedure that we would follow that morning. We were escorted to the airstrip by another young recruit who spoke perfect American English. Our helicopter was being checked by the copilot and the communications person. The helicopter was American made (see Figure 12.10). While we waited for the pilot to arrive, we spoke with more recruits. All of them spoke excellent American English, and were very polite and curious about our purpose. Their flight training forbade them to fly within a certain distance of any volcano because of the danger of a sudden release of dense ash clouds that have downed more than one aircraft. When the pilot arrived, I noticed that he was much older than the others and was treated with formal military respect. Rose and Matías reviewed our purpose and suggested a route to follow, as both of them had taken aerial tours through this area in the past.

We climbed into the helicopter and sat on seats made of tattered cloth panels that were stretched across metal-tube framing. The communications person was the last to climb in. He secured the helicopter's two long sliding doors so that they would stay open during our tour. Rose and Matías had requested this so that we

FIGURE 12.10   **Guatemalan army helicopter used in aerial survey of volcanic hazards. Our escort (left), copilot (center), and pilot (right) deplaning after our tour. November 1998.**

Photo courtesy of William Rose.

could take photographs. I quickly moved to a middle seat, since there were few seats with harnesses to strap myself in.

Moments later, we heard the deep, pulsating rhythm and whine of the blades above. With the doors open, the sound was deafening. We waved to the recruits on the ground and began to ascend. I kept my eyes glued on the control panel of the helicopter. I finally spotted a gauge on the instrument panel that indicated how level we were. We listed about thirty or forty degrees as we quickly veered toward Santa María and Santiaguito.

The land was mostly flat and rose abruptly as we got closer to the volcanoes. Every hue of green was represented here. The pilot flew low to the ground, giving us ample opportunity to see the flooding that was all around this area. He followed the rivers. I could see men breaking rock where the water had receded. Small villages were often hard to spot, since they were scattered and hidden beneath the jungle canopy. More common were isolated single-family, one-room dwellings made of corrugated metal, adobe, and various combinations of scrap materials, both manmade and organic. Fields of sugar cane were everywhere.

We flew over El Palmar and *finca* Filadelfia. From our elevation, it was easy to see how the flooding related to the daily eruptions of Santiaguito. About five rivers emanate from this area. Large gray-brown areas of rocks filled the riverbeds closest to the volcanoes, while flooding still existed further downstream. This pattern of volcanic hazards is common: mud flows tend to occur upstream (*finca* El Faro and El Palmar), while flooding tends to occur farther downstream (*finca* Filadelfia). (See Figure 12.11.)

When we reached Santiaguito, we were at an altitude of over 10,000 feet. The pilot proceeded cautiously. Suddenly, Santiaguito threw out a large puff of vapor, and steaming rocks teemed down its sides towards the rivers below (see Figure 12.12). Even our stoic pilot seemed awed. We rounded Santiaguito and Santa María along their eastern flanks and met a strong air current that shook the helicopter. Within seconds, the instrument panel indicated that we were level once again. We all looked at the pilot with relief.

We headed back and retraced our path at a high altitude and an accelerated speed. We could see the Pacific coast in the distance. Haze was building, as were clouds that showed promise of a typical tropical afternoon storm. We set down on the helipad and walked to Matías's truck. The pilot and copilot joined us, and after our many thanks for a fulfilling and safe journey, we headed out to get some breakfast.

The helicopter tour really put things in perspective for me. Whenever Santiaguito or Santa María erupt in a major way (like the 1902 eruption), which Rose and

FIGURE 12.11   **Aerial view of the Rio Nima I (left) and Rio Nima II valleys, looking south. El Palmar is located at the left edge of the photo. November 1998.**

Photo courtesy of William Rose.

FIGURE 12.12   Aerial view, looking west, of the Santiaguito eruption we witnessed on the helicopter tour. November 1998.

Photo courtesy of William Rose.

other volcanologists believe will happen in our lifetimes, the effect on Guatemala will be profound. Many investments have been made in this region since and because of the 1902 eruption of Santa María. Seeing the geography of this area from the air, and remembering the realities of transportation here, I could not imagine the complexities of evacuation.

Getting Otoniel Matías Official Credentials

The remainder of our trip included more stops to see flooding. Matías knew many of the people in these areas, and he took these opportunities to gather more data on the behavior and effects of flooding and volcanic activity. He also took the opportunity to learn as much as possible from Rose, asking several questions about geology, instrumentation for studying volcanoes, seminars and research on the topic that might increase his knowledge, and so on. Matías's continued education was paramount to volcanic hazard communication in Guatemala, and Rose shared his knowledge and professional connections liberally.

This interchange was also a follow-up to the Santa María Volcanic Hazard Workshop that Rose and Sandoval had orchestrated in 1993. The purpose of the workshop was twofold: (1) to recognize Santa María formally and proactively as a Decade

Volcano, and (2) to provide an arena in which to discuss various interdisciplinary aspects of volcanic hazard mitigation, both generally about risk communication and specifically about risk communication and the Santa María volcano. At this workshop, which was held in Quetzaltenango, Rose introduced Matías to some of the most prominent volcanic researchers in the world. Through these connections, Matías had received scholarships and grants to attend courses and seminars about volcanoes in Switzerland, Hawaii, and other parts of the world. In addition to the complex office politics there, INSIVUMEH has a very limited budget for educational opportunities, even though it is in a country with many active and dangerous volcanoes.

While e-mail and the World Wide Web could offer Matías a wealth of affordable educational opportunities and resources, his access to these is strictly controlled and therefore very limited. In many Latin American countries, knowledge is power, and placing strict limits and controls on access to knowledge, however self-defeating this might seem to U.S. sensibilities, is common practice and, to a large extent, expected by both managers and their staff. Matías does not have a telephone in his home. He owns an old computer that has no modem.

Rose had been frustrated throughout our trip as he searched for ways to give back to Guatemala, for it had given him thirty years of rich volcanic data that awarded him grants, prestige, tenure, and an impressive academic publications list. He had tried direct, official channels as well as indirect ones, such as the Santa María Volcanic Hazard Workshop, which he and Sandoval organized. The grant that funded our research trip to Guatemala was another attempt, this one focused specifically on volcanic hazard communication.

After several days, he concluded that investing in Matías was our best hope. He and Matías discussed the possibility of having Matías attend MTU to receive a master's degree in volcanology. However, Matías does not have the educational credentials that MTU requires for entrance into its graduate program. The irony here, as Rose sees it, is that Matías is in many ways highly educated, even though no formal institution, either MTU or his government employer, INSIVUMEH, officially recognizes his knowledge. As Rose would later explain to me, "Oto's eleven years in the midst of many volcanic crises and his dealings with the people affected are more valuable to volcanic hazards research than many years of academic experience. But, it doesn't help him get respect from within his own agency, because in urban Guatemala, perhaps even more than in the United States, formal degrees really count." A graduate degree would give Matías prestige that would bring him as many accolades as it would agony from inevitable office politics.

Another roadblock to this idea is monetary support. Rose, Matías, and Sandoval, who teaches Spanish at MTU, discussed the possibilities of having Matías teach Spanish courses to fund his education. Salaries at INSIVUMEH and throughout Guatemala are small and the cost of living, even in remote Houghton, Michigan, is far beyond the realm of possibilities for Matías. Although Rose has not given up on this idea, enrolling Matías in MTU's graduate school will require all of his influence as a past department chair.

Joining the conversation, the MTU graduate student offered to upgrade Matías's computer, which would cost significantly less than purchasing a new one.

Several weeks after our return to the United States, Rose sent out an e-mail announcement explaining that buying Matías a new computer—a laptop with a high-speed modem that he could take with him on field trips—was the most sensible solution. Several of us, including many researchers who had attended the Santa María Volcanic Hazard Workshop in 1983 and who had kept in contact with Matías over the years, contributed money to the cause. The laptop was delivered to Matías in February 1999 by a geology graduate student from MTU who was there to do volcanology-related field research. The delivery begins a long and knowledge-filled educational journey for Matías and its resulting volcanic hazard assistance and communication for Guatemala.

Leapfrog Technology on the PanAmerican Highway

When we left Quezaltenango, we decided to drive along the PanAmerican highway through the highlands and back to Guatemala City. This is a beautiful agricultural region of steep rolling hills covered with farmland and surrounded by volcanoes. It is also a killing field; it is where most of the military efforts against guerrilla insurgency took place during the civil war. And to add to its history, it is also where several devastating earthquakes crumbled whole cities, killing and displacing thousands of people.

Driving through villages, we saw many women in traditional Mayan garb carrying dried beans and other foodstuffs in baskets on their heads, corncobs drying in the sun on roofs of corrugated metal, and men building and repairing roads and buildings. Clusters of white calla lilies lined narrow brooks. Chickens, cows, and pigs meandered in the fields and around small dwellings. Life here was focused on basic, day-to-day survival.

I noticed that wild dogs lay alone and in seemingly regular intervals in the breakdown lane, especially on sharp inclines. Matías explained that they were there waiting for the many truckers who drive this road to throw out the remains of their breakfasts, lunches, and dinners.

At one point, we climbed a steep hill and reached a plateau of sorts. Before us was a shocking reminder of the world we were to return to in a few days: four enormous spools of fiber optic cable. Leapfrog technology, such as laying fiber optic cable for digital and voice communication, is a major part of the U.S. national export strategy for places like Guatemala, which are officially called BEMs, or Big Emerging Markets. The spools looked out-of-place and unnatural here.

CONRED: The Hurricane Busters

We returned somewhat reluctantly to the carbon monoxide, traffic, and noise of cosmopolitan Guatemala City. One of our final visits was to an important government agency called Coordinadora Nacional Para La Reduccion de Desastres (CONRED). Rose, Matías, and I met with the executive director of this agency, who was still coping with the aftermath of Hurricane Mitch and all the other hurricanes and tropical storms of 1998. Posters of various disaster-reduction strategies covered the walls. A large whiteboard showed the markings of an intense recent meeting. Maps of volcanoes and rivers had pins marking problematic areas. A large, round conference table surrounded by the most comfortable seats I had seen in Guatemala was the center of this brightly lit and activity-focused command center. It offered a sharp contrast to the office of the governor in Retalhuleu. Through the windows of this office, located in the center of a heavily guarded military airbase and compound, I could see the silhouette of Pacaya, another active volcano, against a colorful sunset.

The executive director of CONRED described the steps they were taking in response to the flooding, mud flows, and mass displacement of people. He was interrupted constantly by telephone calls, fielded by his assistant, always responding to the unknown caller with a sense of urgency and immense authority. Rose explained our purpose and described what we had seen of the flooding and volcanic activity during our week in Guatemala, while the assistant took many notes on a small notepad. The director was not surprised by Rose's observations and conclusions. He, like the director of INSIVUMEH and several others in positions of authority we had met, said that this was the best possible time for natural hazard communication efforts. He, for example, was in the midst of proposing an aggressive program that would recruit and train hundreds of young people throughout the country to work at a grassroots level and educate Guatemalans about natural hazards. He understood too well that natural hazards cannot be prevented, only mitigated. Rose produced several examples of volcanic hazard communications materials from his knapsack. One was a booklet produced in Guatemala that was geared for children. It was filled with colorful cartoons of Volcanito (see Figure 12.13), a cute and happy volcano figure that taught children about the benefits and dangers of volcanoes, as well as how to notice and respond to impending danger. The booklet also contained maps of evacuation routes and shelters throughout the country.

Rose also showed the executive director copies of booklets that we had collected in El Salvador that showed potential as a good way to communicate the risk of volcanic hazards. The booklets were geared not for children, but for their teachers. They provided technical background, many graphics and illustrations, and exercises and projects that the teachers could use in their classes. The booklets also contained references and telephone numbers so that the teachers could learn more and enlist the assistance of experts.

One booklet, for example, was about the dangers of water contamination. Water contamination is a continual problem throughout Central America. Waste management, as we had seen in both rural and outlying urban areas of El Salvador and Guatemala, usually consists of inhabitants' dumping heaps of trash on and over a precipice above a river. The river feeds the water supply farther downstream and is a source for irrigation. Natural disasters, like the flooding from Hurricane Mitch, only compound the problem of water contamination.

At the end of our meeting, the executive director reached into a box and produced T-shirts for Rose, Matías, and myself. On the front of the T-shirt is the word

**FIGURE 12.13   The Civil Defense
(CONE) in Guatemala
uses the Volcanito to
educate children about
volcanic risk.**

Photo courtesy of The Volcanic Hazards Mitigation
Group at the University of Geneva, Switzerland.

Voluntario (Spanish for *volunteer*) and a cartoon of a duck dressed in field clothes pounding the crumbling word *Mitch* with a mallet labeled *CONRED*. Above the mallet are the words *Hurricane Busters*. A fitting end to the trip.

Conclusion: Develop a Community of *Multiplicadores at All Levels*

Our data gathering complete, we spent the three-hour flight from Guatemala City to Houston discussing what we had seen and learned and, most importantly, what could we do next to communicate the risks of volcanic hazards to the people of Guatemala and to the world. Given the way people communicate in Guatemala (mostly oral communication through complex people networks drawn along stark class lines), we agreed that volcanic risk communication and consequent risk mitigation requires a grassroots approach to be successful. We were, after all, just *gringos* in this land of contrasts. We had little influence on anything or anyone, least of all on the indigenous peoples of this country who had a long historic list of reasons for distrusting strangers.

I recalled a lunchtime conversation with Sandoval and Rose many months before, during which Sandoval introduced me to a powerful word and concept in Spanish—*multiplicadores*, which means "people who spread the word in specific fields of knowledge." These are people who have status or influence in the community. As we considered our communication strengths in this situation, we realized that our existing resources and connections consist of an impressive network of volcanologists, university faculty, and students across many disciplines and in many countries, specialists within government agencies and private industry, technical communicators, and so on. All of these people are, in many ways, *multiplicadores*. Our communications strategy, then, began to focus on how to cultivate our existing network into a network of *multiplicadores* to spread the word about volcanic risk.

Multiplicadores *in the Scientific and International Communities*

Rose's and Sandoval's efforts in organizing Santa María Volcanic Hazard Workshop had succeeded in bringing international experts from all over the world to Quetzaltenango to tour the area, share ideas, and mostly to interact with local representatives from various organizations in Guatemala. The workshop was the first step in addressing the Decade Volcano program in Guatemala. The phrase *Decade Volcano* represents the response that members of the International Association of Volcanology and Chemistry of the Earth's Interior (IAVCEI) had to a 1990 United Nations effort called the International Decade for Natural Disaster Reduction (IDNDR). Here is an excerpt from an IDNDR report:

> *Two steps forward, one step back: progress in social development will be eroded if countries do not take natural disasters into account in their development planning. This was one of the key messages emerging from the recent UN-sponsored World Conference on Natural Disaster Reduction, in Yokohama, Japan, from 23 to 27 May 1994.*

Situation

- *Damage inflicted by disasters kill one million people each decade and leave millions more homeless.*
- *Economic damages from natural disasters has tripled in the last thirty years. In the 1960s, disasters cost the world an estimated $40 billion; in the 1970s, the cost was $70 billion; by the 1980s, it had risen to $120 billion.*
- *Before 1987, there was only one disaster the cost of which exceeded $1 billion in insured losses. Since 1987, however, thirteen additional such disasters have occurred (see Table 12.1).*
- *In January 1995, Japan was hit by the latest in a series of 13 major earthquakes since 1923 which have measured between 6.8 and 8.1 on the Richter*

TABLE 12.1   Billion-dollar losses from natural disasters 1983–1994

Event/place/year	Economic losses in US$bn
Hurricane Alicia (USA, 1983)	1.65
Winter storm Herta (Europe, 1990)	1.90
Forest fire (USA, 1991)	2.00
Winter storm Wiebke (Europe, 1990)	2.25
Hurricane Iniki (Hawaii, 1992)	3.00
Winter storm Vivian (Europe, 1990)	3.25
Winter gale (Western Europe, 1987)	3.70
Blizzard (USA, 1993)	5.00
Typhoon Mireille (Japan, 1991)	6.00
Winter storm Daria (Europe, 1990)	6.80
Hurricane Hugo (Caribbean, USA, 1989)	9.00
Floods (USA, 1993)	12.00
Earthquake (USA, 1994)	30.00
Hurricane Andrew (USA, 1991)	30.00

Source: From *Disaster Management to Sustainable Development: How the Public Sector, Private Sector and Voluntary Organizations Can Work Together,* WHO, 1994.

scale. *The city of Kobe suffered a death toll in the thousands and initial estimates of damages and long-term repairs ranged up to $50 billion, according to The New York Times.*

- *Excluded from the above figures are the social and health costs of disasters in terms of lost homes, jobs and hopes—the basics of human life.*

There is a clear link between the 1994 United Nations sponsored World Conference on Natural Disaster Reduction cited above and the World Summit for Social Development to be convened from 6 to 12 March 1995 in Copenhagen, Denmark. The link is to be found in the negative contribution that disasters make to society's worst ills: migration, poverty, disease and environmental degradation.

People everywhere are vulnerable to natural disasters. While industrialized countries suffer greater economic damage in absolute terms, poor countries are impacted more severely in relative terms: GNP lost due to natural disasters is estimated to be 20 times greater in developing countries than in developed countries. Also, deaths from natural disasters are more frequent in poor countries. Japan, for example, averages 63 deaths per year from natural disasters. Peru, with similar natural hazards and only one sixth the population of Japan, averages 2,900 deaths per year.

> *The International Decade for Natural Disaster Reduction (IDNDR), 1990–2000, is essentially a UN-led campaign to reduce the impact of natural disasters. As the 1994 World Conference on Natural Disaster Reduction (a mid-term review of national and international progress toward reducing the impact of disasters) demonstrated, the issues are complex, and the prognosis mixed. (United Nations, 1995)*

But even with this strong link between the scientific and international community, the message of risks of volcanic hazards still is not reaching the people who live and work in the areas surrounding Santa María. Our search, then, focused on how to construct an ongoing, interactive link with the people of Guatemala whose lives were so intricately woven with volcanoes.

Multiplicadores *in Local Government Agencies*

In assessing the potential audiences, we were pleased to find that our connections with official channels tied to volcanic hazard communication were strong and that Rose's years of research and work in Guatemala had rewarded him with much respect in these circles. The official channels, like INSIVUMEH and CONRED, wanted only volcanic data, continued access to volcanic research in their country, and, of course, any equipment and international expertise that could help them lobby for continued government and international funding. But these channels are not enough. They are seeped in the unstable politics of Guatemala, rendering them unpredictable and unreliable.

Multiplicadores *in the K–12 Community*

We considered another audience—children, who are the audience most likely to be affected by volcanic hazards. The current volcanic data confirms this. It is likely, as Rose explained, that Santiaguito and/or Santa María will erupt during the lifetimes of today's children. Children bring home stories to their parents, siblings, and extended families, who in turn share these stories with the community.

Rose had told us several months before of his most gratifying and successful risk-communication effort by showing a photograph of himself communicating with Don Patricio Parouche Herrera (see Figure 12.14), who was an eyewitness to a 1929 eruption of Santa María, that completely destroyed his village and killed hundreds of people, including his neighbors and family. Moments before the photo was taken, Rose had shown Don Patricio an album of photographs taken in the aftermath of the 1929 eruption. In one of the photographs is the image of the partially burned corpse of Don Patricio's neighbor. Surrounding Don Patricio and Rose were several children and some other villagers who listened intently as Don Patricio transformed memories into tales as he moved from photograph to photograph. At the end of this session, Don Patricio, remembering the terrible devastation—at once physical, cultural, and spiritual—agreed to help Rose raise awareness within this community of the dangers of Santa María.

FIGURE 12.14   Rose (far right) and others listening to Don Patricio Parouche Herrera (center) tell the story of the 1929 eruption of Santa Maria. February 1988.

Photo courtesy of Jon Fink.

Multiplicadores *in the Educational Community*

Teachers are most likely to communicate the risks associated with volcanic hazards to children. Teachers are also *multiplicadores*. They help children construct knowledge of the world, learn to use this knowledge, and learn to take responsibility for it.

This theme factors heavily in the recent writings of Fernando A. Muñóz-Carmona, a Colombian who has spent most of his professional career as a geologist, seismologist, and administrator in two volcano observatories and at the Colombian Geological Survey. Muñóz-Carmona wrote about volcanic risk communication:

> *For both experts and the community, it is important to understand how the construction of knowledge is exercised and how the resources derived from it are allocated. It is necessary to shift to a situation where the people involved recognize their power and mobilize those resources present in knowledge, beliefs, culture, and perceptions in everyday activities. . . . The application of the scientific method not only has to continue but has to be encouraged, but, recognizing a participative situation not only in the process of decision-making but in the very process of build-*

ing knowledge. We not only as professionals, but also as members of the community, have to be ready to report to the community any circumstances that can significantly influence the process of risk. However, it is the community itself (which includes the experts) that must take charge of understanding and assuming the responsibilities derived from the experience of risk. Under these circumstances, it is clear that it is the awareness on behalf of the community that they are living in a process (a process of risk) that will create the conditions that will allow for adequate management of volcanic risks and hazards. (Muñóz-Carmona, 1996, p. 6)

One of the efforts that Rose and Sandoval have made as university faculty is to educate their students about the broader social context of volcanology. Rose teaches a course on volcanic hazard communication. Sandoval teaches a course on intercultural communication. Both often guest lecture in each other's courses. This interdisciplinary approach exposes students to a different kind of professional responsibility—a participative, knowledge-building interaction between the experts, the community, and the government about the process of risk. Rose often invites his students to travel with him to do volcanology research. The geology graduate student who joined us in Guatemala was doing research for her thesis on remote sensing of volcanoes like Santa María. She had never been out of the United States and learned as much about the geologic and volcanic situation near Santa María as she did about the culture and social conditions of those who live near the volcano and those who live in the cities and enforce the laws of the country. This kind of experience will stay with her throughout her career, informing her perspective as a professional geologist and perhaps transforming her into a *multiplicadore*.

Multiplicadores *in the Community of Developed Countries*

Muñóz-Carmona's message is taken to yet another level in the U.S. government's *Natural Disaster Reduction Report*, which states quite clearly that natural hazards, like volcanic eruptions, rarely affect only the local population—they affect other nations in complex ways:

Natural disaster reduction is not a domestic matter alone but rather an international challenge for the United States. The Mount Pinatubo eruption occurred half a world away, yet it caused immediate U.S. losses of over $1 billion and triggered a change in U.S. strategic military presence in the western Pacific that will have implications for decades. For many nations of the world, a single natural disaster can significantly reduce that year's gross national product; in a number of regions, these events recur so frequently that they strain the social fabric, not just the economic growth. The resulting unrest contributes significantly to global geopolitical instability. As a world leader, the United States cannot afford to focus its efforts on disaster reduction on a domestic scale only; it must continue to take a global approach. (United States Geological Survey, 1995)

National interest in volcanic hazard communication from countries like the United States offers Guatemala a channel for funding and other aid. With this aid, it becomes more possible for INSIVUMEH and CONRED, for example, to hire and train more staff, purchase modern volcanic monitoring equipment, and develop programs that offer Guatemalans work and an opportunity to educate themselves and other Guatemalans about the risks of volcanic hazards. And as we saw in the cases of Otoniel Matías and the volcano observer at *finca* El Faro, these official *multiplicadores* operated in participative ways with the communities.

The Web as a Community-Building Resource

With these audiences—the scientific community, the international community, developed nations, local governmental agencies, children, teachers, and students—in mind, we sought a communication vehicle through which we could connect *multiplicadores*. The World Wide Web seems like the most economical and wide-reaching communication vehicle, albeit a somewhat problematic one. In many parts of the world, most teachers outside of universities do not have access to the Internet, let alone have access to a computer or possess computer skills. However, we feel that by creating a Web site about volcanic hazards in Guatemala that contains materials for teachers about volcanic hazards and the importance of communicating them to children, perhaps we can entice and enlist yet more *multiplicadores*—university professors, students, and others in Guatemala who have Internet and Web access (like Matías with his new laptop)—to communicate the risks of volcanoes.

Our idea is to create an information repository about volcanic risk in Guatemala. Our hope is that our *multiplicadores* will download the information and distribute it to teachers and other *multiplicadores*, like Don Patricio in Guatemala, who in turn will adapt the material to the language, cultural expectations, and learning styles of their students.

This process of adaptation is formally called *localization* in the business community. Localization is most effective as a local participative process, where local and not foreign talent does the adaptation. Not being familiar with the intimate day-to-day communication practices in the small villages of Guatemala, we are not qualified to do this adaptation. In addition, the people of these small villages view us as strangers, outsiders. Our credentials, while they mean something in the elitist circles of government, business, and higher education, mean nothing in the agrarian world of Guatemala. We are not members of their complex people networks, which take years if not lifetimes to develop, and therefore not credible or trustworthy sources of information. However, people like Don Patricio and the observer at Santa María, as well as teachers in the small schools in this area, are trusted members of these communities. In Guatemala, their words would be valued—in a profoundly cultural way—more than ours.

Some of the material that we will make available on our Web site includes:

- Posters that show areas of the greatest volcanic risk
- Games that include precautions to take and evacuation strategies in the event of a volcanic eruption
- Activities, such as building a model of a volcano and recognizing the different behaviors of volcanoes
- Background information on volcanoes and their benefits and dangers
- Community information about who to contact locally for more information.

Rose would like to get his students involved in this Web site. The students can create many of the materials as well as maintain the Web site over time. Sandoval, as a teacher of Spanish, is another important resource for this effort. He has taught this beautiful and flexible language to many of Rose's students, who then are more likely to travel to places like Guatemala and participate in this complex culture at a more intimate level. As for my contribution, I offer you this story with the hope that you will recognize the potential for your broader role as a technical communicator—that of a multiplicadore—as well as the professional responsibility it carries in this world of immense cultural diversity.

In the best of all possible worlds, we wish for this Web site to become a community-building resource in the spirit of Muñóz-Carmona's reflections. Perhaps one day we will be able to upload to our Web site locally produced content from Guatemala, which may become a resource for a teacher in another country, where volcanoes offer prosperity and take it away.

Background Analysis

This section introduces you to three cultural dimensions that will help you better understand this case study. Note that these cultural dimensions are not exhaustive in their contribution to a thorough analysis of this case. They do, however, highlight key cultural differences in the communication processes of Guatemalans and citizens of the United States.

Orality/Literacy

The literacy rate in Guatemala is an interesting demographic. The most recent profile of Guatemala in the Central Intelligence Agency's *World Factbook* offers these statistics:

Definition: age 15 and over can read and write
Total population: 55.6 percent
Male: 62.5 percent
Female: 48.6 percent (1995 est.)

In contrast, an Internet provider in Guatemala, quetzalnet.com, offers these statistics for comparison:

Literacy Rate: 50 percent
Illiterate Population Over Age 15: 45 percent
Illiterate Female Population Over Age 15: 52.9 percent
Ages of Compulsory Education: 7 to 14

Compounding these differences is the number of languages in Guatemala:

The number of languages listed for Guatemala is 53. Of those, 51 are living languages and 2 are extinct. (Summer Institute of Linguistics, 1996)

Oral communication predominates in Guatemala, particularly in the smaller villages where illiteracy rates are high. Oral communication consists mostly of personal dialogue that often consists of redundancies and other characteristics that sometimes seem annoying to North American ears. Oral communication is quite distinct from written communication. Written communication "restructures consciousness" and "heightens consciousness." Writing allows us to examine the world in an "abstractly sequential, classificatory, [and] explanatory" way (Ong, 1982, p.8). Writing is not a daily part of agrarian life in Guatemala. Therefore, the communication patterns and the thought processes are very different from those in the United States. The style, language use, and persuasive strategies in information written in the United States would not automatically make sense to a villager in Guatemala (assuming that he or she could read). Even within Guatemala, there are enormous differences in language use and the orality/literacy dimension between the wealthy and poor.

Consider, too, that visual communication might be more effective in Guatemala, especially considering the pronounced language issues. In so doing, factor in the cultural differences. Images that represent a message in one country might represent a completely different message in another. Images intended for an indigenous, agrarian population are different from those intended for an educated, often urban, professional population.

Power Distance/Authority Conception

Power distance and authority conception are cultural dimensions well examined in the works of Geert Hofstede and David Victor. Hofstede defines power distance as

The extent to which the less powerful members of institutions and organizations within a country expect and accept that power is distributed unequally. "Institutions" are the basic elements of society like the family, school, and the community; "organizations" are the places where people work. . . . Power distance is thus explained from the value systems of the less powerful members. (1991, p. 28)

In his research of employees at IBM, Hofstede found that Guatemalan power distance was second only to Malaysia, rating a high 95 points on a scale of 100. Victor describes authority conception, a similar concept, this way:

> *Authority itself is primarily symbolic in nature. In other words, authority does not exist in isolation but reflects instead the conception of organization power and leadership common to an organization's members. . . . Since authority conception derives from the collective values of those who vest it, authority itself reflects the cultural values of the organization or society in which the authority is recognized. (1992, p. 169)*

To learn to recognize the extent and nature of authority conception in a target country, Victor suggests that we look at the children's literature of the target country.

> *Considerable understanding of how power is perceived and leaders are treated can be derived from the social guidelines laid out in teaching young people how to behave toward those in power and whether or not they have the right to question authority. (p. 182)*

High Context/Low Context

Edward T. Hall defines high and low context communication this way:

> *A high-context (HC) communication or message is one in which most of the information is either in the physical context or internalized in the person, while very little is in the coded, explicit, transmitted part of the message. A low context (LC) communication is just the opposite; i.e., the mass of information is vested in the explicit code. Twins who have grown up together can and do communicate more economically (HC) than two lawyers in a courtroom during a trial (LC). (1976, p. 91)*

Hall gives this concept of high and low contexting a slightly different twist in a later book:

> *High-context people are well informed and maintain extensive information networks to insure their being abreast of the latest developments; they require a minimum of background information; and they are accustomed to many interruptions and cannot always adhere to a schedule. Low-context people are not well informed outside their own special area of expertise. They are compartmentalized and require lots of background information before they can make a decision. (Hall & Hall, 1990, p. 180)*

Perhaps needless to say, Guatemalans fall on the high-context end of the contexting continuum, while North Americans fall on the low context end. This difference is significant in the cross-cultural and technical communication processes. It leads to the questions: How much information do we supply? What information do we supply?

Questions for Discussion

1. How might technical communicators help volcanologists communicate the risks of natural hazards?

2. Identify the traditional and nontraditional communication methods presented in this case study. Consider effectiveness criteria for each method. Next, identify the primary and secondary audiences that these methods are intended to reach (as suggested in this case study). Rank these methods by their effectiveness. Finally, investigate additional methods that are not presented in the case but that you think might be effective. Discuss your findings.

3. Can we apply the same principles of technical communication in third-world countries? If so, why? If not, how might we adapt technical communication principles to the needs of audiences in the third world? What skills do technical communicators need to communicate effectively to a third-world audience?

4. Consider the role of women in Guatemala. Might they be potential *multiplicadores* of risk mitigation and communication. If so, why and how?

5. Identify the ethical issues in this case study and discuss how they might affect the communication of risk to different audiences in Guatemala.

6. Watch the 1998 film *Dante's Peak* and discuss the risk communication methods used and avoided in the story. Which ones were successful and which ones were not successful? How effective might these methods be in a third-world country like Guatemala?

Writing Assignments

1. Design a Web page for the volcanic hazard communication Web site for Guatemalan *multiplicadores*. See Supplemental Web Sites, following, to choose a volcanic hazard that will form the content of your Web page. Consider creating a system of icons that reflect the cultural context of the indigenous people of Guatemala and that relate to volcanic hazards. For example, we thought that an icon showing the destruction (flattening) of sugar cane fields against the silhouette of a smoking volcano might offer a powerful local image economically and emotionally.

2. Write a letter of introduction to a volcanologist, offering your services as a *multiplicadore*. Explain the value of your services and relate them to the expertise of the volcanologist. Place your explanation in the broader social context. Add your résumé, making sure that you have modified it to support your claims in the letter of introduction.

Additional Resources: Relevant to Issues in the Case

Supplemental Web Sites

For thorough coverage of Santa María, Santiaguito, and the Santa María Volcanic Hazards Workshop, see http://www.geo.mtu.edu/volcanoes/santamaria/.

For demographic and journalistic coverage of Guatemala, see the Washington Post's World Reference for Guatemala, which includes links to the CIA World Factbook, among others: http://www.washingtonpost.com/wp-srv/inatl/longterm/worldref/country/guatemal.htm.

For a U.S. tourism guide to Guatemala, go to http://city.net/countries/guatemala/?page=overview.

For a local look at Guatemala, go to these Web sites: http://infoguat.guatemala.org/Profile.htm and http://www.quetzalnet.com/quetzalNET/Tourism.html.

To learn more about volcanoes and their hazards, see this Web page at the U.S. Geological Survey: http://volcanoes.usgs.gov/. See also the excellent Volcano World Web site at http://volcano.und.nodak.edu/vw.html.

To learn about *multiplicadores*—volcanologists interested in volcanic hazard communication—in other countries, go to the Volcanic Mitigation Team's Web site at: http://www.unige.ch/hazards/volcano/welcome.html.

To learn how to build a model of a volcano, go to http://volcano.und.nodak.edu/vwdocs/volc_models/models.html.

To learn about the threat that natural disasters impose on social development, go to gopher://gopher.un.org/00/conf/wssd/pc-3/bkg/950227122401.txt.

To learn more about the Natural Mitigation Strategy in the United States, go to the Federal Emergency Management Agency (FEMA) at http://www.fema.gov/home/mit/ntmstrat.htm. See also a related Web site at the USGS: http://www.usgs.gov/sndr/report/index.html.

To learn more about the effect that Hurricane Mitch had on Guatemala and other countries in Central America, go to the USAID Web site at http://hurricane.info.usaid.gov/ofda.html.

Journal Articles, Books, and Other Sources

Bennett, E. H. Sanchez, Rose, W. I., Conway, F. M. (1992). "Santa Maria, Guatemala: A Decade Volcano, *EOS. Geophysical Union*, Vol. 73, 521.

Burgos-Debray, E. (Ed.). (1998). *I, Rigoberta Menchú*, A. Wright (Tr.). New York: Verso. This is an account of the life and experiences of Rigoberta Mehchú, an indigenous Guatemalan woman who learned Spanish to help the indigenous peoples of Guatemala.

Doheny-Farina, S. (1996). *The wired neighborhood*. New Haven: Yale University Press. This book offers a thoughtful look at virtual communities and real communities and, more importantly, how they can influence each other in both positive and negative ways.

Freire, P. (1989). *Pedagogy of the oppressed*. M. B. Ramos, (Tr.). New York, Continuum. Freire develops a theory of education for illiterate peasants in the third world. This may serve as a theoretical starting point for volcanic risk communication in the third world.

Goldman, F. (1992). *The long night of white chickens*. New York: Grove Press. This novel is a love story that draws intense intercultural comparisons between a North American and a Guatemalan. The story recreates the political and social realities between the two nations.

Hall, E. T. (1976). *Beyond culture*. New York: Anchor Books.

Hall, E. T., & Hall, M. R. (1990). Understanding cultural differences: Germans, French, and Americans. Yarmouth, ME: Intercultural Press.

Hofstede, G. (1991). *Cultures and organizations: Software of the mind*. New York: McGraw-Hill.

Mader, G. G., & Blair, M. L., with Olson, R. A. (1987). *Living with a volcanic threat: Response to volcanic hazards: Long Valley, California*. Portola Valley, CA: William Spangle and Associates. Written by urban planners, this is a detailed case study about the volcanic mitigation and communication that took place in the early 1980s in Long Valley, California.

In this case study, mitigation efforts describe a volcanic hazard that never occurred. The study explores the consequences leading up to and following the mitigation efforts.

Montejo, V. (1987). *Testimony: Death of a Guatemalan village.* V. Perea, (Tr.). Willimantic CT: Curbstone Press. The true and horrific tale of a Guatemalan village, Tzalal, that is terrorized by the military on September 9, 1992, as recounted by the village school teacher, Victor Montejo.

Muñóz-Carmona, F. A. (1996, August). "Notes about managing volcanic risk and hazards." Paper presented at the Pan Pacific Hazards 1996 Trade Show, Vancouver, Canada, p.6.

Myers, B., Brantley, S. R., Stauffer, P., & Hendley II, J. W. (01, Jan. 1997.). What are volcano hazards? U.S. Geological Survey Fact Sheet 002-97, reprinted online at http://usgs-georef.cos.com/cgi-bin/getRec?un=1997-071847.

Ong, W. (1982). *Orality and literacy,* New York: Routledge.

Hawkins, Janet. (1994, October). "Confronting a Culture of lies." *Harvard Magazine,* vol. 97, no. 1, pp. 49–57.

Rose, W. I. (1992). "Notes on the 1902 eruption of Santa María Volcano, Guatemala." *Bulletin of Volcanology,* vol. 36, 29.

Summer Institute of Linguistics. (1996). *Ethnologue of Guatemala.* Available Internet: http://www.sil.org/ethnologue/countries/Guat.html

United Nations. (1995). *Disasters: Threat to social development.* city: United Nations Department of Public Information. Available: gopher://gopher.un.org/00/conf/wssd/pc-3/bkg/950227122401.txt.

United States Geological Survey. (1995). *Natural disaster reduction: A plan for the nation.* Available Internet: http://www.usgs.gov/sndr/report/international.html.

Victor, D. (1992). *International business communication.* New York: HarperCollins.

List of Contributors

Roger Baumgarte received his Ph.D. in experimental psychology from Bowling Green University in 1973. He currently teaches cross-cultural psychology at Winthrop University in South Carolina. He has also taught at the American University in Paris and the University of Maryland's Asian Division in South Korea. His research focuses on close friendships and how they differ over cultures. He can be reached at BaumgarteR@winthrop.edu.

Philippe Blanchard graduated from the Ecole de Hautes Etudes Commerciales in Lille, France, in 1990, where he specialized in business administration. He has worked in France and the United States, where he implemented fully integrated management information systems. He currently works in Rio de Janeiro, Brazil, in the field of international finance for a worldwide supplier of equipment for the construction of overhead transmission lines. His constant negotiations with customers and suppliers provide him with significant experience with a variety of cultures. In addition, he has done consulting work in Canada and the People's Republic of China.

Deborah S. Bosley, associate professor of English and Director of the University Writing Programs, teaches undergraduate and graduate courses in technical communication at the University of North Carolina at Charlotte. She has published articles on collaboration, international issues in technical communication, gender, and pedagogy. In 1992, she won the Society for Technical Communication Award of Distinguished Technical Communication for the article "Designing Effective Technical Communication Teams," and she received the Nell Ann Picket Award in 1994 from the Association of Teachers of Technical Writing for "Cross-Cultural Collaboration: Whose Culture Is It, Anyway?" Currently, she is the series editor for STC's Series in Technical Communication. In addition to her scholarly focus, she has been a consultant to business and industry for fifteen years. For the past fifteen years, she has been a communications' consultant to such international corporations as IBM,

Hoechst Celanese, and First Union National Bank as well governmental and non-profit agencies throughout the region. Her research includes international technical communication, collaboration, and information design in the health field. Her e-mail address is dsbosley@email.uncc.edu.

Jeutonne Brewer's primary focus is on sociolinguistics. She was audio consultant to the Smithsonian's Remembering Slavery project whose site she and Timothy Flood designed, created, and maintained for the Institute of Language and Culture, Smithsonian Productions: http://www.uncg.edu/~jpbrewer/remember/index.html. She can be reached at jpbrewer@hamlet.uncg.edu.

Ye-Ling Chang specializes in TESOL methodologies, and has recently developed a series of courses featuring electronic exchanges and Web page development as strategies for teaching English in a global setting. Chang's current research is on the use of Web page design for teaching English to second-language writers; some of her projects and those of her students are online at http://140.127.40.7/~engstu/Chang/. She can be reached via e-mail at changyl@mail.nsysu.edu.tw.

Boyd H. Davis, a professor of linguistics at UNC Charlotte; Jeutonne Brewer, associate professor of English at UNC Greensboro; and Ye-Ling Chang, associate professor of English, at the National Kaohsiung Normal University, Kaohsiung, Taiwan (ROC), have collaborated for over a decade to develop on-line educational modules about writing and cross-cultural communications. Davis and Brewer are linguists and have recently published *Electronic Discourse: Linguistic Individuals in Virtual Space* (SUNY, 1997). Davis's recent linguistic work with Ralf Thiede on first- and second-language discourse contact and change in electronic environments is in press. Her current Web site of community language and discourse is at http://www.uncc.edu/english/clc. She can be reached at bdavis@email.uncc.edu.

Sam Dragga is professor of English at Texas Tech University, teaching undergraduate and graduate courses in technical communication. He is a past president of the Association of Teachers of Technical Writing, manager of its e-mail discussion list (ATTW-L), and editor of its Web site (english.ttu.edu/attw). He has twice served as a Technical Communication Delegation Leader for People to People International: to the People's Republic of China (May 1997) and to Russia and the Czech Republic (March 1998). He is co-author of *Reporting Technical Information* (Wiley, 2000), *A Reader's Repertoire* (HarperCollins, 1996), *A Writer's Repertoire* (HarperCollins, 1995), and *Editing: The Design of Rhetoric* (Baywood, 1989) as well as series editor of the Allyn & Bacon Series in Technical Communication. He has also published a variety of journal articles on professional ethics and technical communication. He can be reached at ditsd@TTACS.TTU.EDU.

Frank Driskill, P.E., conducts hazardous operations analyses on large facilities as a senior chemical engineer with Brown and Root Energy Services. He works with project groups, nearly all of which involve engineers from other countries. He has thirty years of experience in refinery and chemical business engineering.

Linda Driskill, Ph.D., is professor of English and Director of the Cain Project in Engineering and Professional Communication at Rice University. She is co-author of two textbooks and has taught technical and management communication courses for engineers and MBA students. Nearly all of her publications in the past five years have involved international or intercultural communication. driskila@rice.edu.

Craig J. Hansen is an associate professor and Director of the BA and MS Technical Communication Programs at Metropolitan State University in St. Paul, Minnesota. He has published works in technical communication, business communication, and composition on topics ranging from the social context of communication technologies to adult literacy. Before becoming an academic, he worked for ten years in the computer industry. His exposure to the pitfalls of intercultural communication came through this work experience and through teaching in an MBA program for Chinese students over several summers. He can be reached at chansen@msus1.msus.edu.

Nancy L. Hoft is currently a Ph.D. student at Michigan Technological University in the Rhetoric and Technical Communication program. She has been a technical writer, artist, trainer, and manager and now specializes in international technical communication. She is the author of *International Technical Communication* (Wiley, 1995), co-author of *The Web Page Design Cookbook* (Wiley, 1996), has written chapters for *International User Interfaces* (Wiley, 1996) and other publications, and was the guest editor of "Global Issues, Local Concerns," a special issue of *Technical Communication* (Society for Technical Communication, May 1999) dealing with issues related to international technical communication. nhoft@worldnet.att.net.

Thomas F. Lannin is an information technology consultant and technical writer in Charlotte, North Carolina, at Metro Information Services. After receiving his Ph.D. in English from the University of California at Riverside, he became the first American Visiting Professor of English and Research Associate at Josai University, Japan, where he guest edited *The Review of Japanese Culture and Society* and helped organize two international conferences. Over the last eight years, he has taught technical communications, literature, and composition classes for The University of Maryland (Asian Division), the University of North Carolina at Charlotte, and Winthrop University. He has traveled extensively throughout Canada, Europe, and the Far East, including four trips to Peninsular Malaysia. His many publications have appeared in periodicals such as *The Fiddlehead, The New Orleans Review, Sanskrit,* and *The Japan Times.* lannin@earthlink.net.

Elizabeth M. Lynn is currently a professor of management communication at Kettering University (formerly GMI Engineering & Management Institute). Previously, she spent fifteen years teaching at City College of New York, Indiana University, the Graduate School of Business at the University of Southern California, and the Graduate School of Management at the University of Michigan-Flint. She has provided extensive management training and organizational development for such companies as Standard Oil (Ohio), British Petroleum-Canada, Pacific Bell, Carter-Hawley-Hale, Heublein, and Hughes Corporation. She holds graduate degrees from Indiana University (Ph.D.), Columbia University, and Villanova University and is listed in *Who's Who in the Midwest, Who's Who of American Women,* and *Who's Who in Education.* She can be reached at elynn@kettering.edu.

Bruce Maylath is an associate member of the American Translators Association, an executive board member of the Council for Programs in Scientific and Technical Communication, and an assistant professor of English at the University of Wisconsin-Stout, where he directs the Program in Technical Communication. His current research takes up translation issues in technical communication. His publications appear in the *Journal for Business and Technical Communication, Research in the Teaching of English,* and numerous other journals and books. He can be reached at maylathb@uwstout.edu.

Jayne A. Moneysmith is an assistant professor of English at Kent State University Stark Campus, where she primarily teaches business and technical writing. Her research focuses on using technology to enhance collaborative writing in both the classroom and the workplace. She can be reached at jmoneysmith@stark.kent.edu.

Barry L. Thatcher is an assistant professor of English and Director of Professional Writing at Ohio University, Athens. His research focuses on rhetoric and professional writing in intercultural contexts, specifically in Latin America and the United States. He is also researching the teaching of professional writing to non-native speakers of English. His affiliations include National Council for Teachers of English (NCTE) and the Association for Business Communication (ABC). His publications include *La creación de una retórica híbrida de América Latina/EUA.* In El Registro del Primer Congreso Internacional de Retórica en Mexico. UNAM: Mexico City. (Summer, 1999). Cultural and rhetorical adaptations for South American audiences. *Technical Communication: Global issues, local concerns;* and in 1994, language theory, culture, and education in Dickens' Hard Times. *Dickens Studies Annual.* thatcher@oak.cats.ohiou.edu.

Emily A. Thrush is an associate professor at the University of Memphis, where she teaches in both the Professional Writing and Teaching English as a Second Language programs. She has consulted on writing projects with companies such as IBM, Georgia-Pacific, the National Asbestos Council, and Burger King. She has delivered teacher training workshops on four continents and published several articles on international issues in professional communication. ethrush@memphis.edu.

Index

Abbott, D. P., 87
Albert, D. P., 90
Albert, R. D., 93
American National Standards Institute (ANSI), 160n.
Attitude, translation quality and, 74–75
Australia, 105
Authority patterns, 7–8. *See also* Hierarchy patterns
power distance and, 105–111, 204–205

Baumgarte, Roger, 7–8, 96–112
Belkin, Lisa, 164
Benjamin, A., 87
Bennett, M. J., 87, 91, 93
Blanchard, Philippe, 7–8, 96–112
Bosley, Deborah S., 1–9
Boswood, T. S., 2
Brewer, Jeutonee, 6, 42–51
Bribery, 108–109, 110–111
Business relationships, 38

Canada, 105
Case studies
issues in, 5–8
nature of, 4–5
using, 4–5
Castañeda, J. G., 93
Cause and effect, 92–93
Central versus individual control, 37–38
Chang, Ye-Ling, 6, 42–51

Chief executive officers (CEOs)
corporate hierarchies and, 7–8, 96–112
language fluency of, 75–78
China
sign revision process, 6, 10–18
technical documentation, 6, 19–26
Cognitive disonance, 75
Colombia, risk-based design of pipeline, 8, 148–173
Condon, J. C., 92
CONRED (*Coordinadora Nacional Para La Reduccion de Desastres*), 194–196, 202
Cornejo-Polar, Antonio, 87–88
Corporate hierarchies in Latin America, 7–8, 96–112
abstract, 96–97
background for analysis, 105–109
case analysis, 109–111
case background, 97–105
Crisis situations
cultural misunderstandings in, 7, 52–63
Estonia sinking, 8, 127–147
natural hazard communication, 8, 174–208
Cross-cultural team-building
abstract, 42–43
case background, 43–50
continuing usage issues in, 50
cross-cultural communication in, 45
gender pronouns in, 6, 42–51
in risk-based pipeline design, 149–151, 152–158

Cultural misunderstandings in crisis situations, 7, 52–63
abstract, 52–53
background for analysis, 58–59
case analysis, 59–61
case background, 53–55
scenario, 53–58
Culture, defining, 2–3
Czech Republic, Teaching English as a Foreign Language (TEFL), 6, 27–41

Davis, Boyd H., 6, 42–51
Denmark, 105
Disaster communication. *See* Natural hazard communication
Dragga, Sam, 6, 10–18
Driskill, Frank, 8, 148–173
Driskill, Linda, 8, 148–173

Ecuador, communication patterns in, 7, 81–95
Emergencies. *See* Crisis situations
Environmental issues
balancing security with, 167–172
communicating risks of natural hazards, 8, 174–210
Estonia, sinking of, 8, 127–147
abstract, 127–128
background for additional analysis, 140–144
case analysis, 135–139
case background, 128–133
described, 133–135
Ethical considerations
in risk-based pipeline design, 159–165
in user manual translation, 70–73

First, Do No Harm (Belkin), 164

Geertz, C., 2
Gender pronoun usage, 6, 42–51
Gift-giving, 108–109, 110–111
Group-centeredness versus individualism, 38, 89–90, 105
Group versus individual control, 37–38
Guatemala
as high-power-distance country, 205
volcanic risk communication in, 8, 174–208

Hall, Edward T., 2, 3, 6, 7, 88–89, 92, 205
Hansen, Craig J., 6, 19–26
Hazard communication. *See* Natural hazard communication
Hierarchy patterns, 7–8
in Chinese culture, 25
in Latin American culture, 7–8, 96–112
High-context cultures
characteristics of, 35, 88–89, 205
South American communication patterns, 7, 81–95
Teaching English as a Foreign Language (TEFL), 6, 27–41
user manual translation and, 7, 64–80
Hofstede, Geert, 7–8, 89, 90, 96, 105–111, 157–158, 204–205
Hoft, Nancy L., 3, 8, 175–210
Hurricane hazard communication, 176, 180, 194–196

Individualism versus group-centeredness, 38, 89–90, 105
Individual versus group or central control, 37–38
In-groups, 89–90
INSIVUMEH (*Instituti Nacional de Sismología, Vulcanología, Meteorología e Hidrología*), 176, 178–180, 183, 188, 195, 202
International Maritime Organization (IMO), 129n., 130n., 136, 137n., 139, 141–142
Internet, in community-building process, 202–203

Job appraisal systems, 108, 110

Keesing, R., 2
Kohlberg, Lawrence, 164–165
Korea, cultural misunderstandings in crisis situations, 7, 52–63
Kras, E., 93

Lannin, Thomas F., 8, 113–126
Latin America
corporate hierarchies in, 7–8, 96–112
high-context culture of, 7, 81–95
as high-power-distance culture, 106, 205
risk-based design of pipeline, 8, 148–173

South American communication patterns, 7, 81–95
   volcanic risk communication, 8, 174–208
Level of knowledge, translation quality and, 75
Lovitt, C., 2
Low-context cultures
   characteristics of, 35, 205
   South American communication patterns, 7, 81–95
   Teaching English as a Foreign Language (TEFL), 6, 27–41
   user manual translation and, 64–80
Lynn, Elizabeth M., 8, 127–147

Malaysia
   as high-power-distance culture, 106, 205
   virtual university project, 8, 113–126
Managers
   corporate hierarchies and, 96–112
   language fluency of, 75–78
Matías, Otoniel, 176, 181–182, 187, 188–196
Maylath, Bruce, 7, 64–80
Michigan Technical University (MTU), 175, 193–194
Moneysmith, Jayne A., 7, 52–63
Monochronic time frames, 92
Moral reasoning, 164–165
Multiplicadores, 8, 196–203
   in community of developed countries, 201–202
   concept of, 199
   in educational community, 200–201
   in K-12 community, 199–200
   in local government, 199
   in scientific and international communities, 197–199
   World Wide Web and, 202–203
Muñóz-Carmona, Fernando A., 200–201

National Disaster Reduction Report, 201–202
Natural hazard communication, 8, 175–210
   abstract, 174–175
   background analysis, 203–205
   case background, 176–196
   community of *multiplicadores* in, 196–203
   losses from natural disasters, 198

Nepotism, 108, 110
NetRider, 7, 52–63

Ong, W., 206
Oral versus written communication, 6, 37, 87–88, 203–204

Particularist values, 91
Pastor, R. A., 93
Politeness, in Chinese culture, 24–25
Polychronic time frames, 92
Porter, Kit, 130
Power distance (PDI), 105–111, 204–205
   high-PDI cultures, 106–109
   low-PDI cultures, 105–106, 107
Problem solving
   time and, 91–92
   whirlpool approach to, 7, 93–94

Relativism, 3
Risk-based pipeline design, 8, 148–173
   abstract, 148–149
   analyzing risks, costs, and ethical issues in, 159–165
   background for analysis, 157–158, 163–165
   balancing security and environmental effects in, 167–172
   case background, 149–151
   identification of people in case, 151–152
   stakeholder culture and hazard mitigation, 152–158
Risk management
   passenger ship traffic and, 131–133, 136–137, 140–141
   in risk-based design of pipeline, 8, 148–173
   volcanic hazard communication, 8, 174–208
Rose, William, Jr., 174, 176, 179, 181–182, 184, 185, 187, 188, 190–194, 195–196, 199, 201, 203

Sandoval, Ciro, 174, 176, 180, 190, 194, 201
Santa María volcano (Guatemala) hazard communication, 8, 174–208
Scollon, R., 45
Scollon, S. W., 45

Security. *See also* Risk management
  balancing environmental effects with,
    167–172
Sexist language. *See* Gender pronoun usage
Shared knowledge, 38–39
Sign revision process, 6, 10–18
  abstract, 10
  background for analysis, 14–16
  case background, 10–14
  sign content, 12, 13, 15
SOLAS Convention, 130–131, 132, 142, 143
South American communication patterns, 7,
    81–95
  abstract, 81
  background for analysis, 86–94
  case background, 82–86
Stewart, E. C., 87, 91, 93

Taiwan
  gender pronoun usage in, 6, 42–51
  technical documentation plan, 6, 19–26
Tannen, D., 35
Teaching English as a Foreign Language
    (TEFL), 6, 27–41
  abstract, 27
  background for analysis, 33–37
  case analysis, 37–39
  case background, 27–33
Team-building. *See* Cross-cultural team-
    building
Technical communication
  curriculum adjustments in, 1–2
  Estonia, sinking of, 8, 127–147
Technical documentation
  abstract, 19
  background for analysis, 23–25
  case background, 20–23
  joint Taiwan-U.S. plan, 6, 19–26
Thatcher, Barry L., 7, 81–95
Thrush, Emily A., 6, 27–41
Time
  problem solving and, 91–92
  translation quality and, 74

Translation
  and sinking of the *Estonia*, 8, 127–147
  South American communication patterns
    and, 7, 81–95
  of technical documentation, 6, 19–26
  of user manuals, 7, 64–80
Trompenaars, Franz, 89, 90, 157–158

United States
  joint U.S-Taiwan technical documentation
    plan, 6, 19–26
  as low-power-distance culture, 105
  Malaysian virtual university project, 8,
    113–126
  Teaching English as a Foreign Language
    (TEFL), 6, 27–41
Universal values, 3, 91
University of Memphis, 6, 27–41
University of West Bohemia, 6, 27–41
User manual translation, 7, 64–80
  abstract, 64
  background for analysis, 73–78
  case background, 64–69
  client company/translation company
    relations, 67–73
  ethical considerations, 70–73

Values, 3, 91
Version control, translation quality and, 74
Victor, David, 204, 205
Virtual university in Malaysia, 8, 113–126
  abstract, 113–114
  background for analysis, 116–123
  case analysis, 123–125
  case background, 114–115
Volcanic hazard communication, 8, 174–208

Whirlpool approach, 7, 93–94
World Maritime University, 129, 129n., 130
World Wide Web, in community-building
    process, 202–203
Written versus oral communication, 6, 37,
    87–88, 203–204